The State and Underdevelopment in Spanish America

Westview Replica Editions

The concept of Westview Replica Editions is a response to the continuing crisis in academic and informational publishing. Library budgets for books have been severely curtailed. Ever larger portions of general library budgets are being diverted from the purchase of books and used for data banks, computers, micromedia, and other methods of information retrieval. Interlibrary loan structures further reduce the edition sizes required to satisfy the needs of the scholarly community. Economic pressures on the university presses and the few private scholarly publishing companies have severely limited the capacity of the industry to properly serve the academic and research communities. As a result, many manuscripts dealing with important subjects, often representing the highest level of scholarship, are no longer economically viable publishing projects--or, if accepted for publication, are typically subject to lead times ranging from one to three years.

Westview Replica Editions are our practical solution to the problem. We accept a manuscript in camera-ready form, typed according to our specifications, and move it immediately into the production process. As always, the selection criteria include the importance of the subject, the work's contribution to scholarship, and its insight, originality of thought, and excellence of exposition. The responsibility for editing and proofreading lies with the author or sponsoring institution. We prepare chapter headings and display pages, file for copyright, and obtain Library of Congress Cataloging in Publication Data. A detailed manual contains simple instructions for preparing the final typescript, and our editorial staff is always available to answer questions.

The end result is a book printed on acid-free paper and bound in sturdy library-quality soft covers. We manufacture these books ourselves using equipment that does not require a lengthy make-ready process and that allows us to publish first editions of 300 to 600 copies and to reprint even smaller quantities as needed. Thus, we can produce Replica Editions quickly and can keep even very specialized books in print as long as there is a demand for them.

About the Book and Author

The State and Underdevelopment
in Spanish America: The Political Roots
of Dependency in Peru and Argentina
Douglas Friedman

Challenging the dependency theory approach to the origin of underdevelopment in Spanish America, this book argues that internal political and economic factors led the nations of the region to become dependent and underdeveloped during the nineteenth century. Dr. Friedman focuses on Peru and Argentina in the aftermath of their wars of independence to show how underdevelopment and dependency resulted from a crisis of the state brought about by the loss of legitimacy of Spanish colonial rule.

Class conflicts had been effectively managed by the colonial state; its collapse, Dr. Friedman demonstrates, created conditions of intense inter- and intra-class conflicts, chiefly political in nature, which weak post-independence governments found impossible to restrain. Left with little authority, legitimacy, or control over internal resources, the fledging Peruvian and Argentine states turned to external sources for the capabilities with which to begin the process of consolidating their internal power. By the last half of the nineteenth century, both Peru and Argentina had chosen a course that led to their integration into the international economy as dependent nations.

Douglas Friedman is assistant professor of political science at the College of Charleston in Charleston, South Carolina.

The State and Underdevelopment in Spanish America

The Political Roots of Dependency in Peru and Argentina

Douglas Friedman

Westview Press / Boulder and London

A Westview Replica Edition

Copyright © 1984 by Westview Press, Inc.

Published in 1984 in the United States of America by
     Westview Press, Inc.
     5500 Central Avenue
     Boulder, Colorado 80301
     Frederick A. Praeger, Publisher

Library of Congress Catalog Card Number: 84-50658
ISBN 0-86531-824-7

Printed and bound in the United States of America

10 9 8 7 6 5 4 3 2

For Virginia and Malachy

Contents

ix

Acknowledgments

Any work of this kind is rarely the result of individual effort alone. Intellectual and personal debts are incurred all along the way and, while I of course accept full responsibility for the finished product, I would like to mention some of those who consciously or unconsciously have had a part in this work.

Although I have been highly critical of the dependencia approach, the works of Andre Gunder Frank and Fernando Henrique Cardoso have had and continue to have a powerful influence on my thinking. Anyone interested in economic and political development in the Third World must first come to grips with their important theses. I am also deeply indebted to authors such as Nicos Poulantzas, Hal Draper, Erik Olin Wright and Alan Wolfe whose works on the Marxist theory of the state have informed the theoretical sections of this book.

An earlier version of this work (my doctoral dissertation) received stimulating and helpful criticism from my teachers and fellow students at the City University of New York. I would in particular like to thank Lenny Markovitz, Ken Erickson, Ralph della Cava, Mel Redman, Mesfin Araya, Hobart Spalding and Ben Rivlin for their support and encouragement.

Dean Birkenkamp and Victoria Yogman at Westview's Replica department could not have been more supportive. Any improvement in the readability of the text is a result of their editing and their attempt to teach me how to write clearly. Unfortunately I learn somewhat slowly and thus any lack of clarity is a result of my own stubborness.

Vincent Gilchrist, who did the word processing, deserves special thanks for easing my anxieties about using this new technology. However, I don't think I am yet ready to discard my trusty typewriter.

Virginia has had to suffer through the writing and re-writing of this book twice now and again I would like to let her know that those who do not type also serve. Her support made this task so much easier. Even little Malachy played his part--for everyone needs pleasant distractions!

Douglas Friedman

Part One

Dependency, Colonialism, and Crisis

1
Spanish American Underdevelopment: Dependency Theory, the State, and Class Conflict

In the late nineteenth century, the Spanish American countries emerged from a period of relative economic stagnation or decline and almost constant civil war into a period of economic growth and relative political stability. Economically, this period was characterized by the emergence of "classic export economies" in which agro/mineral products were exchanged in international trade for manufactured goods, capital, and infrastructure investment. Politically, this period was characterized by the emergence of the "oligarchies," small groups of landowners, merchants, urban politicians, bureaucrats, and intellectuals who formed a solid class base for governing, whether in liberal democratic or authoritarian guise.

The fact that agro/mineral export growth and relative political stability arose at approximately the same time has led recent interpretations of this period to suggest that, (1) political stability in late nineteenth century Spanish America resulted from prosperity created by agro/mineral export growth;[1] (2) both the growth of agro/mineral exports and political stability in nineteenth century Spanish America can be explained primarily by external factors, as the industrial development of Western Europe and the United States sparked world demand for Spanish American agro/mineral products;[2] and (3) the underdevelopment and dependency of Spanish America was caused by a world capitalist economic system controlled by Western Europe and the United States.[3]

Such interpretations, in my estimation, are flawed because they ignore the role of internal factors in the creation of Spanish American agro/mineral export growth and political stability. By examining class conflicts and the consolidation of the State in two Spanish American countries, this study will show that that agro/mineral export growth was a result of the search for political stability and thus, that underdevelopment and dependency have their origins in factors internal to Spanish America.

3

UNDERDEVELOPMENT, DEPENDENCY THEORY, AND NINETEENTH CENTURY SPANISH AMERICA

To ask why the Spanish American countries had agro/mineral export economies by the late nineteenth century is to ask the more important question of why they became underdeveloped and dependent. The term "underdeveloped" is used here in a very specific sense. It does not mean that these countries were left undeveloped; obviously economic development occurred throughout the nineteenth century--more land was cultivated, people were put to work, production was extended, wealth was created, etc. Yet at the close of the nineteenth century, Spanish America was well behind Western Europe in economic development. Of course this lag could be explained by Western Europe's "head start," but what about the United States which began from a comparable position to Spanish America in the early nineteenth century, or Japan which still had a feudal system in the mid nineteenth century? By the late nineteenth century, both nations were progressing quickly towards advanced industrial capitalism, far outdistancing economic development in Spanish America.[4]

Of the various explanations for Spanish American underdevelopment and dependency, the one that has prevailed in recent years is "dependency theory."[5] Although developed by neo-Marxists such as Andre Gunder Frank[6] and Fernando Henrique Cardoso,[7] dependency theory has been accepted by non-Marxists like Peter H. Smith, who argues that the approach has ". . . great potential as an explanatory tool . . ." which he hopes ". . . political history in the 1980s will pursue."[8] Dependency theory was conceived by its authors as a response, critique, and alternative to "modernization theory,"[9] notable in the writings of Jacques Lambert, Gino Germini, Frank Jay Moreno, W. W. Rostow and others, who argued that underdevelopment in Spanish America resulted from an "original" undevelopment, which could only be overcome through greater contact--trade, investment, technology, and values--with more developed nations.[10] These authors contended that in Spanish America there existed "dual" economies and societies in which relatively developed modern capitalist sectors stood in opposition to undeveloped feudal or "traditional" sectors. Development, they concluded, was a process of a diffusion of modern economic, social, and political values from the developed modern sectors to the traditional ones. In the same way, economic, social, and political intercourse with the advanced Western countries would greatly facilitate the "modernization" of Spanish America.

Frank began his attack on modernization theory by rejecting these notions and arguing quite the opposite. He contended that what the modernization theorists took to be the traditional characteristics of Spanish America were in fact the results of economic, social, and political contact with the advanced industrial countries. Development and underdevelopment, he argued, were opposite sides of the same coin of world wide capitalist development.[11] In Frank's formulation, Spanish America has been part of an expanding world capitalist system

4

since the sixteenth century and therefore must be defined as capitalist. The structure of its economies, societies, and polities have been determined by its incorporation into that system, which Frank defines as an international system of trade. Accordingly, Spanish American countries were forced to become complements of the European economies, producing raw agricultural and mineral goods in exchange for manufactured articles from Europe.[12]

The dependentistas contend that the structuring of Spanish American economies by the world capitalist system during the last 500 years has left Spanish America "dependent." While the dynamic "metropolitan" countries could determine their own economic, social, and political direction because their economies generated economic growth autonomously, those of Spanish America were determined externally because the impetus for their economic growth lag outside their borders. Thus, the rhythm of the international economy, which is sensitive only to the needs of the advanced industrial nations, determined the economic development (and therefore to a large extent the social and political development) of Spanish America. According to Fernando Henrique Cardoso and Enzo Faletto,

> . . . the situation of underdevelopment is produced historically when the expansion of early commercial capitalism and later industrial capitalism ties the backward regions into the international market, and these regions become suppliers of essential raw materials for the advanced countries as well as purchasers of their industrial goods. Therefore, internal development in the countries of the periphery is shaped according to the needs of the metropolitan powers that dominate them.[13]

To argue that a capitalist world economy causes underdevelopment and dependency is no better an explanation than the argument that tradition causes underdevelopment. If the capitalist world economic system was responsible for integrating the Spanish American economies into that system as agro/mineral exporters, then why did it not integrate, for example, the United States, Germany, or even France in the same manner? Why did the capitalist world economy differentiate between Peru and the United States? The answer obviously cannot be found in focusing on an undifferentiated "world capitalist system," but this is precisely what the dependentistas would have us believe. For them, Spanish America, Western Europe, and the United States all had fundamentally the same type of economy--capitalist. Since all were capitalist, any explanation citing fundamental differences between the Spanish American economies, societies, and polities and those of Western Europe and the United States is absurd. In other words, capitalism creates dynamic industrial economies in one part of the world, and dependent underdevelopment in the other.

By arguing that capitalism created development and underdevelopment at the same time, the dependentistas have eliminated capitalism as an explanation for either. Yet, isn't the question of development in reality a question of the development of capitalism as we understand it? The prodigious increase in material wealth and production in the modern era results from the capitalist system of production, which requires continued progress and expansion for its very survival. The reproduction of the existing system is not enough; it must continually expand, generating more production, higher profits, greater efficiency, higher consumption, more technologically developed production tools, etc.[14] It is, of course, a highly exploitative system but nevertheless has produced greater surpluses than any previous economic system.

The basic weakness of dependency theory is its mistaken assumption that capitalism is simply a national and international system of commodity exchange in which profit, i.e. capital, is acquired through trade.[15] Is capitalism simply trade, and can trade create development? The problem of the definition and origin of capitalism is not new. Marx pointedly criticized the classical economists for arguing that market forces and relations were what defined capitalism,[16] and in the 1950s Paul Sweezy and Maurice Dobb debated just this issue on similar grounds. Sweezy argued that the expansion of trade in sixteenth century Western Europe was responsible for the rise of capitalism, while Dobb contended that changes in the relations of production, i.e., the change from feudal coercive labor systems to capitalist free wage labor, explain the origin and growth of capitalism.[17] Dobb here more closely follows Marx who, while taking note of the importance of a rising world market for commodities in that era, defined capitalism as a system of production.[18]

While it is true, as the dependentistas contend, that capitalism has to do with producing for a market and the making of profit, focusing on these factors leaves its material basis hidden. Capitalism is better defined by the relationship between wage labor and capital, which must be produced and reproduced for commodities and capitalist profit to be created. Capitalism, therefore, is a mode of production not a system of trade or market relations.[19] The uniqueness of the capitalist mode of production is in the tensions inherent to the system which compel capitalist enterprises to constantly revolutionize the means of production and, under the threat of extinction, to accumulate or "die."[20]

With regard to Spanish America, Geoffrey Kay, following Marx,[21] has convincingly argued that the nature of trade and investment in Spanish America up to the end of the nineteenth century could not have created capitalist relations of production because of the dominance of merchant's capital. As Kay notes,

. . . historically, merchant's capital has never been able to effect this transition to capitalism proper itself. Its dependence on the non-capitalist class that is directly responsible for the exploitation of labor leads it to support this class at the very moment is is undermining it. This is fully apparent in the effect it has on production . . .

6

merchant capital is trading capital and the surplus it seizes is used to expand trade not the forces of production.[22]

Where merchant's capital hold sway, Marx argues,

This system presents everywhere an obstacle to the real capitalist mode of production and goes under with its development. Without revolutionising the mode of production, it only worsens the conditions of the direct producers, turns them into mere wage workers and proletarians under conditions worse than those under the immediate control of capital, and appropriates their surplus labor on the basis of the old mode of production.[23] (author's emphasis)

Kay's point is echoed and confirmed by Ernesto Laclau who contends that Spanish America was not capitalist in the period under discussion, nor could its participation in capitalist world markets make it so. He argues that although commodities were produced for the world market, they were produced under non-capitalist relations of production--slave labor, share cropping, debt peonage, and virtual serfdom--which could hardly generate the dynamic possibilities of industrial capitalist production. For Laclau, the failure of Spanish America to "develop" was the result of the non-capitalist nature of its economies.[24]

Laclau's position does not, however, dispute the dependentista assertion that an unequal relationship has existed between the Spanish American economies and the advanced industrial economies. But it does dispute the basis of that unequal relationship. As John Weeks has argued, ". . . in many or even most cases where there is a net flow of surplus out of the backward countries into the advanced countries in commodity or money form . . . this is a consequence of backwardness, not its cause."[25] In other words, a surplus was transferred from the underdeveloped countries to the developed countries because their economies were not capitalist, not, as the dependentistas claim, because they were capitalist.

There is no doubt, as Colin Leys has pointed out, that dependency theory is flawed by its genesis as a critique of Western modernization theory. In arguing the opposite of modernization theory, the dependentistas accepted the main explanatory variable of their opponents--international trade.[26] By doing so they have almost ignored the internal factors that structured the Spanish American economies and led to their being intergrated into the nineteenth century world economy as agro/mineral exporters.[27] This deficiency in dependency theory does not mean that we have to return to the static analyses of modernization theory. Rather, what is needed is a dynamic analysis of the internal political and economic processes, and their interactions. These are the forces that shaped the Spanish American economies and their external links. Such an analysis requires a focus on four significant factors: (1) economic class conflict; (2) political conflict and the

7

development of the State; (3) the State and economic development; and (4) the role of the world economy in economic development. Below I will discuss the theoretical basis for this focus and outline its application to an analysis of nineteenth century Spanish American underdevelopment and dependency.

ECONOMIC CLASS CONFLICT

The Marxist theory of class conflict offers an explanation of major historical changes based on an analysis of the antagonisms between and within classes in any class divided socio-economic formation. In other words, it is an explanation based on factors internal to that society. For Marx, classes are determined principally by the position of individuals in the production process. As Poulantzas notes, "The economic place of the social agents has a principal role in determining social classes."[28] Relations between classes are inherently conflictual because of their exploitative character as the class of owners extract the economic surplus produced by the workers. Relatons within classes may also be conflictual as, for example, capitalists compete with one another for markets, labor, and financial resources;[29] or fuedal lords compete with one another for land and serfs;[30] or proletarians compete with one another in the labor market.[31] For Marx, these structural antagonisms, internal to any society divided by classes, create tensions in the economic, and ultmately the political level of society. These tension, then, produce change or maintain stability.

To understand either these changes in or the stability of a given mode of production one must analyze class conflicts in their historical setting. Robet Brenner, for example, follows Marx in explaining the decline of feudalism and the rise of capitalism in Western Europe by focusing on the changes in the relations of production as a result of class conflict between lord and serf. For Brenner,

> . . . the origins of capitalist economic development as it first occurred in England, are to be found in the specific historical process by which, on the one hand, serfdom was dissolved (thus precluding forceful squeezing as the normal form of surplus extraction) and, on the other hand, peasant property was short circuited or undermined (thus opening the way for the accumulation of land, labor and means of production).[32]

These two conditions were met, on the one hand, by peasant resistance to increased appropriation of their surplus by the lord, and on the other hand, by the success of the lords and/or rising capitalist farmers in defeating the peasants' attempt to appropriate the land for themselves. The result was, on the one side, the free laborer, and on the other, the capitalist farmer, who by innovation in production could dramatically increase his surplus through the use of free wage labor.[33] Elsewhere, the

8

results of similar class conflicts may be different. In France, for example, the peasantry won control of the land, impeding the development of a modern capitalist agriculture.[34]

Economic class conflicts in nineteenth century Spanish America have largely been ignored by observers of that period because they rarely broke out into open, and thus observable, violence. That these class conflicts did in fact exist, however, can be inferred from the structural position of individuals in the production process.[35]

The overall structure of early nineteenth century Spanish American economies was largely determined by the needs of the Spanish State. In the preceding colonial period, the economy was geared to provide the Spanish State with revenue from the silver mines to enable it to continue its territorial wars in Europe. Economic activities other than mining were largely ancillaries to the mines--trading, agriculture, stock raising, crafts--or necessary for the support of outlying defense posts, as in the River Plate area. The distribution of land, labor, and trading rights was firmly in the hands of the colonial bureaucracy, which tended to regulate this distribution in the interest of the crown.[36] Conflict within the elite over the distribution of these resources was displaced to the colonial bureaucracy which could effect a change in their allocation. Creoles, Spaniards and even Indians were more than willing to bribe, patronize, or in any other way influence bureaucratic officials to make distributions in their favor. Corruption thus became institutionalized within colonial society, from the local corregidor to the viceroy, both as a means of affecting the distribution of scarce economic factors and as a way for local crown representatives to augment their meager pay.[37]

Relations between creoles and their laborers (Indians, mestizos, and slaves) were generally exploitative but also were severely restricted by the policies of the crown. Royal bureaucrats regulated the supply and the use of much of the available labor. This policy was directly related to the crown's interest in preserving the Indian labor force for work in the mines and needed support activities. The Spanish State further restricted creoles by making the lucrative trade between the colonies and Spain an official preserve of peninsular Spaniards, leaving creoles only the intra-colonial and contraband trades, both largely illegal.

The Bourbon dynasty, which replaced the Hapsburgs in 1700, gradually changed Spanish State policy towards the colonies in the latter half of the eighteenth century. The new policies, while promoting a more general economic growth throughout the colonies, increased tensions and conflict between creoles and the bureaucracy, peninsulares, other creoles, and their laborers. The Bourbons, attempting to restructure the depressed Spanish economy along the lines of France, sought to intergrate the Spanish American colonies into Spain's economy as mercantile capitalist colonies.[38] This policy of freer trade attempted to produce a colonial trade advantageous to the development of industry in Spain. Rather than remaining content to receive

9

declining revenues from the depleted silver mines, the Bourbon administration sought to increase crown revenues by taxing agricultural production and trade for export.[39] Some hard-pressed creoles intensified the exploitation of their laborers, legally or illegally,[40] fueling rural and urban revolts from below (the two most celebrated were the rural revolt in Peru under Tupac Amaru II in 1780,[41] and the urban revolt of the Communeros in Colombia in 1781).[42] Others, particularly those involved in trade, profited by the elimination of impediments to their participation in trade with Spain while Spanish and some creole merchants and bureaucrats suffered the loss of their monopoly.[43]

The Wars of Independence ended mediation of the Spanish State in the conflicts between creoles and peninsulares, creoles and creoles, and creoles and their laborers. These groups now directly confronted one another as each sought its own advantage. Many peninsular Spaniards gathered up what wealth they could and left for Spain, creating a severe capital shortage and disorganization of credit in the new nations. Creoles, standing now in direct competition with one another over the distribution of land, labor, and trade began creating petty alliances, generally based on kin relations, which later formed a basis for caudillism.[44] The most serious economic conflict arose over the distribution and control of labor because labor, systems (relations of production) differed amongst agricultural landowners, stock raising landowners, miners, and urban employers.[45] Where those who relied on coercive methods of labor recruitment prevailed, those who depended on the sale of labor power in a free market suffered.

The Wars of Independence severely damaged the caste system that prevented the social rise of the mestizos during the colonial era. The wars armed the mestizos and released them from subservience to the creoles. They entered the scramble for control over land and labor either under their military mestizo leaders or in the retinue of competing creole landowners. Though mestizos provided the manpower for intra-creole warfare, they also represented a potential threat from below. Thus, creole landowners sometimes allied with and sometimes opposed this force.[46]

The Wars of Independence also seriously disruped landowner control over the Indian masses and Black slaves who constituted the bulk of the labor force in Spanish America. Much of the administration and distribution of labor had been performed by the Spanish colonial bureaucracy. When this bureaucracy became defunct or was in disarray because of the wars, the labor force disappeared from the commercial mining and agricultural regions. The disruption of trade and transport and the difficulty of acquiring funds and tools led many agricultural regions to fall back into subsistence production, usually to the advantage of the Indian laborers.[47] During the colonial era, the Spanish administration protected creole landowners from the rise of a competing Indian landowning elite by redistributing Indian lands to displaced Indians. This policy also benefited the crown by

10

creating new Indian villages which increased the tribute rolls, and thus crown revenue. With the abandonment of this policy by liberal governments in the nineteenth century, hacendados tried to grab as much land as they could to prevent the rise of such an Indian elite.[48] Also in this period the curacas, the local Indian elite who recruited Indian labor for the haciendas, virtually disappeared. The encroachment of Indian subsistence agriculture on hacienda lands gave the Indians possession of much of the land. It is for this reason that the history of the hacienda, from this period until the early twentieth century, is a history of the hacendados' struggle to reappropriate this land and of the Indians' resistance.[49] The intense competition between landlords for labor and the opportunity for workers to escape to alternative labor systems (wage labor, sharecropping, urban employment) put the landlords in a precarious position.

Thus, in the aftermath of the Wars of Independence, serious economic conflicts existed among sectors of the dominant owning classes and between the dominant owning classes and their subordinate laboring classes. Though these conflicts formed the material basis for Spanish America's turn towards agro/mineral export economic growth, and will be analyzed in their national settings later in this study, they do not explain that development.

POLITICAL CONFLICT AND THE STATE

Focusing on economic class conflict as an explanation for the "development of underdevelopment" is clearly inadequate in itself. To attempt to explain so complex a phenomenon in this way would simply substitute one form of economic determinism (that of the social relations of production) for another (the capitalist world economy of the dependency model). Economic conflicts between and within classes are but one factor, albeit an important one, in analyzing the development of any society. They are not immediately translated in their economic form to other important arenas of conflict and struggle.

In most cases, although classes may be defined at the economic level--social relations of production--the focal point of intra-class conflict will be the State. Political conflicts in general are directed at the State because of the central position of the political system in not only legitimating, but also maintaining or transforming social, economic, and political relationships between classes, regions, and cultures within a nation.[50] Through law, administration, and coercion, the political system performs a "regulatory" role which can either preserve or substantially transform these relationships.[51] For Marx, this is why State power is the object of all revolutions.

The most common error in attempting to relate political conflicts to economic class conflicts is dissolving the former into the latter. Marxist studies have been notorious for reducing the State and political conflicts to mere epiphenomena of the economy. Thus, in explaining a political conflict or

11

issue one is required to always refer directly back to the economic conflict or issue "behind it."[52] Structuralist political scientists tend to dissolve the State and politics in a similar manner, though in their case, into the whole of society's conflicts. As Roy Macridis and Bernard Brown critically observe,

. . . the government is at its best a filter mechanism through which interests express themselves and at its worst a simple transmission mechanism. The role of the State is reduced to the narrow confines of an organization that channels, reflects and expresses commands and instructions that come from "elsewhere."[53]

Both approaches therefore reject the specificity of the State and politics which remain superfluous to what are essentially economic or societal conflicts.

To reduce the State and politics to economics or sociology is to entirely miss the point that while economic and social relations condition and set limits to political conflicts, they do not always determine them. This is because the role of the State in reproducing or transforming these relations is specifically political.[54] Once economic antagonisms, both between and within classes, are translated into the political level of the State they become "political" issues and are expressed and defined by the individuals involved as political issues. Although the basis for these issues and the parameters within which they will be fought out are ultimately set by the economic level--the social relations of production--they in themselves have a "relative autonomy" and may develop on other than an economic basis. As Stuart Hall suggests,

The level of the political class struggle, then, has its own efficacy, its own forms, its specific conditions of existence, its own momentum, tempo and direction, its own contradictions internal to it, its "peculiar" outcomes and results.[55]

To a greater or lesser extent, the State provides the political requisites or preconditions for the reproduction or transformation of economic relations. For example, under feudalism the political Estates system provided the basis for the lord-serf relationship, and under capitalism, the legal-political definition (and the State's protection) of private property rights and the wage labor contract provide the preconditions for the capital-wage labor relationship. Thus, the struggle against feudalism and capitalism are always essentially political struggles, the one against the Estates system, the other against absolute private property rights.

Political struggles then seek to influence the State's role in reproducing or transforming social, economic, and political relations by affecting the very organization of the State, its constitution, and the balance of class forces which form its supports. Political struggles even question the definition of the public and private spheres. How these spheres are defined (as a result of political conflict) and what legal-political relations result will determine whether the State reproduces or transforms existing economic and social relations.

Although the dependentistas may interpret nineteenth century Spanish American history solely in terms of its integration into the international economy, for Spanish Americans the most prominent feature of that era was intense political conflict. In Spanish America during the colonial era, economic and political power were fused not in a decentralized nobility as with feudalism, but in the bureaucratic apparatus. Royal officials controlled the distribution of land and labor, while legal corporate entities controlled trade. The Bourbon reforms of the late eighteenth century were, in large part, an attempt to change this system by reducing direct political control of the economic sphere.[56] The political conflicts within the new Spanish American nations in the nineteenth century were fought, to a great degree, over the continuation of this process. Whether one's position in society was to be defined politically as in a caste or Estates system, or economically, as in a class system, was a major facet of the conflicts. There were miners, merchants, landowners, bureaucrats (particularly lawyers), artisans, and clerics whose position in society required a political definition. Other merchants, miners, landowners, bureaucrats, artisans, and clerics, those whose political status prevented them from rising in the social structure, found that a change to a class definition could greatly improve their position.[57]

This transformation had economic effects but was, in the last instance, the result of political conflict. The object of the conflict was the State and its role. Here I will only briefly outline the four major political conflicts in nineteenth century Spanish America that will be examined later in their national context; (A) the conflict between liberals and conservatives; (B) the conflict between church and State; (C) the conflict between centralism and federalism (regionalism); and (D) the issue of caudillism.

(A) <u>Liberals vs Conservatives</u>: The major conflict in nineteenth century Spanish America is generally regarded as the struggle between liberals and conservatives.[58] This conflict is seen as either the result of the clash between the ideas of the Enlightenment and Spanish scholasticism[59] or, as in most recent accounts, over strictly economic issues. In the latter view, conservatives are represented as the old colonial landowners who struggled against the commercialization and open politics of liberal merchants, intellectuals, and bureaucrats.[60] This view has rightly been challenged because no clear polarization of political forces based on occupation can be established.[61] According to Frank Safford, included within conservative ranks were merchants, intellectuals, and bureaucrats as well as landowners. Liberal ranks similarly included individuals representing all of these groups.[62]

It would perhaps be better to approach the conflicts between liberals and conservatives from their respective positions on the role of the State in regulating class conflict and maintaining the position of the elite vis-à-vis the lower classes.[63] From this view, conservatives generally favored the direct intervention of the State in inter class relations through State regulation of the lower classes by the legal system and the police. Liberals, on the other hand, generally favored the indirect intervention of the State, preferring to have the State legalize their own regulation of the relations between themselves and their working classes--with the State acting in a "nightwatchman" capacity.[64]

Though these positions were generally held, their complexity in actual political practice cannot be minimized. For example, between 1851 and 1854, Colombian Liberals courted and received a great deal of support from artisans who were still organized in closed corporate guilds. The Liberal alliance with this "feudal caste" did not belie their opposition to a monopolistic-corporatist society, rather it was necessitated by their electoral competition with rural Conservatives who controlled a superior voting force of dependent peasants. Thus, as Urrutia argues,

> In theory, the Liberals were being inconsistent when they defended the colonial form of economic organization in Cauca, but in practice they were consistent since they only wanted to destroy the colonial institutions that created a barrier to bourgeois accumulation of wealth.[65]

But, when the democratization fostered by the Liberal regime became an obvious threat to all the owning classes, a large fraction of the Liberals left the Liberal government and joined with the Conservative opposition. This alliance of a fraction of the Liberals, known as golgotas, and Conservatives made use of the universal suffrage enacted by the Liberals to mobilize the peasantry in a conservative reaction. This alliance gained State power and consequently crushed the democratic artisan movement and its Liberal supporters.[66]

(B) Church vs State: The issue of secularization formed a three way political conflict. During the colonial era the church acted as a political arm of the Spanish State, keeping creoles in line through the Inquisition and restricting their use of Indian labor.[67] With the coming of independence, the church was freed from the patronato of the Spanish crown (the Pope had ceded control over the Spanish colonial church to the crown in sixteenth century) but became the object of intense political struggle. A struggle over whether or not the church would function in its traditional political role.

Conservatives generally favored the reintegration of the church into the State apparatus as a social control mechanism and ideological prop. Thus, they favored retention of church control over education and the exclusivity of the Roman Catholic Church

14

in the nation. Liberals generally wanted to reduce the church to political impotence, favoring secular mechanisms of social control and ideology which they could control directly or through the State. These positions were not, of course, hard and fast. Many times conservatives would favor an independent church to protect it from the liberals when they were in power. Within the church itself, some members of the clergy wished to continue the colonial church-State relationship, albeit with the church having greater control over its own internal organization, and some felt that internal autonomy could only be achieved through some kind of church-State separation.[68]

Attacks against the church usually took the form of the appropriation of church lands, and the abolition of its corporate privileges and role in the control over and protection of the Indian. Although these attacks have been interpreted as having been motivated by economic gain,[69] their essential aim was political. As J. Lloyd Mecham argues,

> The basis of this early opposition to the Roman Catholic organization--not the Roman Catholic religion--was largely political. The abolition of tithes, suppression of religious orders, confiscation of ecclesiastical property, and like measures, were as a rule, acts of vengeance wreaked upon the clergy by their political opponents. . . . if they regarded clerical wealth as an evil, it was because this wealth made the church powerful politically.[70]

Thus, the weakening of the church's political power had the aim of weakening a major prop of the conservative vision of society.[71]

(C) Centralism vs Federalism: The conflict between centralists and federalists causes great consternation for those who opt for an economic or ideological analysis. Though liberals generally favored political decentralization and conservatives favored political centralization, these were political rather than economic or ideological positions. The shift of some liberals to centralism and some conservatives to federalism (most notably in Argentina and Colombia)[72] should be related to their political aims rather than their economic opportunism or ideological confusion.

The initial attack of the liberals against centralism derived from their desire to reduce the State's regulation of social and economic life. Their triumph was usually short lived because it created the basis of conservative resistance in the form of semi-sovereign regional or provincial governments. With conservatives in control, these governments acted as centralized States within their own borders. Liberals switched over to centralism in order to reverse this trend. The reduction of direct State intervention through the setting up of federal type administrations did not, therefore, guarantee that the centralized State form would not reappear in regional governments.[73]

15

(D) The Rise of the Caudillo: In nineteenth century Spanish America, the emergence of the caudillo, a local political boss at the head of an armed retinue of men, was the result of three separate but related political problems. (1) The arming of mestizos during the Wars of Independence created a general breakdown of the caste system which had been slowly dying out in the crisis-ridden late colonial era.[74] A few mestizos actually rose to great social and political heights as a result of their participation in the armies of independence. After the wars were over, there were great difficulties in paying for war-service and in reintegrating the soldiers into the productive system. The problem of demobilizing this mass of armed and war experienced men in an era of contracting economic resources plagued those areas which had provided the bulk of armed forces for the wars (Argentina, Gran Colombia, and later Peru).[75] (2) Local conflicts between landowners, merchants and mine owners gave the caudillo led bands lucrative employment and a means of rising in the social system by confiscating the opposition's property.[76] (3) The lack of owning class political hegemony allowed the caudillo to use his control over the masses to insert himself into elite conflicts. Caudillos served in the employ of liberals and conservatives, frequently gaining control of the State, plundering the treasuries, confiscating the property of some rich creoles, but rarely solving the political crisis. Caudillism of this type receded and became the subject of derision once the class hegemony of the elites was cemented in the late nineteenth century.

THE STATE AND ECONOMIC DEVELOPMENT

It is clear from the preceding discussion that the major conflicts in Spanish America during the nineteenth century were essentially political and focused on the problem of State building. Yet, even though political conflicts in general are directed at the State, the State is rarely the tool of any class or class fraction. The State has a "relative autonomy" from warring classes and derives from this an independent economic role and economic effect.[77]

As Marx and Engels recognized, the State arises with the development of class society.[78] The irreconcilable conflict between producer and non-producer requires an agency which is above the struggle and can manage it in the interest of the ruling sector of that society. The State is thus always a class State which, while tending to the interest of the dominant class, is not always slavish in its service.[79] The State receives its role from its structural position in society, rather than from the social class position of those who occupy its apparatuses.[80] A given set of conflictual relationships must be managed, and civil order or peace maintained,[81] but how those who occupy the apparatuses of the State will achieve these goals depends on the given historical setting.[82]

16

In assuming the role of wielding public power in a class divided society, the State normally achieves a "relative autonomy" not only from the dominated classes but from the dominant classes as well.[83] This autonomy may approach absolute autonomy as with the absolutist State in Western Europe during the seventeenth and eighteenth centuries, the State under the two Bonapartes in France, and the Bismarkian State in Germany.[84] Relative state autonomy occurs in both normal and exceptional or crisis periods. For Marx, greater state autonomy occurs when the formation of a dominant ruling class is impossible or is impeded by disunity and conflict within the dominant class. Concretely, this happens when classes representing more than one mode of production create a rough oppositional balance in a society.[85] The failure of any class to impose its vision of society on the State leads to the greater independence of the State vis-à-vis these classes. Thus, both Marx and Engels described absolutism in the West as the result of a balance between the feudal aristocracy and the rising bourgeoisie.[86] Though the absolutist State was the class State of the aristocracy, it could not and did not base its power on the aristocracy.[87] Greater State autonomy also comes about when a heterogeneous ruling class cannot raise itself to the level of hegemonic political power. Here the hegemonic crisis results from the structurally determined conflicts between members of the same class. For example, Marx believed that because the bourgeoisie was so split by internal conflicts, it could not rule without the State organizing its hegemony.[88] Thus, he explained the State of Louis Bonaparte as arising from the inability of any sector of the French bourgeoisie to provide hegemonic leadership for their class rule. Louis Bonaparte could step in as the representative of the peasantry, which was not a party to the conflict, circumvent the conflict- ridden bourgeoisie, and impose political stability, which was ultimately in the interest of the bourgeoisie.[89] Thus, while the State may be "for" the ruling class, it may not be "of" the ruling class.

Thus, in performing its major tasks--creating internal order and competing with other States internationally--the State maintains a relative autonomy from dominated and dominant classes. As Theda Skocpol argues, "Indeed, attempts of state rulers merely to perform the state's "own" functions may create conflicts of interest with the dominant class."[90] Further, while not directly economic themselves, these State functions form the basis of the State's crucial economic role.

The State's economic role is an effect of, and secondary to, its purely political role. This can best be illustrated by the role of the absolutist State in the development of capitalism in Western Europe. While in some cases its policies stimulated trade, manufacturing, and the acquisition of colonies, its objective was primarily the enhancement of State power vis-à-vis the internal classes and other competing States.[91] In the era of the rise of the absolutist States, the conflicts at the dynastic level were, for the most part, still feudal. In effect,

17

conflicts were territorial, attempts to increase the amount of land and the number of people under a State's jurisdiction in a world where these resources were the most important. Intra-class conflicts within the aristocracy over the control of land and people in many cases led to inter-class warfare between the aristocracy and the peasantry who rose in rebellion against the rising exploitation of a ruling class at war.[92] This general turmoil had the effect of freeing the monarchies from their subservience to the nobility. The monarchies used this "relative autonomy" to build strong absolutist States, raising intra-class conflicts from regional to international conflicts, and clamping down hard on the peasantry.

While the State was managed in the interest of the nobility, its policies in doing so were often a boon to the bourgeoisie. Where territorial conquest failed as a policy for increasing the internal and external power of the absolutist State, absolutist monarchies attempted to appropriate the "finite" resources of their enemies through trade and manufacture.[93] Thus, though the aim of the absolutist monarchies was political--to reduce intra and inter class conflict under the aegis of a strong central State--the effects of this policy, in some cases, was to move their economies along the road to capitalist development.[94] That the same political goal could have just the opposite economic effect is apparent in the case of Spain. Successful in its territorial conquests which were fueled by the great specie wealth of its American colonies, the absolutist State there had no need to stimulate home production and trade. Spain's bourgeoisie and economy withered away under the Hapsburgs while the class position of the aristocracy remained secure.[95]

State policies encouraging trade and, more importantly, manufacturing in the interest of State power, some analysts argue, has not been atypical in the development of capitalism worldwide. The bourgeoisie itself, it seems, has not created capitalist economies without State aid or interest. John Merrington, for example, notes the reluctance of the commercial bourgeoisie in seventeenth century Europe to invest in industry, opting rather for "usurious forms of rent and tax farming" which simply reinforced feudal forms of production, although on a commercial basis.[96] Frances Moulder agrees and adds that,

. . . the commercial bourgeoisie has repeatedly shown itself reluctant to invest in modern industry without government prodding and encouragment. In Japan after the Restoration, there was little interest by bourgeois investors in investing in large scale modern industry. Industrial investment was forthcoming only after vigorous state effort to prove its potential profitability and to eliminate risk. It appears that Japan's bourgeoisie would have remined commercially oriented in the absence of government interest and would have doomed the nation to industrial backwardness.[97]

while Stuart Bruchey claims that in the case of the United States,

. . . if growth depended on industrialization, the latter
depended on the national market, and a national market upon
large capital sums for improved transportation. If these are
valid assessments, I cannot see how a place of central
importance in American economic growth can be denied the role
of government, because of its contribution to the formation
of a national market . . . This is one reason I have
emphasized the "American Revolution" which permitted the
development of an independent state that could further
national capitalist development.[98]

A similar dynamic of class conflict and relative State
autonomy, I will argue, created the export economies of late
nineteenth century Spanish America. How this occurred in
specific Spanish American countries will be the subject of a
later section, but the general outline of the analysis can be
presented here.

The failure to resolve fundamental political conflicts in
Spanish America in the aftermath of the Wars of Independence was
the failure of the political process and the State to fashion a
common State principle out of the various political positions
held by sectors of the dominant classes. The initial base of
most of the new Spanish American States was external, as
recognition of the State by other States in the international
community generally "preceded the institutionalization of a State
power acknowledged within the national territory itself."[99]
Two notable exceptions, of course, were Chile and Paraguay. In
Chile, Portales unified the dominant classes in the late 1820s
and so provided Chile with early political and social
stability.[100] In Paraguay, the absence of a strong landowning
and/or merchant class gave Dr. Francia free reign to create a
stable, though isolated, autarkic regime.[101] Both though,
rejoined the general flow of Spanish American history by polar
opposite paths, Chile through victory in war, Paraguay through
defeat.

Elsewhere throughout Spanish America, a succession of
liberal, conservative, and caudillo regimes failed to create
civil order among the dominant classes. Shortly after each
faction had captured power, difficulties arose as its vision of
social organization, its social and economic policies, and its
position on the role of the State were found by the opposition to
be untenable. The problem for each faction that took power was
how to reconcile the interests for whom they had taken power with
the structural position of the State. Effective functioning of
the State called for unity among the various fractions of the
dominant class. Yet with each fraction considering its
differences with the others irreconcilable, the State became the
focus of disunity, not class unity and rule. If the State was to
guarantee the interest of any fraction of the dominant classes it
had to be considered legitimate by all, or a large number of
those fractions. Armed force was rarely an effective alternative
to agreement. Assurance had to be made to the opposition that it
would not be eradicated, that the State would guarantee its

19

social and economic position too.

The early Independence governments found agreement among the owning classes only at the most general level. Each fraction sought the protection, if not the enhancement of its position. Those who, like miners and plantation owners, relied on coerced or slave labor sought a strong highly centralized State. Those who relied on less troublesome methods of labor control and recruitment, favored a less powerful, less expensive, less centralized State.[102] Since control over taxable wealth and people (Indian tribute was collected by the landowner) was the club with which some sectors of the dominant classes attempted to bludgeon their governments, many governments tried to free themselves of their influence by borrowing abroad.[103] Thus, in the period immediately after the Wars of Independence, many Spanish American governments became deeply indebted to foreign (mainly English) creditors, adding international pressures to their already considerable internal pressures.[104] In Peru, the State's control of the guano mines substantially freed it from landowner pressure and allowed it to build up an independent (though contentious) political support among guano merchants and coastal landowners. Revenues from guano even allowed the State to declare an end to Indian tribute, substantially weakening the national political power of the recalcitrant sierra landowners.[105]

Borrowing abroad and government production monopolies were, in the long run, relatively poor solutions. Borrowing brought only debt which led back to the problem of internal taxation, while a government production monopoly, as in Peru, created its own problems.[106] Thus, throughout most of Spanish America between 1825 and 1890, civil war, authoritarian caudillo government, regional secession, and political instability were the rule rather than the exception. General anarchy and instability prevailed until a solution could be found to intra-class conflict within the dominant classes.

Such a solution was arrived at (as it was the path of least resistance) in the active encouragement of export production by Spanish America States. Rather than attempting to create a unity based upon the economic intergration of the dominant classes which would exacerbate an already violent confrontation, the policy of export expansion tended to insure their social and economic isolation at the level of production. Linking each growth sector of the economy to an external market led to reduced tensions between dominant classes and created a basis for their unity and political hegemony. Even a few industrialists could be integrated into the new order if, as in Argentina, their markets were protected by the relatively high transport cost for imported lower class consumption goods, and their import of manufacturing machinery was assisted by low import tariffs.[107] The State itself did not have to upset dominant class relations over the issue of internal taxation as it derived the bulk of its revenues from its control over the customs house.[108]

Thus, the export expansion of late nineteenth century Spanish American nations emerged as a political solution to the problem of dominant class cohesion. Its effect--creating what later have been characterized as underdeveloped or dependent economies-- though recognized by some in Spanish America in the 1880-1930 period, was generally ignored until the collapse of foreign markets in the 1930s also brought about the collapse of oligarchic unity.

SPANISH AMERICA AND THE WORLD ECONOMY

In rejecting the dependency theory focus on the inter-national economy as the main explanatory variable I am not discounting the effects of the world economy on Spanish American development in the nineteenth century. There is broad agreement in the literature on Spanish American development that the export economies would not have emerged without the creation of world market demand for their agro/mineral products.[109] Some writers even go as far as explaining the movement for independence as having been chiefly motivated by the desire to form export links with the dynamic center of world trade in that period, England.[110] Nevertheless, while I agree that it is indisputable that by the end of the nineteenth century the Spanish American economies had been firmly integrated into the world economy as raw agro/mineral porducers and manufactured goods consumers, the evidence does not support the view that the world economy was the cause.

That the Spanish American countries would orient their economies exclusively toward agro/mineral export growth was not a forgone conclusion in the immediate aftermath of the independence struggles. Upon independence, most Spanish American governments attempted to follow a path of balanced economic development. It was accepted that agriculture and mining were the most important economic activities (as they were in most of the world in the early nineteenth century, even in the industrializing European nations), and that export trade was desirable. However, the establishment of modern industry was also seen as an important, if not crucial, goal. Manuel Camilo Vial, Minister of Finance in the Bulnes administration in Chile (1841-1851), expressed what many in Spanish American governments believed,

I am far from believing . . . that in order to be rich a people must produce everything; but I am persuaded that to be prosperous, free and civilized, it has to possess an extensive industry and, if possible, a varied one. What have been the purely agricultural peoples, and in the present time, what are they? There is no nation in which agriculture dominates everything, and in which slavery or feudalism shows its odious face, which does not follow the march of humanity among the stragglers. In Europe, for example, what figure does Poland or Ireland cut? . . . That future threatens us also, if we do not promote industry with a firm had and constant will.[111]

21

In this period, therefore, most Spanish American States actively aided the establishment of manufacturing. In Colombia, tariff protection of artisan production, State loans to manufacturing enterprises, and limited industrial monopolies only ended in the 1850s.[112] In Mexico, a national credit and loan bank, established in 1830, financed the development of a modern textile industry whose production soon outdistanced internal demand. The development bank subsequently financed woolen mills, carpet factories, and iron and paper manufacture.[113]

By 1860, most Spanish American States had abandoned, or were quickly abandoning, the goal of industrial development. Rather than attempting to foster the growth of agro/mineral export development and industrialization, the States shifted to the encouragement of agro/mineral export production exclusively. Protective tariffs were, for the most part, dismantled, colonization schemes aimed at creating a sector of small capitalist farmers/consumers were abandoned, capital from State revenues or foreign loans made available only to activities which expanded export production, and labor supplies were directed by the State to the export sectors.[114] Thus, in the second half of the nineteenth century, the Spanish American economies grew but did not "develop."

The shift in State policy toward active encouragement of export production through trade liberalization, monetary policy, infrastructure investment, and land and labor policies can only be explained through an examination of the internal Spanish American political scene in the nineteenth century. In the following pages, such an examination will be made in an effort to bring to light the internal determinants of nineteenth century Spanish American underdevelopment and dependency.

NOTES

[1]See for example the collection of essays in Ronald Chilcote and Joel Edelstein, eds., Latin America: The Struggle with Dependency and Beyond (New York: Wiley, 1974). Also see Andre Gunder Frank, Capitalism and Underdevelopment in Latin America (New York: Monthly Review Press, 1967): and Andre Gunder Frank, Dependent Accumulation and Underdevelopment (New York: Monthly Review Press, 1979), 164-171.

[2]Ibid.

[3]Ibid.

[4]For the United States see Stuart Bruchey, The Roots of American Economic Growth (New York: Harper, 1965). For Japan see Frances V. Moulder, Japan, China and the Modern World Economy (London: Cambridge University Press, 1977).

⁵The dependency approach has generated a large number of theoretical and empirical studies on Latin America as well as Africa and the Caribbean. For the uninitiated there are several good reviews of dependency theory literature, see Philip O'Brien, "A Critique of Latin American Theories of Dependency," pp. 7-27, and David Booth, "Andre Gunder Frank: An Introduction and Appreciation," pp. 50-85 in Beyond the Sociology of Development, Ivar Oxaal, Tony Barnett and David Booth, eds. (London: Routledge and Kegan Paul, 1975); and J. Samuel Valenzuela and Arturo Valenzuela, "Modernization and Dependency," Comparative Politics X, Number 4 (July 1978), 535-557. Perhaps the best critique from the left is in John G. Taylor, From Modernisation to Modes of Production (London: Macmillan Press, 1979), 71-98. Non-Marxist critiques of dependency theory have centered around the testing and empirical validity of the theory; see Richard Fagen, "Studying Latin American Politics: Some Implications of a "Dependencia" Approach," Latin American Research Review XII, Number 2 (1977), 3-26; and David Ray, "The Dependency Model of Latin American Underdevelopment: Three Basic Fallacies," Journal of Inter-American Studies XV, Number 1 (February 1973), 4-20.

⁶See Frank, Capitalism and Underdevelopment.

⁷See Fernando Henrique Cardoso and Enzo Faletto, Dependency and Development in Latin America (Berkeley: University of California Press, 1979).

⁸Peter H. Smith, "Political History in the 1980s: A View From Latin America," Journal of Interdisciplinary History XII, Number 1 (Summer 1981), 13 & 18.

⁹Modernization theory has been the dominant approach among "establishment" social scientists. Major works include, Talcott Parsons, The System of Modern Societies (Englewood Cliffs, Prentice Hall. 1971); S. N. Eisenstadt, Tradition, Change and Modernity (Englewood Cliffs: Prentice Hall, 1969); B. F. Hoselitz, Sociological Factors in Economic Growth (Glencoe, Illinois: Free Press, 1966); D. Lerner, The Passing of Traditional Society (Glencoe, Illinois: Free Press, 1958); and C. E. Black, The Dynamics of Modernization (New York: Harper, 1966). On attitudinal change as the key to modernization see David McClelland, The Achieving Society (New York: Van Nostrand, 1961). On the economic aspects of modernization see Arthur Lewis, The Theory of Economic Growth (London: Allen and Unwin, 1955) For the political aspects see W. W. Rostow, Politics and the Stages of Growth (London: Cambridge University Press, 1971); and David Apter, The Politics of Modernization (Chicago: University of Chicago Press, 1965).

¹⁰See Jacques Lambert, Latin America: Social Structures and Political Institutions (Berkeley: University of California Press, 1967); Frank Jay Moreno, Legitimacy and Stability in Latin America: A Study in Chilean Political Culture (New York: New York University Press, 1969); Gino Germini, "Stages of Modernization

in Latin America," in Latin America: The Dynamics of Social Change, eds. Stefan A. Halper and John R. Sterling (New York: St. Martin's Press, 1972), 1-43; and W. W. Rostow, The Stages of Economic Growth (London: Cambridge University Press, 1960).

[11]Frank, Capitalism and Underdevelopment, 3-20, 221-227; and Andre Gunder Frank, Lumpenbourgeoisie: Lumpendevelopment (New York: Monthly Review Press, 1972), 3-17.

[12]Frank, Capitalism and Undervelopment, 3-12, 20-28. A major argument in Frank's original formulation was that the main reason for the poverty of Spanish America was its decapitalization by the "metropolitan countries." This thesis will not be discussed here as it raises questions that are not relevant to this study and because Frank has somewhat retreated from this position recently, see Frank, Dependent Accumulation. For critiques of this position see Elizabeth Dore and John Weeks, "Class Alliances and Class Struggles in Peru," Latin American Perspectives IV, Issue 14, Number 3 (Summer 1977), 4-17; and Charles Bettelheim, "Appendix I," in Unequal Exchange, Arghiri Emmanuel (New York: Monthly Review Press, 1972), 271-322.

[13]Quoted in Joseph A. Kahl, Modernization, Exploitation and Dependency in Latin America (New Brunswick: Transaction Books, 1976), 157.

[14]Karl Marx, Capital, 3 vols. (New York: International Publishers, 1967), I:244-245. Also see Martin Murray, "Recent Views on the Transition from Feudalism to Capitalism," Socialist Revolution (Spring 1976), 83.

[15]Immanuel Wallerstein, "The Rise and Future Demise of the World Capitalist System," Comparative Studies in Society and History XVI, Number 4 (September 1974), 399.

[16]Many of Marx's most pointed criticisms of these economists on the issue of trade can be found in Karl Marx, A Contribution to the Critique of Political Economy (Moscow: Progress Publishers, 1970); Karl Marx, The Economic and Philosophic Manuscripts of 1844 (New York: International Publishers, 1964); and Karl Marx, Grundrisse, trans. Martin Nicolaus (Harmondsworth, England: Penguin, 1973).

[17]This debate arose with the publication of Maurice Dobb, Studies in the Development of Capitalism (New York: International Publishers, 1947). The debate was fought out in the pages of Science and Society during the 1950s but the whole debate can be found in Rodney Hilton, ed., The Transition from Feudalism to Capitalism (London: New Left Books, 1976).

[18]Marx, Capital, III:337.

[19]Ibid., 791.

[20]Robert Brenner, "The Origins of Capitalist Development: A Critique of Neo-Smithian Marxism," New Left Review Number 104

24

(July-August 1977), 31-33. Also see Murray, 64-91.

[21]Marx, Capital, III:331-333.

[22]Geoffrey Kay, Development and Underdevelopment: A Marxist Analysis (New York: St. Martin's Press, 1975), 95.

[23]Marx, Capital, III:334-335.

[24]Ernesto Laclau, Politics and Ideology in Marxist Theory (London: New Left Books, 1977), 15-34.

[25]John Weeks, "Backwardness, Foreign Capital and Accumulation in the Manufacturing Sector of Peru: 1954-1975," Latin American Perspectives IV, Issue 14, Number 3 (Summer 1977), 126.

[26]Colin Leys, "Underdevelopment and Dependency: Critical Notes," Journal of Contemporary Asia VII, Number 1 (1977), 94.

[27]Cardoso and Faletto do give class relations and class conflict some attention and argue that they have a "relative autonomy" but they are forced to the same position as Frank when they argue that these class relations and conflicts receive their ultimate determination from the capitalist world economy. See Kahl, 136; Cardoso and Faletto, xvi, 15.

[28]Nicos Poulantzas, Classes in Contemporary Capitalism (London: New Left Books, 1975), 14. The best critique of Marxian class theory is Frank Parkin, Marxism and Class Theory: A Bourgeois Critique (New York: Columbia University Press, 1979).

[29]Karl Marx, "The Poverty of Philosophy," in Karl Marx Selected Writings, ed. David McClellan (London: Oxford University Press, 1977), 210.

[30]Perry Anderson, Lineages of the Absolutist State (London: New Left Books, 1974), 30-31.

[31]Karl Marx and Frederick Engels, "The Communist Manifesto," in Selected Works, 3 vols. (Moscow: Progress Publishers, 1967), I:116.

[32]Brenner, 78.

[33]Ibid.

[34]Ibid.

[35]Stuart Hall, "The 'Political' and the 'Economic' in Marx's Theory of Classes," in Class and Class Structure, ed. Alan Hunt (London: Laurence and Wishart, 1977), 28-36. Also see Nicos Poulantzas, Political Power and Social Classes (London: New Left Books, 1973), 57-73.

[36]Stanley Stein and Barbara Stein, The Colonial Heritage of Latin America (New York: Oxford University Press, 1970), 45-59.

[37]Charles Gibson, Spain in America (New York: Harper, 1966), 107-111, 143-159. Also see William P. Glade, The Latin American Economies (New York: Van Nostrand, 1969), 65-66.

[38]Brian Hamnett, Politics and Trade in Southern Mexico, 1750-1821 (Cambridge: Cambridge University Press, 1971), 28, 40; and John Lynch, The Spanish American Revolutions, 1808-1826 (New York: Norton, 1973), 9-14.

[39]Sergio Villalobos R., "Opposition to Imperial Taxation," in The Origins of the Spanish American Revolutions, 1808-1826, eds. R. A. Humphreys and John Lynch (New York: Knopf, 1965), 124-127; and Oscar Cornblit, "Society and Mass Rebellion in Eighteenth Century Peru and Bolivia," in Latin American Affairs (St. Antony's Papers #22), ed. Raymond Carr (London: Oxford University Press, 1970), 40-41.

[40]Frederick Stirton Weaver, "Political Disintergration and Reconstruction in Nineteenth Century Spanish America: The Class Basis of Political Change," Politics and Society V, Number 2 (1975), 167.

[41]Cornblit, 39-44.

[42]Lynch, 231.

[43]Hamnett, 56-120.

[44]Eric Wolf and Edward Hansen, "Caudillo Politics: A Structural Analysis," Comparative Studies in Society and History Number 9, (1967), 170-171.

[45]Weaver, 172-174.

[46]Wolf and Hansen, 172-173 & 176-177.

[47]Charles Griffin, "Economic and Social Aspects of the Era of Spanish American Independence," Hispanic American Historical Review XXIX, Number 2 (May 1949), 170-187.

[48]Karen Spalding, "Hacienda-Village Relations in Andean Society to 1830," Latin American Perspectives II, Issue 4, Number 1 (Spring 1975), 118-119.

[49]Juan Martínez Alier, "Relations of Production in Andean Haciendas: Peru," in Land and Labour in Latin America, eds. Kenneth Duncan and Ian Routledge (Cambridge: Cambridge University Press, 1977), 141-142.

[50]Nicos Poulantzas, State, Power, Socialism (London: New Left Books, 1978), 26-28; Maurice Godelier, "Infrastructure, Societies and History," New Left Review Number 112 (November-December 1978), 84-96; and Poulantzas, Political Power, 100-101.

[51]Poulantzas, Political Power, 44-50. American political scientists have ascribed a similar "regulatory" role to the State

or political system, see David Apter, "A Comparative Method for the Study of Politics," American Journal of Sociology LXIV, Number 3 (November 1958), 221-237.

[52]For example see T. B. Bottomore, Elites and Society (Harmondsworth, England: Penguin, 1964); and G. William Domhoff, Who Rules America? (Englewood Cliffs, N.J.: Prentice Hall, 1967). For a good summary of this approach and some of its problems from a sympathetic point of view see John Mollenkopf, "Theories of the State and Power Structure Research," Insurgent Sociologist V, Number 3 (Spring 1975), 245-264.

[53]Roy C. Macridis and Bernard E. Brown, eds., Comparative Politics: Notes and Readings, 5th ed., (Homewood, Ill.: Dorsey Press, 1977), 10. Not discussed here, but also important is the "pluralist" notion of the State which sees the State as neutral, open to access by various interest groups which compete for its favors. A good recent discussion of the "pluralist" view in comparison to others can be found in Alfred Stepan, The State and Society (Princeton: Princeton University Press, 1978), 1-17. Examples of its application are David Truman, The Governmental Process (New York: Knopf, 1951); Arthur Bentley, The Process of Government (Chicago: University of Chicago Press, 1908); Robert Dahl, A Preface to Democratic Theory (Chicago: University of Chicago Press, 1956). For an example of its application to Spanish America see José Luis de Imaz, Los Que Mandan (Albany: State University of New York Press, 1970). Two useful critiques of this view are Peter Bachrach and Morton Baratz, "Two Faces of Power," American Political Science Review LVI (December 1972), 947-952; and Peter Bachrach, The Theory of Democratic Elitism (New York: Little, Brown, 1967).

[54]Poulantzas, Political Power. This work is the first contemporary attempt to develop a Marxist political science. Poulantzas here develops the concept of the "specificity of the political." For a close reading of Marx's views on the State and politics see Hal Draper, Karl Marx's Theory of Revolution: State and Bureaucracy (New York: Monthly Review Press, 1977). Also see Göron Therborn, Science, Class and Society (London: New Left Books, 1976), 407; Eric Olin Wright, Class Crisis and the State (London: New Left Books, 1978), 9-29; and Hall, 22-24, 47-50.

[55]Hall, 46. Also see Ian Roxborough, Theories of Underdevelopment (Atlantic Highlands, New Jersey: Humanities Press, 1979), 120.

[56]Lynch, 7-18.

[57]Hamnett, 95-120.

[58]As for example in John Johnson, Political Change in Latin America: The Rise of the Middle Sectors (Stanford: Stanford University Press, 1958), 15-26.

[59]As in the various essays in Arthur P. Whitaker, ed., Latin American and the Enlightenment (Ithica: Cornell University Press, 1961).

[60]Johnson, 15-26.

[61]Frank Safford, "Bases of Political Alignment in Early Republican Spanish America," in New Approaches to Latin American History, eds. Richard Graham and Peter H. Smith (Austin: University of Texas Press, 1974), 80-88.

[62]Ibid., 82.

[63]Hamnett, 154-155.

[64]Weaver, 173-176.

[65]Miguel Urrutia, The Development of the Colombian Labor Movement (New Haven: Yale University Press, 1969), 37.

[66]Ibid., 37-44.

[67]Weaver, 194.

[68]Tulio Halperin-Donghi, The Aftermath of Revolution in Latin America (New York: Harper, 1973), 100-102.

[69]As in Rudolfo Stavenhagen, Social Classes in Agrarian Societies (New York: Doubleday, 1975), 100-101.

[70]J. Lloyd Mecham, Church and State in Latin America (Chapel Hill, North Carolina: University of North Carolina Press, 1934, 1966), 416, 417.

[71]Ibid., 417-418.

[72]Harry Bernstein, Modern and Contemporary Latin America (New York: Russell and Russell, 1965), 202-262, 605-627; and Lynch, 342-343.

[73]As in Argentina. See Bernstein, 202-261.

[74]Wolf and Hansen, 168-169; and Marco C. Vazquez, "Immigration and Mestizaje in Nineteenth Century Peru," in Race and Class in Latin America, ed. Magnus Mörner (New York: Columbia University Press, 1970), 74-77.

[75]Lynch, 344-345.

[76]Wolf and Hansen, 170-171, 172-173, 176.

[77]Roxborough, 120-121.

[78]Frederick Engels, The Origin of the Family, Private Property and the State (New York: International Publishers, 1972), 22-237. One social science most concerned with the State, its origin, and definition, has been anthropology. Where in the last thirty years economics, sociology and political science have

largely ignored the subject, anthropologists have fought a running battle which has, for the most part, divided into two opposing camps - those who support a conflict theory of State origins as with Morton Fried, The Evolution of Political Society (New York: Random House, 1967), and those who support an integration theory of State origins as with Elman R. Service, Origin of the State and Civilization (New York: Norton, 1975). While Fried argues, similarly to Marx and Engels, that stratification, in terms of access to and control of scarce resources, is the essential condition for the emergence of the State, Service emphasizes the cooperative or coordinating and integrative aspects of the State, arguing that once a society has reached a certain level of complexity the State is needed to perform essential services. While anthropologists tend to see these two positions as mutually exclusive, Draper (237-264) has found that Marx and Engels held both positions without being contradictory. Draper argues that they did not see the State as "simply a class plot" but as, at bottom, based on the need to perform indispensable functons for the social whole. At the same time though, that same complexity which makes a State form necessary to serve the "common" needs of society also leads to differentiation and inequality within society and thus the rise of social classes, one of which will constitute itself as the "ruling class." This ruling class, whether exclusively economic or political (or theocratic?), is served by the State in its function as the maintainer of the social order. For an excellent overview of the anthropological debate see Ronald Cohen and Elman R. Service, eds., Origins of the State: The Anthropology of Political Evolution (Philadelphia: Institute for the Study of Human Issues, 1978).

[79]Draper, 237-262.

[80]See recent Marxist studies of the State, Poulantzas, Political Power; Poulantzas, Classes; Poulantzas, State; Hall; Anderson; Godelier; and Wright. Also see Ralph Miliband, The State in Capitalist Society (New York: Basic Books, 1969); and Thomas Bamat, "Relative State Autonomy and Capitalism in Brazil and Peru," Insurgent Sociologist VII, Number 2 (1977), 74-84.

[81]Theda Skocpol, States and Social Revolutions (Cambridge: Cambridge University Press, 1979), 30.

[82]Poulantzas, Political Power, 245-252.

[83]Draper, 237-262.

[84]Ibid., 311-463. Also see, Karl Marx, "The Eighteenth Brumaire of Louis Bonaparte" in Selected Works, 3 vols. Karl Marx and Frederick Engels (Moscow: Progress Publishers, 1969), I:398-487.

[85]A "mode of production" as defined by Laclau, 34-35., is "a totality of interconnecting relationships composed of 1) a

determinate type of ownership of the means of production; 2) a determinate form of appropriation of the economic surplus; 3) a determinate degree of development of the division of labor; 4) a determinate level of development of the productive forces." A society, or social formation, may incorporate numerous modes of production at the same time, one generally dominating the others. Also see Poulantzas, Political Power, 15-16.

[86]Draper, 478-479.

[87]Anderson, 428-430.

[88]Draper, 321-338; Poulantzas, Political Power, 228-252; and Roxborough, 122.

[89]Marx, "Eighteenth Brumaire," 478-479, 484-486; and Draper, 403-409.

[90]Skocpol, 30.

[91]Anderson, 15-42.

[92]Gianfranco Poggi, The Development of the Modern State (Stanford: Stanford University Press, 1978), 30-31; and Draper, 468-469.

[93]Carl Friedrich, The Age of Baroque, 1610-1660 (New York: Harper, 1952), 12-14.

[94]Anderson, 15-42.

[95]Immanuel Wallerstein, The Modern World System, text ed., (New York: Academic Press, 1976), 115-142; Anderson, 60-84; and Karl Marx, Revolution in Spain (New York: International Publisher, 1939), 25-26.

[96]John Merrington, "Town and Country in the Transition to Capitalism," in The Transition from Feudalism to Capitalism, ed. Rodney Hilton (London: New Left Books, 1976), 184. Also see Robert DuPlessis, "From Demesne to World System: A Critical Review of the Literature on the Transition from Feudalism to Capitalism," Radical History Review III, Number 4 (Winter 1977), 12.

[97]Moulder, 21.

[98]Bruchey, 213.

[99]Oscar Oszlak, "The Historical Formation of the State in Latin America," Latin American Research Review XVI, Number 2 (1981), 8.

[100]Bernstein, 478-497.

[101]B. C. MacDermot, "Historical Introduction," The British in Paraguay, 1850-1870, J. Pla (Surrey, England: Richmond Publishing Company, 1976), i-xxv. Also see Ricard Alan White,

Paraguay's Autonomous Revolution, 1810-1840 (Albuquerque: University of New Mexico Press, 1978).

[102]Weaver, 176.

[103]William Lofstrom, "Attempted Economic Reforms and Innovations in Bolivia Under Antonio José de Sucre, 1825-1828," Hispanic American Historical Review L, Number 2 (May 1970), 279-299.

[104]Weaver, 181.

[105]Ronald Berg and Frederick Stirton Weaver, "Toward a Reconstruction of Political Change in Peru during the First Century of Independence," Journal of Inter-American Studies XX, Number 1 (February 1978), 73-74.

[106]Ibid., 75-76. For a discussion of these see Chapters 5 & 6 below.

[107]Frederick Stirton Weaver, "American Underdevelopment: An Interpretive Essay on Historical Change," Latin American Perspectives III, Issue 11, Number 4 (Fall 1976), 41-42.

[108]Griffin, 185.

[109]For example see Glade; Frank, Capitalism and Underdevelopment and Celso Furtado, The Economic Development of Latin America (London: Oxford University Press, 1970).

[110]For example see Cardoso and Faletto, 34.

[111]D. Martner, Historia de Chile (Santiago: 1929), page 198; quoted in Alcira Leiserson, Notes on the Process of Industrialization in Argentina, Chile and Peru (Berkeley: University of California Press, 1966), 21.

[112]Frank Safford, "Foreign and National Enterprise in Nineteenth Century Colombia," Business History Review XXXIX (Winter 1965), 503-526.

[113]Eduardo Galeano, Open Veins of Latin America (New York: Monthly Review Press, 1973), 199.

[114]Glade, 232-241.

2
State and Economy in Colonial Spanish America

If the heritage of Spanish colonialism weighed heavy on the emerging republics of the nineteenth century Spanish America, capitalism was not one of its legacies. A chief error of the dependency theorists has been their assertion that Spanish America has been "capitalist" since the sixteenth century.[1] To argue this is to discount the true imprint of the Spanish colonial enterprise which, as I will show presently, had little to do with the instituting of capitalism in the Americas. Rather, the colonial period laid the foundation for Spanish American underdevelopment by instituting and maintaining distinctly non-capitalist forms of production.

Further, these non-capitalist forms of production, largely maintained and reproduced by the policies and representatives of the Spanish State, created the basis for major constitutional crises throughout Spanish America in the independence period. The struggles that ensued over the role of the State in the societies, economies, and polities of the new Spanish American countries, not the effects of the international economy as the dependentistas claim, were chiefly responsible for the creation of the export economies in the late nineteenth century.

Although it is not within the scope of this study to present a comprehensive reivew of the colonial era, this very brief account is offered with the aim of highlighting two important aspects of colonial society; (1) its non-capitalist origin and nature, and (2) the important role of the State in the regulation and maintenance of its non-capitalist forms of production.

THE COLONIAL ENTERPRISE: CAPITALIST OR NON-CAPITALIST?

If the British Empire can be said to have arisen in a fit of absentmindedness, as much can be said of Spanish colonial expansion in the fifteenth and sixteenth centuries. Spain, emerging from a seven centuries long reconquest of the Iberian Peninsula, and consolidating the first absolutist State in Europe, was an expansionist power in the tradition of the late middle ages.[2] Neither Spain itself, nor the society it ruled over in America were ever capitalist. No doubt, in the case of both, some capitalist elements were present, yet they were hardly dominant and, in the case of Spain in the sixteenth century, were under severe attack.

Capitalism, as discussed earlier, is a system of production in which the free laborer has access to the means of production only through capital.[3] The means of appropriating the surplus of the laborer is purely economic as the laborer is forced to work for the capitalist because he has no other means of providing for his subsistence. The lack of a formally "feudal" system in either sixteenth century Spain or colonial America should not immediately define them as capitalist. Non-capitalist systems do not all conform to the characteristics of European feudalism, although they are certainly closer to that form than the capitalist. Manfred Kossok, for example, claims that Spain and colonial America were of a feudal "type."[4] The existence of commercialization and the absence of formal se for him, does not indicate a transition to capitalist forms of production. Commercialization is rather an indication of the rise of merchant capitalism which, as we have seen, rarely affects the form of production. Similarly, Witold Kula, in his study of Polish feudalism, found that the commercialization of a large part of production in no way destroyed feudalism and, in Eastern Europe, became an integral part of it.[5] As Kossok notes, even the abolition of serfdom only indicates, ". . .not the elimination of feudalism as a system, but only of certain forms of feudal domination."[6] The instituting of extra-economic means of labor exploitation in colonial Spanish America indicates, in his opinion, the absence of capitalist relations of production.[7] Jaime Vicens Vives, in his major study of Spanish economic development, similarly concludes that Spain was not "capitalist," but also argues that it was not formally feudal.[8] The many trappings of Western European feudalism that abounded in Spain during the medieval period were in all likelihood borrowed from the French who, at various points, assisted the Spanish militarily during the reconquest.[9] Rather than feudalism or capitalism, the combination of social and economic elements of Spain's unique medieval history created (except in Catalonia which may be characterized as "feudal") what Vicens Vives calls a "seigniorial" society.[10]

The uniqueness of Spanish seigniorialism derives from the Christian Spaniards' long struggle to reconquer the Iberian peninsula from the Moors. Political power became, from the first, more centralized in the monarchy (although there were several) than under feudalism proper because greater coordination was needed under a constant war footing for the national/religious enterprise.[11] This centralism must, however, be understood as only a "relative" centralism in that the realms of Spain were not unified until the reign of Isabel and Ferdinand.[12] More importantly, this centralism was also conditioned and limited by the decentralized nature of the actual reconquest. Individual knights, groups of knights, untitled persons, religious orders, town militias, and foreign adventurers, receiving authorization from the monarchs, were instrumental in reconquering the peninsula in exchange for certain rights, privileges, grants of land and, most importantly, booty.[13] The monarchs received ultimate sovereignty and ownership of the conquered lands but granted all that had been conquered, less, most times, a quinto (royal fifth) of the booty.[14] As Mario Góngora notes, "The Reconquest led to the formulation of a system of political justice which placed great emphasis on the concepts derived from the royal duty of rewarding and granting favors to men who had distinguished themselves in war."[15] Though these, especially in Castile, became "lords of the land" their jurisdiction over the land and its people was "a jurisdiction limited by the power of the monarchy."[16]

Although the conditions of labor during the reconquest were fluid because Castile was underpopulated and needed to re-populate newly captured lands, by the period of the conquest of America Spain was still a predominantly agrarian nation with more than 80% of its population peasants working under servile conditions of labor on land owned largerly by the aristocracy and church.[17] Thus, the hallmark of this "seigniorial system" was the non-alienation of ultimate political sovereignty by the monarchs, coupled with non-capitalist social relations of production.[18]

The town middle classes or bourgeoisie were always relatively weak owing to their small numbers (not more than 3-5% of the population) and to the fact that many were Jews or conversos (Jews or their forbears who had "converted" to christianity) who were either persecuted or emigrated during this period.[19] Their traditional histroical role as an ally of the monarch against the aristocracy in the consolidation of an absolutist State[20] led, in the Spanish version of that alliance, to the destruction of the autonomy of the cities and towns and to the predominance of the aristocracy under the auspices of the absolutist State.[21] With the growing perdominance of the aristocracy economically and socially, the bourgeoisie took on aristocratic values and ceased to be an enterprising, ascending bourgeoisie.[22] Industry, which had made some gains in the early sixteenth century with the advent of the American trade, fell into ruin under the weight of a seigniorial economic structure.[23] The discovery of the great riches in America gave the final blow to the Spanish bourgeoisie, as Ronald Glassman relates,

. . . at precisely the point when other European kings fell back upon the merchant classes in their need for monetary wealth for internal and external expansion, the Spanish kingship got a miracle, the delivery of unbelievably enormous and endless sources of wealth, with no strings attached.

Therefore, the Spanish kings did not have to encourage the development of the internal economy, for they had been blessed with an external source of wealth. Not only did they not have to develop and encourage internal economic development, but they preferred not to develop it (as all

35

other European kings would have preferred not to), for . . . this meant that the only remaining class of potential political foes to the kingship could be reduced or ignored . . .

Thus the Spanish internal economy was allowed to disintegrate, and the Spanish commercial classes slowly and imperceptibly began to disappear as a force in the realm.[24]

It is within the context of this type of political, economic, and social structure that the Spanish conquest of America must be understood. The original aim of the monarchy in this age of conquest was not colonization (Spain was still relatively underpopulated) but conquest and trade--the crown would share with the individual conqueror the booty or trade secured. Upon the discovery of the Indies, the objective of the State, according to Góngora was, ". . . to establish in the Indies entrepots for the trade of gold, on the Portuguese model and as a crown monopoly, keeping overseas only a small garrison of soldiers and the indispensible minimum of settlers . . ."[25]

If the intent of the crown was fairly traditional, so too were the intentions and organization of the conquistadores. These conquistadores came to the New World with relatively the same social and political organization under which they had fought the re-conquest in Spain--"a nucleus of conqueror--the caudillo or military leader, and his compañia, or followers."[26] The conquistador, holding in his hand a capitulación, a grant from the monarch stipulating his rights and rewards for the conquest, rewarded his followers and paid due homage to the monarch by giving each their rightful share of the booty.[27] The conquests of America were not "private" enterprises, although they may have been financed as such. They required the permission of the crown and were forced to conform to the goals of the Spanish State.[28]

The conquistador was under no illusion that he was there to create a "new" society. Most were members of the lower aristocracy who claimed the social prestige of their class but lacked the economic means to enjoy it because of the system of primogeniture.[29] These relatively impoverished knights sought a way back into the upper reaches of castillian society through success in plunder. As James Lang argues,

This was not a movement of a counter culture. Cortés and Pizarro came to the New World to acquire the resources to re-enter the old one with enhanced status and prestige.[30]

and,

These men are not institutional entrepreneurs or the harbingers of social change. They are attuned to the aristocratic, seigneurial ideal.[31]

In fact, the conquest of America can be seen as a rebirth of the reconquest of Spain itself in that it revived conquest as the principal means of upward social mobility. According to Glassman,

> In Spanish America, as in the reconquest of Spain, the possibility of (1) heroism in battle (2) conquest of Indian controlled lands and treasures (Moslem land and treasure in Spain), and piratical and bandit acquisition of wealth reproduced a situation in which everyman could become enobled, and where enormous numbers of men did received titles or the power that comes from territorial control. The spirit of 'hidalgo,' and the would be 'hidalgo' re-emerged from the corpses of the Indian aristocracy, as it once had emerged from those of the Moslems. Land, slaves and titles were available once again. The New World had opened the door to the Old.[32]

Given these roots, it is not surprising that neither the crown nor the conquistadores instituted a capitalist regime in America. While a classically "feudal" system was not imposed, neither did they create small farmer settler colonies. What emerged as the pattern of social, economic, and political development unsurprisingly mirrored the seigniorial system extant in Spain.

Spanish American society and economy was dominated throughout the colonial era by the State. Mercantilism, as Magali Sarfatti notes, tended towards two varieties, one, a ". . . monopolistic mercantilism, where the purely fiscal orientation prevails and where new industries, based on the concession of a monopoly by the State, are submitted to strict State control," and the other, a ". . . national mercantilism, which builds up a protectionist system for the national industries that already exist."[33] Spanish mercantilism tended towards the first form, the most unlikely to produce industrial capitalism.[34] Thus, while economic exploitation was entrusted to private individuals, the remarkable achievement of the Spanish crown in the opinion of Sarfatti
". . . was to superimpose regulations on the system of production to control access to the means of production and place a toll on the results."[35]

Yet, although unprogressive in this sense, the State's control over the society and economy of Spanish America did secure the crown's goal of directing a large part of the enormous bullion wealth of the colonies into its coffers. Direct bureaucratic intervention into the society and economy also had the benefit of reducing tension between competitors for the available resources--land, labor and trade. The bureaucracy itself became the focus of that competition. While corruption and poor administration were the result of such policy, the benefits were many in terms of creating attachment to the imperial system and providing the social control mechanisms necessary for the exploitation of servile labor.

ENCOMIENDA AND ITS ANTECEDENTS

Immediately upon their arrival in the Indies, the conquistadores set to imposing servile labor conditions upon the native inhabitants. From this it is immediately apparent that the men who came to America had no intention of working the land themselves. The Spaniards, after surviving for a while on the hospitality of the natives of Hispaniola enslaved them after they revolted against the increasing demands of their "guests." Columbus imposed a tribute tax upon the whole native population over the age of fourteen, and those unable to pay (of which there was a large majority) were forced to provide labor service free.[36] By 1499, the "choice" of tribute tax or labor service had effectively been suppressed in favor of labor service parcelled out to individual Spaniards, as this better assured them control over the fruits of native labor.[37]

The crown did initially halt the practice of private compulsory labor dues (compulsory labor in crown mines was never at issue), but this would have left the Spaniards to fend for themselves and, given their aristocratic values and aspirations, they violently protested. The crown demured to the needs and wishes of the conquistadores by re-evaluating its position and formally legalizing compulsory forced labor in 1503.[38] Under Governor Ovando, this began to take the form of encomienda, a conditional grant of native forced labor to particularly meritorious conquistadores. The encomendero was obliged to "take care" of his native charges, instructing them in Christianity and civilization, and protecting their persons and properties.[39]

The grossly increasing exploitation of the native population of Hispaniola quickly led to depopulation and a cry by the Spaniards for new sources of labor. Estimates of native population decline on the Island show a drop from a high of one million when the Spanish arrived to scarcely five hundred by 1570.[40] Expeditions were sent to neighboring islands to secure the needed labor, leading to the rapid depopulation of many of the Caribbean Islands.[41] The continuing decline of available forced labor then led to expeditions to the mainland in search of both labor and riches as new "conquistadores" arrived from the peninsula regularly only to find colonial society now closed. These new "conquistadores," seeking lucrative positions, clamored for new conquests.[42]

This medieval Spanish form of conquest and colonization did not radically alter with the conquest of the mainland. There, in the Andes and the Valley of Mexico, the Spaniards found relatively developed native empires lording over fairly complex systems of production. In Peru, the Inca Empire ruled over an estimated sixteen million people stretching from southern Colombia to northern Chile along the Andean cordillera.[43] The Incan social, economic, and political system was characterized by groups of independent village communities or ayllus, organized by lineage, and linked to the central Incan authority through a complex bureaucracy subordinate to that, and only that, authority. The independent villages produced communally on lands designated for the village, the sun god, and local gods. Indian villages also owed the State a certain amount of labor service, predominately for public works, e.g. roads, temple building, and irrigation projects. Much of the surplus collected by the central authorities (that not used for the support of the royal family, the bureaucracy, the army, the priests or to feed, house, and clothe laborers doing public service) was redistributed to the villages in the form of largesse from the Inca.[44]

The Aztecs of Mexico were, at the village level, similarly organized. Differences, though, existed in their political, social, and economic system. Central administration was fairly lax as compared to the Incas. Local authorities (chiefs, village headmen, etc.) held power in the absence of an imperial bureaucracy. All that was required of the local authorities was that they deliver their share of the tribute demanded by the Aztec aristocracy. Economically the system was not redistributive (at least not at the imperial level) as it was with the Incas, and trade and economic differentiation had begun to appear before the arrival of the Spanish conquistadores.[45]

Two factors greatly facilitated the relatively easy conquest of these two advanced Indian empires. First, in both empires, internal dissension greatly assisted the Spaniards. The Aztecs had only recently conquered many tribes on their periphery and, groaning under their heavy tribute exactions, these tribes gladly assisted Cortés' attack of the Aztec capital. In Peru, a dynastic struggle within the Inca royal family permitted a small band of Spaniards under Pizarro's leadership to play both sides against each other, leading to the defeat of both.[46] Second, the apparent absence of popular uprisings (except in the very centers of both empires--Cuzco and Tenochitlán) which was a result of the sedentary nature of both populations and the insularity of the villages vis-à-vis the empires themselves. These independent villages had been the object of conquerors before the Incas and Aztecs and regarded the Spaniards at first as deliverers, and later simply new overloads to bear.

Marx's assertion that the conqueror must conform to the forms of production and exchange of the conquered was never so borne out than in the Spanish conquest of the Inca and Aztec Empires.[47] After the Spaniards had stripped the American Indian Empires of all the precious metals they had lying about, they were forced to confront their own survival in their new land. Rather than changing the modes of surplus extraction extant, the Spaniards inserted themselves at the pinnacle of the hierachic structure of tribute collection and distribution through the use of encomienda.[48] The encomienda[49] was, in the early stages of Spanish colonialism, the primary method of extracting the surplus wealth and labor of the native population. On the continent, it became a conditional grant of the tribute of Indian communities to a particularly meritorious Spaniard. The tribute, received in kind or cash, was ordinarily what the Indians were required to pay the Spanish king (before him the Inca or Aztec king) as their overlord.[50] Certain kinds of direct labor services were also extracted by the encomendero although such practices were not condoned by the crown and were ultimately outlawed. In some areas, particularly Chile which suffered from extreme labor shortage, encomienda was extremely harsh in that tribute was extracted mainly through labor services. Arnold Bauer relates how Haurpe Indians from Cuyo ". . . were brought in chains through Andean passes and assigned to various agricultural tasks around Santiago. Often the indios huarpes were rented by their encomenderos to other Spaniards . . ."[51]

The encomienda was not a grant of land, nor did it form the legal basis for the large landed estates or haciendas that were to arise in the seventeenth century.[52] Grants of land (merced) were made by the Spanish towns upon their founding according to the status of the individual settler. Land was also granted and sold by the crown in the sixteenth and seventeenth centuries.[53] Encomenderos were forbidden to own land or to live within the confines of their encomienda. Encomiendas could include the tribute of Indians who lived on their own community lands, crown lands, or lands owned by other Spaniards.[54] Although usurptions of Indian lands by encomenderos and others occurred throughout the colonial period, control of land, except that in the immediate vicinity of Spanish towns (for the provisioning of those towns), was less important than the control of labor in the first century and a half of colonization.[55]

The encomenderos' aim was not to institute a new system of production, but to live well off of the old Indian system.[56] The encomendero was still, in a sense, a military leader who provided for his retinue of soldiers through the tribute he received from his encomienda Indians.[57] His responsibilities to the crown were military, social, and economic--further conquest, the Catholization of his Indian charges, and the provisioning of the crown with as much gold and silver as he could find.[58] The encomendero was not an independent "lord." As Claudio Véliz notes, although the Indians were commended to a Spaniard, he did not therefore receive judicial authority over them as a feudal overlord. The encomenderos were ". . . informal civil servants representing the monarch, acting on behalf of the central government with limited tenure, and liable to have their duties terminated at the royal will."[59]

The encomienda was geared to the survival of the indigenous non-capitalist mode of production and social and political organization (relations within the village and between the village and the Spaniards were mediated through the village headman or curaca). First, the crown did not want the American conquerors to become an hereditary aristocracy (the one it had to contend with in Spain was already one too many) and thus restrictred the encomendero in his tenure and use of Indian labor.[60] Second, the crown had an interest in the survival of the indigenous system which produced the labor for the silver mines, and tribute for the State and church.[61] But the encomienda system, this hybrid public/private system of surplus extraction, did not survive past the early 1700s (for various

40

reasons it lasted well into the eighteenth century in Chile and Paraguay) and divided into the "private" hacienda and "public" corregimiento.[62]

By the end of the sixteenth century, and throughout the seventeenth century, the encomienda form of surplus extraction began to change radically until it was finally abolished in1718. This change did not include a transformation to capitalist forms of surplus extraction, but rather was a reorganization of non-capitalist forms. Several developments led to this unplanned reorganization, (1) the dramatic decrease in the Indian population throughout the sixteenth century, (2) the creation of a large market for agricultural produce with the development of silver mining on a grand scale, and (3) the crown's policy of decreasing both the power and profitability of encomienda.

Perhaps of all of these the dramatic decline of the Indian population was most important. A number of factors have been cited as the cause for this demographic disaster, but it is generally agreed that the introduction of European diseases, particularly small pox, typhus, malaria and yellow fever, to which the Indians had little immunity, was the chief cause.[63] Compounding the decline by disease were the intensified labor requirements in the silver and mercury mines and in producing agricultural products for Spanish consumption which took time away from subsistence production. According to Rolando Mellafe, it seems that Indian labor drafts for the building of new Spanish towns, and the usurption of some of the best Indian agricultural lands for the building sites of these towns, also greatly contributed to the demographic decline.[64] Although there is some dispute as to the loss in actual numbers, recent research has estimated a decline in Mexico from 25-30 million at the time of the conquest to about 1 1/2 million by the middle of the seventeenth century. The decline in Peru appears to have been somewhat less dramatic as the population of the isolated altiplano communities of Upper Peru seems to have fared much better.[65] With such a great decline of population and thus production, encomenderos were finding it more and more difficult to support themselves and their numerous dependents solely on the basis of Indian tribute.

The enormous increase of mining activity in both Mexico and Peru had a twofold effect in hastening the decline of encomienda. First, the mines reduced the number of Indians available to encomenderos because of the deaths within the mines, and also because Indians subject to mining drafts fled their communities to reside on the properties of Spaniards (and the church) who in return for their labor would shield them from such labor drafts.[66] Second, as the mines created greater demand for foodstuffs, transport, and mining tools, private farms or haciendas arose to which encomienda Indians, subject to mine labor, could escape and find security.[67]

Nevertheless, royal policy was an equally important factor in the demise of the encomienda system. The crown very early sought to control the aristocratic pretensions of encomenderos by first restricting their use of encomienda Indians and second,

restricting their tenure as encomenderos and their ownership of
land. The encomendero was further restricted in not being
allowed to administer justice to his Indians, a function which
the crown delegated to local corregidores or alcaldes mayores who
were not allowed to be encomenderos. More effective than any of
these was the crown imposed decline in encomendero tribute
income. In 1568, the crown ruled that large encomiendas were to
be limited to an income of 2,000 pesos per year, the remainder
going to the crown.[68] By constantly increasing the State's
share of the tribute collected by the encomendero, the crown made
the holding of an encomienda in the highly populated regions
extremely unattractive. In Peru, encomienda was abolished--"all
encomiendas began to revert to the crown upon the death of the
owner"--in 1718.[69] The best an encomendero could hope for then
was a pension from the crown.

CORREGIMIENTO AND HACIENDA

Actually, encomienda type surplus appropriation did not
disappear with the end of encomienda. The aim of the crown was
not to destroy the system, but to preserve it by gaining greater
control over it since it was the basis of the bulk of the revenue
the Spanish state extracted from the colonies. As Robert Keith
has noted, the system of corregimiento was simply encomienda by
another name--with one important difference. Rather than a
private Spaniard holding it, the corregimiento was an encomienda
held by the crown and administered by it representative.[70]
Corregidores de indios (or alcaldes mayores in Mexico), appointed
for a relatively short term of office, the crown believed, would
ensure the survival of the indigenous population and the social
and economic organization which preserved it. This, however, was
not obtained in the long run.[71] The office of corregidor, as
most offices during the latter Hapsburg period, was sold by the
crown in an effort to fill a treasury impoverished by war. Those
who bought the offices were usually poorer Spaniards or creoles
who borrowed heavily from local merchants in order to pay the
fee. To recoup this debt and make their sinecures pay,
corregidores developed the repartimiento de mercancias (forced
distribution of goods) whereby Indians were forced to purchase a
certain amount of goods (useful or useless) from the
corregidor.[72] In order to pay for these goods, the Indians
were forced to produce goods that they could sell in Spanish
markets or to the corregidor. A good deal of the commodities
circulating in Spanish markets were thus produced in this
manner.[73]
Corregidores, while serving as a conduit for merchants in the
sale and collection of goods, and the State in the collection of
tribute, also acted as labor recruiters for local haciendas
(although this practice was illegal). As the king's
administrative and judicial representative, the corregidor
dispensed justice to the Indians in his district and was
responsible for maintaining the separation of the Indians from

Spaniards and mestizos who, the crown felt, would (and did) abuse the Indians.[74] But while charged with protecting their Indians from Spaniard and mestizo freebooters, corregidores were not averse to handing over any number of their charges to local hacendados who required additional labor on their lands--for a price.[75]

The hacienda, a large private estate-farm, received its impetus with the decline of encomienda. As the Indian population declined, and opportunities for gain in the provisioning of the mines grew, land ownership became highly important.

Land itself was a concession given away or sold by the political authorities. From the first, grants of land were made by the founder of a Spanish town and later, by the town council or cabildo.[76] All ultimate ownership of land in America was held to belong to the crown. At various periods viceroys, governors and audencias were authorized to either grant or sell land for the benefit of the crown. Ownership of land gave rise to all sorts of disputes as gaining clear title, given the counter claims of Indians (whose lands were usually being usurped) and competing hacendados or the church, was extraordinarily complicated. Thus, the colonial courts, officials and lawyers (letrados) were enormously important to any landlord (or aspiring landlord).[77] Obviuously, having connections to, or the ability to bribe royal officials was extemely important. Further, the state sanctioned practice of entail and primogeniture ensured the reproduction of the system of large landholding.[78]

More "free" in comparison to encomienda Indians, hacienda Indians produced for the hacendado in much the same way they had produced for the encomendero. Although haciendas were more market oriented, particularly those that provisioned large urban areas or mining centers, they were, neverless, in no way harbingers of an emerging capitalist economy. Each hacienda, regardless of its connection to the market, strove for the ideal of self sufficiency. Diversification only served as a means to monopolize many small markets and thereby control supply and price. Even the most highly commercialized sugar plantations grew their own food--maize, vegetables, wheat and cattle--with an eye towards monopolizing the entire production process.[79]

The hacienda attracted labor by offering the Indians a better situation than they could obtain either as encomienda or/and community Indians. In Peru especially, the increasing burden of tribute (in Peru, tribute was assessed to villages and thus the decrease of the Indian population only increased the per capita tribute the remaining Indians had to pay; in Mexico, tribute was an individual responsibility) forced many to seek succor on haciendas. The hacendado offered the Indian a small plot of land to work in exchange for his labor. Even later, when the crown required hacendados to pay their Indians a "wage" in addition to a plot of land, wages were paid (if they were paid at all) in kind.[80]

Labor relations on haciendas were varied. For the most part, the hacendado required a small permanent work force which, at harvest times, could be expanded fairly easily. The permanent work force, those attracted to year round residence on the hacienda, were either serf-like yancononas as in Southern Peru, sharecroppers who owed the hacienda certain portion of their harvest, or wage laborers (though very few were permanent workers) who were paid a wage well below subsistence and therefore had to depend on support outside the hacienda. Much of the seasonal labor the hacienda required was provided through the mita or repartimiento--forced labor (though paid) directed to the haciendas by crown officials.[81] Even in the later colonial period, according to James Lockhart, resident and non-resident labor was provided through the pre-colombian system of periodic obligatory work. Hacendados continued to enjoy the free personal services of Indians in having their produce delivered to market and in the provision of house servants.[82]

The hacienda was able to attract additional seasonal labor in two ways. One, which seems to have been more predominant in Mexico, was to put pressure on Indian villages in their vicinity by usurping their lands and thus forcing the Indians to send labor to the hacienda to supplement the decreased community resources. The other was by the State putting pressure on Indian villages through tribute, payment required by the church, labor drafts for the mines, and forced sale of goods by corregidores. All of these exactions forced Indians to seek added income in seasonal labor on haciendas. In fact, Karen Spalding claims that the State "forced the Indians to sell their labor to the Spaniards," through only cheap below-subsistence labor, because it was not in the interest of the hacendados, who could not fully support such a large labor force, or the State, which needed the Indians' labor and tribute, to fully destroy indigenous systems of social reproduction.[83]

MITA AND REPARTIMIENTO

Obviously, forms of enforced labor did not end with encomienda. In both major areas of Indian population, systems of forced labor recruitment lasted well into the eighteenth century. Forced labor, generally called mita in Peru and repartimiento in Mexico, was distributed by royal officials, corregidores or jueces repartidores, to mines, haciendas, textile factories, churches and church lands, and towns.[84] Thus, some degree of influence with the political authorities was necessary to acquire this labor. Though nominally "wage labor," the need to make such employment obligatory indicates that proletarianization, that is, the inability of the worker to survive without selling his labor, had not really gone very far.

In Peru, the mita was a labor draft in which certain Indian villages were required to send a given number of mitayos to the mines, haciendas, or public works such as roads irrigation, town building, etc.[85] Until 1609, mitayos were unpaid, but thereafter they received a small daily payment.[86] Forced labor in the silver mines of Potosí and the mercury mine at

44

Huancalevica was especially onerous as thousands died from overwork.[87] Given unrelaxed mita conscription in the same geographic area, it has been estimated that the mita produced 11,199 laborers in 1573, but only 1,674 one hundred years later.[88] Of course, this decline was not entirely the fault of overwork in the mines, but it nevertheless was the reason so many Indians fled these particular areas to seek shelter on Spanish haciendas.

In Mexico, forced labor was somewhat milder because a repartimiento for the mines was not the fashion. But Indians, Negroes, vagabonds and all people of color were required to make themselves available daily for labor drafts. The laborer could in theory "choose" his employer, but he nevertheless had to work.[89] Debt peonage seems to have appeared earlier, and been more widespread in Mexico, as hacendados sought to acquire a fixed labor force by making the Indians legally bound to them through debt. As the Indians attempted to pay off their debts, the small below subsistence "wage" they received only sent them deeper into debt.[90] However, as recent research into this aspect of colonial (and nineteenth century) social relations indicates, to the Indians, their debt slavery was relatively unimportant in that being a permanent tenant on a hacienda may have been the best possible existence for an Indian.[91]

MINES, OBRAJES AND GUILDS

The silver mines of Peru and Mexico were of chief importance to the Spanish crown and therefore received careful attention from the colonial bureaucracy. Although bullion remittances never exceeded the revenue raised through taxation in Castile, they were of greater value because of their liquidity and therefore more useful in the crown's international adventurism.[92] The crown sought, therefore, not only to increase silver production, but also to assure that the resources necessary for the exploitation of the mines were available to the miners.

The mines, though worked by private individuals, were rarely sold outright. Usually, they were granted as concessions to Spaniards and creoles, the crown retaining ultimate ownership.[93] Concessions were of relatively short duration and thus the exploitation of the mines, particularly in the early flush days, was rapacious and investment minimal. The crown held ultimate control over mining not through ownership of the mines, but by monopolizing the production and distribution of one essential input—mercury. Mercury, needed in the amalgamation process which reduced silver bearing ores to relatively pure silver, was produced and distributed as a state monopoly.[94] In addition, all bullion had to be delivered to government smelters to be assayed, cast into bars, stamped and taxed. A small tax of one and one half percent was assessed for the cost of this service while the _quinto_ was assessed and collected for the crown.[95] Although much of the silver produced in America never reached government offices to be taxed (being hidden or leaving as contraband), much that did revert to the crown during its periodic financial crises when it simply confiscated all private bullion coming from America.[96]

Mining itself was a precarious industry. A concessionaire might get rich very quickly, but many more ended in ruin. Miners were notoriously short of capital and were usually at the mercy of merchant money lenders or aviadores who advanced them just enough to buy necessary equipment and mercury, but not enough to expand or modernize production.[97] The aviadores were, of course, only middlemen who linked the mining economy to the large Lima and Mexico City merchants.[98]

Given the importance of the mines to the crown, they were granted preferential treatment in the distribution of labor by royal officials. The mita in Peru, as discussed above, provided the bulk of the labor for the mercury mine in Huancavelica and the silver mines in Potosí during the sixteenth and early seventeenth centuries. In Mexico, it seems repartimiento did not provide the needed workforce and thus a combination of slave labor and "free" wage labor was utilized.[99] It should be noted that while the crown progressively limited the types of industries allowed to use mita or repartimiento labor, the last to lose this privilege was mining.[100]

What manufacturing existed in America during the colonial era was mainly in the manufacture of coarse textiles, usually destined for Indian workers in the mines. Textiles were produced in workhouses called obrajes which were found everywhere in the colonies (although Querétaro in Mexico, and Quito in Peru were centers of production) and worked by servile labor. Exploitation of Indian labor in the obrajes was particularly brutal and, although steps were taken early to reduce or abolish Indian servitude in them, all regulations were ineffective.[101] Indians, including women and children six to eight years of age, were kidnapped and forced to work long hours in dark unhealthy textile mills.[102] According to Góngora, miners and obraje operators were virtually in the same boat, they were "fundamentally dependent on the power of the state" for access to the labor inputs of their industries.[103]

Most other kinds of manufacturing in the colonies, if they did not use servile labor, did not alternatively take capitalist form. Neither did they escape (or want to escape) State regulation. Most manufacturing (except cottage industry in the counrtyside) was organized into craft guilds or gremios.[104] Craftsmen producing shoes, furniture, glass, leather goods, pots, candles, etc., organized into guilds in order to prevent conpetition.[105] Guild labor, as well as the production process, was meticulously regulated by guild ordinances which were given the force of law by the State. Economic and political at the same time, guilds represented the monopolistic corporatist pattern of Spanish colonial society.[106]

The slave plantation is often defined as a capitalist institution by those who misunderstand the difference between commercialization and capitalism.[107] Capitalism, it should be remembered, is a form of production constituting the combination of capital and free wage labor--of which slavery forms no part. Slave systems, however, enjoyed great stimulus under the dominance of the commercial bourgeoisie which, as Genovese observes, ". . . supported the existing system of production."[108] Its relationship to the growth of capitalism is ambiguous. Slavery, as Marx showed, fed the "original accumulation of capital" in Western Europe, though not exclusively or predoninantly.[109] As soon as industrial capitalism becomes dominant though, we find forces attempting to abolish the slave trade, e.g. Britain[110] or/and slavery itself, e.g. the United States.[111]

Slavery was an early system of labor in colonial Spanish America and it certainly did not presage the coming development of capitalist relations of production. Columbus' first inclination was to enslave the Indians he found on the Caribbean Islands. The crown, however, quickly eliminted this practice except for Indians taken in a "just war." Thus, Indian slavery existed only in Chile, Argentina and Northern Mexico where hostile Indian tribes could provide its justification.[112] For the most part though, slavery meant Black slavery and was closely regulated by the imperial bureaucracy.

Black slavery was not without precedent in Spain itself. In fact, Black slaves seem to have accompanied the second voyage of Columbus and were prohibited, unsuccessfully, by the crown from migrating to America in the Instrucciónes of 1501.[113] The importation of Black slaves was extremely important to the colonization of the Caribbean Islands as Spaniards sought servile replacement labor for their enterprises, particularly sugar and gold production, when the Indian population dwindled.[114] On the mainland, the tropical and coastal areas received the bulk of imported slaves as the highland areas of both Peru and Mexico were fairly densly populated and thus did not present labor shortage problems.[115] Strangely enough, the greatest advocate for the introduction of Black slavery into Spanish America was the church which sought to protect the Indians from the more onerous types of labor.[116]

The slave trade to America originally began as a crown monopoly, although concessions for the importation of small numbers of slaves were made to individual colonists as payment for some meritorious act.[117] The crown administered monopoly was soon abandoned and, until the late sixteenth century, the supplying of salves was contracted out through the sale of licenses. This form became successful not only as a means of supplying all the colonies with slaves, but also as an added source of income for the crown.[118] Even after the asiento or monopoly form of provisioning slaves was revived in 1580, the crown profited from the trade by collecting import duties and a bonus for every slave imported. This practice was not abandoned until 1773.[119]

Although Black slaves could be found throughout the colonies, their concentration in particular areas, generally those of cash crop production (and often coastal cities), put the onus of social control on the lower Spanish bueaucracy. Any system of production in which the laborers' position in the social relations of production is juridically defined, as in slavery, requires an active role for the State. As Mellafe notes, the regulation of the relations between freeman and slave was a major function of State bureaucrats who maintained ". . . strict social controls, aimed at maximum economic yield and the preservation of a stratified, hierarchical society . . ."[120] Laws regulating slavery were promulgated by the crown and administered by its representatives. Purchase and sale of slaves, legal ownership, manumission, the rights of slaves and their punishment for crimes (including running away and/or becoming renegades or cimarrones) were all within the purview of the State bureaucracy.[121]

Regulation and social control by the State and its agencies here, as in many other areas, deteriorated as the colonial period wore on. As slave revolts became more and more common by the eighteenth century, slaveowners had to fall back upon their own resources in order to control their workforces. At the same time, a growing floating population of vagabond mestizos and escaped slaves made rural colonial America particularly unsafe.[122] This rootless mass would create problems of social control throughout the late Bourbon and independence periods.[123]

ESTATE, CORPORATION AND CASTAS

Spanish American colonial society, like that of Spain, was organized in a hierarchy of estates and corporations, not social classes. Societies based on social class, where social status is derived from one's economic position, and societies based on estate and corporation, where social status is derived through political-legal definition, differ fundamentally in the role played by the State. In the former, ownership of property, wealth, and/or success in economic pursuits denote social status--the State's role is in simply guaranteeing these founts of social status. In the latter, the State holds a central position in the ascription and recognition of social status. In order to maintain or increase one's social status, recognition by the State is indispensable. Therefore, in the case of the estate/corporate society the role of the State is direct, while in class society it is indirect.[125]

Colonial Spanish America never had an "estate system" proper because the political-representational function of estate was absent.[126] But, as Lyle McAlister argues, the ethnic-cultural groups of the American colonies tended to constitute an estates system.[127] For McAlister, the fact that social status was juridically defined in the case of Spaniards (white peninsulares and creoles), Indians, and castas indicates an estate system,

48

even though it developed in an "ad hoc fashion."[128] This hierarchic system was accepted throughout the colonial period as the natural order of things so, as McAlister argues, "Social unrest took the form of drives to improve the status of the individual and the group, not efforts to change the system."[129]

Spaniards were accorded specific rights (fueros) including exemption from tribute and the right to hold positions in the higher corporations, bureaucracy, clergy, and military. Similarly, Indians were accorded a specific juridical status in that they were subject to the tribute while exempt from the sales tax (alcabala), the inquisition, and the regular courts. Castas, who I will deal with below, similarly had a juridically defined status.[130] In addition, a corporate structure was superimposed upon the system of estates, as it was in medieval Europe. Social status and one's "place" in society was often defined by one's corporate membership in guilds, the church, universities, the army or militia, and the municipalities which conferred upon their members a special juridical status.[131]

The social hierarchy of early colonial days quickly became problematic with the rapid intermingling of the races and thus required State regulation. Although it was crown policy to prevent this intermixing, it was impossible to halt.[132] As women formed a very small part of the white emigration to the colonies in the early years,[133] and only approximately one-third of the Black slaves imported were women,[134] intermixing was inevitable on the part of both Black and white men with Indian women.

Although these were not the only forms of race mixture given the various combinations that could occur once race mixture got underway, they did form the basis of a society graded hierarchically in terms of "whiteness."[135] A quite complex formal-legal system of discrimination based on caste was instituted which existed until the end of the colonial era (and informally up to this day).[136] This "pigmentocracy" received official sanction and included restrictions on the right to wear certain clothing, membership in guilds and other corporations, positions in the bureaucracy, access to schools and universities, and the holding of ecclesiatic positions.[137]

Far and away the largest group of castas were the mestizos who were, for the most part, a complex mixture of the white, Indian and sometimes Black races. Mestizos fairly soon became the majority of the population throughout the colonies as the white population did not grow as dramatically, the Indian population declined, and the Black population was restricted by the slave trade.[138] Having literally no place in colonial society--being neither white and having the privileges of that status, nor Indian and having the protection (for what it was worth) of the crown and access to communal lands, the mestizos were seen by both Spaniards and Indians as a degraded race.[139] For the white creoles, they were both useful and dangerous. Useful as intermediaries between them and their slaves or Indians in the capacity of foreman or slavedrivers, and dangerous because of their unrootedness and tendency towards vagrancy and

unlawfulness.[140]   Mestizos aspired to white creole status and
thus shunned "legitimate" work in a society that always seemed
labor poor. This disgruntled mass was later to form the backbone
of the armies of independence and the basis of support for the
caudillos of the early nineteenth century.[141]

THE CHURCH

The Roman Catholic Church in colonial Spanish America served,
up till the middle of the eighteenth century, as the Spanish
State's chief agency of social control and as adjunct to the
bureaucracy. In fact, since the Spanish crown acquired the
patronato in 1508 (a concession granted by the Pope giving the
Spanish monarch the right to appoint individuals to
ecclesiastical positions, collect church tithes, and review and
approve all church policy--including that emanating from the Pope
himself), the church in Spanish America was always an arm of the
State.[142]
The chief contribution of the church to Spanish rule in
America was its role in identifying obedience to the State with
obedience to religion. For the Indians of Peru and Mexico, this
was particularly potent in that their own indigenous State
organizations evinced a similar combination of State and
religion. Their "conversion" to christianity by the church did
much to legitimize the authority of the secular Spanish
administration. While the Indians often rebelled against the
secular administration, the clergy's authority always stood
firm. Always the representative of the crown, the clergy was
given the responsibility of protecting the Indians from rapacious
Spaniards and creoles, even though these often complained that
the clergy monopolized the services of the Indians for their own
purposes.[143]
To a large degree, where State authority and church authority
began and ended was unclear. The role of the church as an arm of
the imperial bureaucracy infused secular authority with religious
justification and sanctions.[144]   So identified was religion
with the State that "treason against the State was equated with
heresy . . ."[145] The Inquisition, exported from Spain by the
crown and under its sole direction, acted as a defender of the
State, censoring not only religious materials, but political and
philosophical ideas found dangerous to the political order.[146]
While hardly the heinous institution history has branded it (at
least in America),[147] the Inquisition did provide the crown
with an effective deterrent to creole opposition. Useless and
counterproductive as Henry Charles Lea may characterize it,[148]
the Inquisition was extremely effective. Even if it did nothing,
its presence and occasional actions were enough to cause
Spaniards and creoles (who were solely under its jurisdiction) to
walk the straight and narrow.[149]
The church performed many social functions that ingratiated
all classes to it. Almost all education in the colonies was
administered by the church through its monastaries, colegios,

50

universities, and schools of the regular and secular clergy.[150] In addition, the church was the chief founder of hospitals, poorhouses and other charitable institutions.[151] But of all the important social functions of the church, nothing compared with its role as colonial banker. The church grew to be the richest institution in America from years of receiving donations of land and money from the faithful, Charles Gibson arguing that its ownership of one-half of the land in the colonies would not be an unreasonable estimate.[152] The church, with an enormous income from its haciendas, plantations, and sale of services, was able to land out money, usually to landowners living well beyond their incomes, and thus came to hold mortgages on an enormous amount of land.[153] By these mortgages, much land was encumbered by dues to the church (a certain portion of the loan was to be repaid out of the operating income of the hacienda) while creoles were enabled to live in an "aristocratic" style.[154] Thus, the economic relationship between the hacienda and the church was symbiotic--the hacienda provided incomes for the church in the form of annuities, mortgages, gifts, and tithes, while the church provided the hacendado with ready cash in the form of loans.[155] When, in the late eighteenth century, the Bourbon State took over these mortgages and attempted to liquidate them in order to fill the royal coffers, panic struck the colonies and many hacendados were ruined.[156]

COMMERCE

Trade between Spain and the colonies was a monopoly of the State. The function of trading with the colonies was delegated to the consulado of Seville, a corporate merchants guild which served as another bureaucratic arm of the monarchy, and, at the same time, profited from holding the trade monopoly. Similar merchant guilds were organized in Lima and Mexico City.[157] In addition to the merchant guilds, the crown set up the Casa de Contratación (Board of Trade) which regulated trade in the interest of the State and restricted it to the priviledged few. All trade was routed through a very few ports to allow tight control of who traded and what they traded. This facilitated the collection of royal taxes and prevented the illegal export of bullion. Only official ports could receive ships and goods from Spain and send ships and goods back. Veracruz (an entrepot for Mexico City), Portobello (a transfer point for goods on their way to the west coast), Callao (an entrepot for Lima), and Cartegena (another transfer point for goods proceeding to or from Lima) were the only cities duly authorized. In effect, trade could be officially conducted only through the Lima and Mexico City consulados.[158] This monopoly of the larger merchants of the consulados, usually peninsulares, discriminated against local creole merchants and consumers who were gouged by the high prices they were forced to pay for goods from Spain. High profits were built into the system as these merchants profited by keeping supply short and prices high.[159]

Merchant groups in America and Spain were not two separate groups. Having personal contacts, preferably familial, with members of the Seville consulado was generally a prerequisite to membership in the American consulados. These trading families maintained their privileged position by financing loans to the crown and jobs for colonial bureaucrats who either had to buy their offices or were required to leave a security payment with the crown.[160] Local trade, on the other hand, was fairly open. It seems that almost everyone--hacendados, bureaucrats and clergy--in the upper reaches of colonial society engaged or invested in trade, even though many may not have wanted to be identified as merchants.[161]

While the Spanish colonies were highly commercialized for this era, the fact that buying and selling was engaged in to such an extent should not seduce the observer into the believing that a bourgeois society was emerging. As Góngora argues in the case of the particularly enterprising new Basque, Cantabrian and Navarrese merchants, they ". . . were passionately interested in acquiring titles of nobility and were full of enthusiasm for genealogy, . . . and they frequently acquired titles of nobility or the habits of the military orders. The "bourgeois" life style was still alien to their collective consciousness. Their habits of thrift and diligence were at all times typical for an immigrant class, and never in our opinion, developed the characteristics which would make it possible for us to describe these merchants as a "bourgeois class."[162] They, like all others in colonial society, aspired to the seigniorial ideal.

BUREAUCRACY

With the economic and social life of the colonies so closely regulated by the crown, the state bureaucracy became the focal point of a highly politicized society. Practice, however, rarely followed form in the colonial bureaucracy. But whether it was corrupt, influenced by Spaniards or colonials, followed or did not follow royal instructions and decrees is immaterial.[163] What must never be lost sight of is that this bureaucracy mediated social relations throughout the colonial era. Regardless of what individuals thought of the practices of various members of the bureaucracy, they still recognized its legitimacy through the crown.

Prior to the Bourbon reforms, the colonial bureaucracy was a system of hierarchic yet overlapping authority. A common structure of authority was reproduced at all levels of administration in an executive and judicial body melded together--King and Council of the Indies; Viceroy and Audencia; Governor (or Corregidor) and Cabildo.[164] Each nominally judicial body shared power with the executive, but the executive was always superior and the ultimate decisions were his. All decisions, however, even those of the viceroy, had to be submitted to the Council of the Indies and needed the ultimate approval of the king.[165] Although the viceroys were the superordinate authorities in the colonies, many subordinate officials were not their choice and therefore could not be removed by them. The fact that any official could independently petition the king directly created havoc with the authority of the viceroys,[166] while the overlapping of administrative responsibility created conflicts that could only be solved by appeal to the King and Council.[167]

Of more interest here is the local administration which had to deal with the everyday life of colonial America. Provincial governors and corregidores (they were generally synonymous, if not in title, then in function and powers) were appointed either by the monarch or viceroy, with the consent of the Council. These administrators combined in their hands the distribution of local justice and the local police power.[168] The corregidores of both Spanish and Indian towns presided over the cabildo and were given the authority to intervene in its affairs.

Although originally appointed by the viceroy and audencia, corregidores and other local officials were later chiefly appointed by the monarch as, in an attempt to supplement the hard pressed treasury, more and more colonial offices were sold.[169] As such offices were sold, they came to be seen more and more as means to grow rich. Favoritism towards wealthy colonials grew rampant because it was clear that local officials could help or hinder one's access to the great resources controlled by the bureaucracy. Higher bureaucrats were not immune from this sort of practice as, according to Stanley and Barbara Stein, ". . . they strove for consensus among conflicting groups on the basis of bribery not equity. In this fashion, powerful interests in effect manipulated viceroys who found in colonial office economic opportunities lacking in the metropolis."[170]

Two important points should now be clear from the above brief description of the Spanish American colonial regime. One is the absence of capitalist production. The other is the important role played by the State bureaucracy in the regulation and distribution of land, labor and trade.

The goals of the crown in the settling of the Americas were always geared to the needs of the Spanish State. From the earliest settlement of the Caribbean Islands as simple trading entrepots to the discovery and exploitation of the vast silver mines of New Spain and Peru, there was never any movement to create in America, or Spain for that matter, a capitalist economy. Many commentators have, in fact, pointed to the debilitating effects of the large bullion infusions on the nascent capitalist sectors in Spain after the American discoveries.[171] For the varied forms of social relations of production--tribute, unpaid personal service (or serf) labor, forced "wage labor," slave labor, debt peonage, and guild labor--to be considered "capitalist" is to define capitalism as a useful concept out of existence. As Gongora points out, ". . . eighteenth century society (in Spanish America) cannot be described as "bourgeois" in any sense of the word, if one bears in mind, for example, that in addition to this more or less compulsory attachment to the land Negro slavery still persisted as an institution . . ."172

For those who point to the extensive commercialization of Spanish colonial society as an indication of the presence of capitalism, we need only to point out the conditions of labor under which the commodities traded were produced and the limited extent of exchange. As indicated above, the bulk of goods produced in Spanish America for trade, either to Spain or within the colonies, were produced under non-capitalist relations of production. Legal trade, and a good deal of contraband trade dealt in the transfer of bullion for European goods, while internal trade dealt in the provisioning of mines or cities that were basically administrative centers devoid of any production themselves.173 Most people provided for themselves and had access to means subsistence, no matter how tenuous or inadequate. The reports from various areas in the colonies of labor shortages in the eighteenth century, coupled with reports of widespread vagrancy, indicate a very low level of proletarianization.174 Although large numbers of Indians were tied to the market economy through the need to raise cash for taxes and goods forced upon them by corregidores, and many produced goods sold in Spanish markets, a great many always maintained, in some measure, their own communal social relations of production. They became "market creatures" only to the extent that they had to.

Spaniards and creoles were interested in profit and becoming wealthy, but the compulsion to profit was dramatically different than would appear in a capitalist economy. In a society in which a seigniorial ideal prevailed, to make it, to be successful, required one to approximate the aristocratic ideal of becoming a lord of the land.175 Wealth acquired in trade, mining, farming, graft, tribute, and bureaucratic employment went into the purchase of land and titles of nobility to enhance one's social status, or the purchase of bureaucratic positions as a means to the other two. The logic of interminable accumulation as an end in itself, the hallmark of a capitalist ethic, never pervaded Spanish colonial society.

The varied systems of social relations of production which existed in the colonial era were made possible by the Spanish imperial bureaucracy. State regulation and distribution of privileged access to the important resources and trade of the colonies prevented competition for these from breaking out into open conflict between the various owning classes by displacing it to one between the colonists and the bureaucracy. Further, the reproduction of the various labor systems required the intervention of the State at some point. It must be remembered that the colonial elite was always relatively small in numbers in relation to the large, mostly alien population. Thus, force and ideology were the primary means of extracting surplus labor. These were provided by the bureaucracy through law, the church and police (militia and army).

Regardless of how corrupt and tied to creole interests the bureaucracy became during the seventeenth century, its legitimacy was never challenged by colonials or Spaniards. Disputes with and within the bureaucracy occurred quite naturally in a system in which overlapping hierarchies, shared jurisdiction, and a combination of subservience and autonomy prevailed,[176] as well as where redress was sought by appeal to another or higher authority, or the paying off of crown officials to look the other way.[177] As John Leddy Phelan suggests, the flexibility inspired in the expression "I obey but do not execute" permitted the bureaucracy wide latitude in adjusting their actions to local conditions without, however, delegitimizing the system.[178]

This flexibility was, in fact, the secret to the longevity of Spanish rule in America. Its undermining by Bourbon reformism in the late eighteenth century was to create much of the tension that vented itself in the Wars of Independence and upheavals of the first half of the nineteenth century.[179] This flexibility created a highly centralized bureaucratic regime which overlaid a regional power structure that retained a good deal of autonomy. As O. Carlos Stoetzer claims, "The Spanish Empire in America was actually built on the federative basis of its many towns and provinces."[180]

Regional autonomy was not alien to the Spanish political experience. Spain, the first of the centralized absolutist states, was itself only nominally centralized. As the Steins relate, "The marriage of Ferdinand and Isabella, often considered the birth of the modern Spanish state, resulted not in the unification of the kingdoms of Aragon and Castile but in condominium in which the two parts of the "Spanish Crown" co-existed as separate entities with separate laws, taxation systems, coinage and trading patterns."[181] Similarly, the Basque provinces, although associated with Castile, retained ". . . recognition of local privileges including freedom from Castilian taxation and military recruitment and most striking of all, maintenance of a customs frontier which gave the "tax exempt provinces" the status of foreign nation in trade with Spain."[182]

What made this regionalism possible for so long, according to Perry Anderson, was "The supply of huge quantities of silver from the Americas . . ."[183] The Spanish State, unlike other absolutisms in Western Europe could ". . . dispense with the slow fiscal and administrative unification which was a pre-condition for absolutism elsewhere. The stubborn recalcitrance of Aragon was compensated by the limitless compliance of Peru."[184] Herein lies the secret to the Spanish State's relative autonomy from powerful, geographically based elites.

The basis for regionalism in Spanish America, as in Spain, was the town cabildo. The town has always been central to Spanish development and the same is true of the colonies.[185] Urban development in Spain has its origins, not as in Northern Europe with trade and the rise of the bourgeoisie, but in conquest and the need to administer newly acquired areas. The town was the outpost of the central power and its liberties were sanctioned as privileges from the king who permitted some amount of self government.[186] Indeed, this balance of central State authority and local autonomy crystalized only in the Spanish town. In the colonies, the first act of the conquistadores was

55

to establish a town and municipal government from which to administer the newly conquered territory. All social, political, and economic life revolved around the town as it provided the basis for the exploitation of the surrounding countryside.[187] Much like medieval Italian City States, the colonial town included more than just the town proper, its administrative and economic authority extending deep into the surrounding area.

During the first half of the sixteenth century, the cabildos wielded enormous power.[188] Their decline in the subsequent period, usually associated with the sale of offices and the system of corregimiento,[189] does not indicate the triumph of the central bureaucratic administration in controlling regional autonomy, but rather the co-opting of that administration to regional interests. It is no surprise, therefore, that cabildos re-generated in the latter half of the eighteenth century when the collusion of powerful local interests and the colonial bureaucracy was attacked and reformed by the Bourbon monarchy.[190]

The seventeenth century decline in mining and trade with Spain, coupled with the rise of fairly self-sufficient and prosperous economies in the colonies, is often cited as an indication that the colonies wrested their economies from the clutches of the Spanish crown.[191] Such conclusions misunderstand the objectives of the Spanish State. The colonial economies always served the interests of the Spanish State. That interest in the sixteenth century was the quest for European imperium. When that failed in the seventeenth century, the goal became holding (unsuccessfully) what it had won in the previous century.[192] War was expensive and, although the burden of taxation was felt most in Castile, it was bullion from America that made these adventures possible.[193]

In retrospect, it is easy to see that the Spanish State did not effectively exploit the colonies in the interest of the Spanish economy. However, by exploiting the colonies through contracting out its resources to individuals and groups, the State was satisfied that by their efforts it would be able to skim sufficient revenues off the top. This technique had worked admirably during the reconquest and, in America, closer crown supervision never allowed the rise of an aristocracy as had occurred in Spain. The State was interested only in mining and the wealth it produced and thus tightly controled that sector.[194] Its indifference to all other production and areas of the empire is clear. Paraguay was, for the most part, given over to the administration of Jesuit missionaries, much to the chagrin of the other colonists and bureaucrats alike. Chile provided Peru with a buffer against hostile Indian tribes to the south. Argentina held Spanish claims to the Atlantic coast against the Portuguese while also serving as a dam to prevent Peruvian silver from illegally leaving America. The Caribbean Islands served as stratigic way stations for the silver flotilas. The fact that prosperous economies grew in some of these neglected areas as a result of inattentiveness or, in the main areas of colonization, by supporting the mining economy, was a result of crown policies, not their abrogation.

That Spain did not participate in this prosperity through colonial imperialism is related more to the fact that it could not, given the underdevelopment of its own economy which had been ravished by the bullionist policies of the State, than to the colonials' control of their own economies. This becomes clear in the eighteenth century when, through the Bourbon economic and administrative reforms in Spain, Spain began to develop the kind of economy that could take economic advantage of its colonies. With the adjustment of the Spanish economy through the actions of the Bourbon State, Spain instituted a new policy of imperialism in America based on modern trade imperialism, not solely the extraction of precious metals..

NOTES

[1]Andre Gunder Frank, Capitalism and Underdevelopment in Latin America (New York: Monthly Review Press, 1967), 20-28; and Fernando Henrique Cardoso and Enzo Faletto, Dependency and Development in Latin America (Berkeley: University of California Press, 1979), xiv-xv.

[2]Charles Verlinden, The Beginings of Modern Colonization (Ithica: Cornell University Press, 1970), x-xxi, 3-32, 33-41.

[3]See above Chapter 1.

[4]Manfred Kossok, "Common Aspects and Distinctive Features in Colonial America," Science and Society XXXVII (Spring 1973), 14.

[5]Witold Kula, An Economic Theory of the Feudal System (London: New Left Books, 1976).

[6]Kossok, 14.

[7]Ibid.

[8]Jaime Vicens Vives, An Economic History of Spain, trans. Frances M. López-Morillas (Princeton: Princeton University Press, 1969), 100-101.

[9]Ronald Glassman, Political History of Latin America (New York: Funk and Wagnalls, 1969), 7-8.

[10]Vicens Vives, 100-101.

[11]Richard M. Morse, "The Heritage of Latin America," in The Founding of New Societies, ed. Louis Hartz (New York: Harcourt, 1964), 144-145.

[12]This unity was more apparent than real in that unity

existed only at the level of the monarch himself.

[13]Angus MacKay, Spain in the Middle Ages (New York: St. Martin's Press, 1977), 45-50.

[14]Mario Góngora, Studies in the Colonial History of Latin America (Cambridge: Cambridge University Press, 1975), 2.

[15]Ibid., 3.

[16]Vicens Vives, 101.

[17]Ibid., 295.

[18]Claudio Véliz, The Centralist Tradition of Latin America (Princeton: Princeton University Press, 1980), 35; and Morse, 145.

[19]Vicens Vives, 298.

[20]Perry Anderson, Lineages of the Absolutist State (London: New Left Books, 1974).

[21]Glassman, 3-73.

[22]The monarch's control over the American trade could also have something to do with this, see Ibid., 62.

[23]Vicens Vives, 338-339, 341.

[24]Glassman, 76.

[25]Góngora, 5.

[26]Ibid., 4.

[27]Ibid., 5-6.

[28]Morse, 139.

[29]Ibid., 127.

[30]James Lang, Conquest and Commerce: Spain and England in the Americas (New York: Academic Press, 1975), 11.

[31]Ibid., 12.

[32]Glassman, 80.

[33]Magali Sarfatti, Spanish Bureaucratic-Patrimonialism in America (Berkeley: Institute of International Studies, University of California Press, 1966), 18.

[34]Ibid., 17-18.

[35]Ibid., 49.

[36]Charles H. Haring, The Spanish Empire in America (New York: Harcourt, 1947), 39.

[37] Ibid.

[38] Ibid., 40.

[39] Ibid.

[40] Rolando Mellafe, Negro Slavery in Latin America (Berkeley: University of California Press, 1975), 19.

[41] Haring, 42.

[42] Góngora, 7.

[43] Arlene Eisen, "The Indians in Colonial Spanish America," in Sarfatti, 99.

[44] For a more detailed account see Nathan Wachtel, The Vision of the Vanquished (New York: Barnes and Noble Books, 1977), 61-81.

[45] For a more detailed account see Jacques Soustelle, Daily Life of the Aztecs (Stanford: Stanford University Press, 1961), xiii-xxiv.

[46] Charles Gibson, Spain in America (New York: Harper, 1966) 35.

[47] Karl Marx and Frederick Engels, "The German Ideology," in Selected Works 3 Vols., (Moscow: Progress Publishers, 1967), I:72.

[48] Elman R. Service, "Indian-European Relations in Colonial Latin America," American Anthropologist LVII (June 1955), 418; and Robert G. Keith, ed. Haciendas and Plantations in Latin American History (New York: Holmes and Meier, 1977), 6.

[49] There has been some discussion recently over the propriety of calling early grants of Indian labor dues "encomienda" as opposed to the term "repartimiento", used predominantly in the sixteenth century. The term "repartimiento" was first used by Colombus on the Island of Hispaniola. See Robert G. Keith, "Encomienda, Hacienda and Corregimiento in Spanish America: A Structural Analysis," Hispanic American Historical Review LI, Number 3 (August 1971), 432-446; and James Lockhart, "Encomienda and Hacienda: The Evolution of the Great Estate in the Spanish Indies," Hispanic American Historical Review XLIX (August 1969), 411-429.

[50] Góngora, 133.

[51] Arnold J. Bauer, Chilean Rural Society From the Spanish Conquest to 1930 (Cambridge University Press, 1975), 7.

[52] Gibson, 48-67. Also see Rudolfo Stavenhagen, Social Classes in Agrarian Societies (New York: Doubleday, 1975), 96.

[53]Stavenhagen, 97. Also see Eisen, 102.

[54]Eisen, 102; and Gongora, 133.

[55]Gibson, 151.

[56]Keith, Hispanic American Historical Review, 435.

[57]Haring, 42.

[58]Góngora, 133.

[59]Véliz, 52.

[60]Gibson, 58-62.

[61]Karen Spalding, "Hacienda-Village Relations in Andean Society to 1830," Latin American Perspectives II, Issue 4, Number 1 (Spring 1975), 110.

[62]Lockhart, 422.

[63]Magnus Mörner, Race Mixture in the History of Latin America (Boston: Little, Brown, 1967), 31-33; and Ralph Davis, The Rise of the Atlantic Economies (Ithica: Cornell University Press, 1973), 54.

[64]Rolando Mellafe, The Latifundio and the City in Latin American History. The Latin American in Residence Lectures, #2 of the Series. (Toronto: University of Toronto Press, 1970-71), 18.

[65]Shelburne F. Cook and Woodrow Borah, Essays in Population History: Mexico and the Caribbean 2 Vols. (Berkeley and Los Angeles: University of California Press, 1971-1974), I:376-410; and Nicholás Sanchez-Albornoz, The Population of Latin America: A History (Berkeley and Los Angeles: University of California Press, 1974), 39-66.

[66]Lockhart, 423.

[67]Keith, Haciendas and Plantations, 9.

[68]Haring, 53.

[69]Eisen, 113; Góngora, 141-142; and Haring, 66-67.

[70]Keith, Hispanic American Historical Review, 439-444; and Lockhart, 423.

[71]Góngora, 95-96.

[72]Ibid., 96.

[73]Spalding, 110.

[74]Haring, 132-133; and Mörner, 46.

[75]Spalding, 115.

[76]Haring, 240.

[77]Ibid., 240-241.

[78]Ibid., and Gibson, 155.

[79]Lockhart, 424-425.

[80]Góngora, 152.

[81]Spalding, 114-115.

[82]Lockhart, 423.

[83]Spalding, 114-116.

[84]Góngora, 143-147.

[85]Lang, 19.

[86]Eisen, 107-108.

[87]Bernard Moses, "Flush Times in Potosí," in Papers on the Southern Spanish Colonies in America (Berkeley: University of California Press, 1911), 6-7; and Arthur P. Whitaker, The Huancavelica Mercury Mine (Cambridge: Cambridge University Press, 1941), 3-21.

[88]Phillip Means, The Fall of the Inca Empire (New York: Scribners, 1932), 192.

[89]Haring, 60.

[90]Ibid., 62.

[91]Mörner, 95.

[92]Stanley Stein and Barbara Stein, The Colonial Heritage of Latin America (New York: Oxford University Press, 1970), 44-45; and John Lynch, Spain Under the Hapsburgs, 2 Vols. (New York: Oxford University Press, 1969), II:71-72.

[93]Haring, 258.

[94]Ibid., 245.

[95]Ibid., 260.

[96]Lynch, 165-166.

[97]John Fisher, "Silver Mining and Silver Mines in the Viceroyalty of Peru, 1776-1824: A Prolegomenon," in Social and Economic Change in Modern Peru, Center of Latin American Studies, eds. Rory Miller, Clifford Smith and John Fisher (Liverpool: University of Liverpool Monograph #6, 1976), 15-16. Also see Góngora, 163.

[98]Fisher, 15-16.

[99]Gibson, 122; and Haring, 62-63.

[100]Góngora, 148.

[101]Haring, 243.

[102]Ibid., 66; and John C. Super, "Querétaro Obrajes: Industry and Society in Provincial Mexico, 1600-1810," Hispanic American Historical Review LVI, Number 2 (May 1976), 197-216.

[103]Góngora, 109.

[104]Gibson, 127.

[105]Ibid.

[106]Haring, 251-253.

[107]For exemple see Immanuel Wallerstein, The Modern World System Text Ed. (New York: Academic Press, 1976).

[108]Eugene Genovese, The Political Economy of Slavery (New York: Random House, 1965), 19.

[109]Karl Marx, Capital 3 Vols. (New York: International Publishers, 1967), I:713-760. Marx does mention the slave trade as one of the sources of the "primitive accumulation of capital" (p. 751), but he lays greater stress on the expropriation of the rural peasantry in Europe as the prime source (pp. 713-744).

[110]Eric Williams, Capitalism and Slavery (New York: Russell and Russell, 1944), 135-168.

[111]Genovese, 19-36.

[112]Morse, 147; Haring, 52-54; Bauer, 7; and Góngora, 130-131.

[113]Mellafe, Negro Slavery, 9-14.

[114]Ibid., 17-19.

[115]Ibid., 29-31.

[116]Gibson, 115.

[117]Haring, 203.

[118]Ibid., 204.

[119]Ibid., 204-205.

[120]Mellafe, Negro Slavery, 100.

[121]Ibid., 101-106.

[122]Ibid., 109-110.

[123]Ibid., 108-111.

[124]The caste system in colonial Spanish America should not be confused with the caste system in India. As Mörner argues, it ". . . was not divided into strictly endogamous groups; some verticle social mobility existed and the system enjoyed no explicit religious sanction." Mörner, 53.

[125]See Oliver Cromwell Cox, Caste, Class and Race (New York: Monthly Review Press, 1959), 8-9.

[126]Gianfranco Poggi, The Development of the Modern State (Stanford: Stanford University Press, 1978), 42-49.

[127]Lyle N. McAlister, "Social Structure and Social Change in New Spain," in Readings in Latin American History 2 Vols. ed. Lewis Hanke (New York: Crowell, 1966), I:160.

[128]Ibid.

[129]Ibid., 166.

[130]Ibid., 160-162.

[131]Ibid., 156-157, 166. Also see Howard J. Wiarda, "Corporatism and Development in the Iberic-Latin World: Persistent Strains and New Variations," in The New Corporatism, eds. Frederick B. Pike and Thomas Stritch (Notre Dame: University of Notre Dame, 1974), 18-19.

[132]Mellafe, Negro Slavery, 112.

[133]Haring, 201; and Morse, 129.

[134]Mellafe, Negro Slavery, 117.

[135]For examples of these very complex orderings see Ibid., 114; and Morner, 58-60.

[136]Mörner, 54.

[137]Ibid., 42-45; and McAlister, 166.

[138]Gibson, 117.

[139]Mörner, 57.

[140]Ibid., 75-76.

[141]Ibid., 53-70.

[142]Haring, 168-169; and Gibson, 76.

[143]Sarfatti, 31.

[144]Gibson, 80.

[145]Stein and Stein, 76.

[146]Haring, 190.

[147]Salvador de Madariaga, "The Church and the Inquisition in the Spanish American Colonies," in The Conflict Between Church and State in Latin America, ed. Frederick B. Pike (New York: Knopf, 1964), 53-64.

[148]Henry Charles Lea, "The Inquisition in Colonial Peru," in The Conflict Between Church and State in Latin America, ed. Frederick B. Pike (New York: Knopf, 1964), 38-52.

[149]The fact that the Inquisition kept records on the racial ancestry of some of the most notable creoles best explains this and the attack and looting of the offices of the Inquisition bythe populace in Lima when, in 1813, the Spanish Cortes abolished the Inquisition. See Timothy Anna, The Fall of the Royal Government in Peru (Lincoln: University of Nebraska Press, 1979), 90-91.

[150]Haring, 208-218.

[151]Ibid., 181-182.

[152]Gibson, 83-84.

[153]Arnold J. Bauer, "The Church and Spanish American Agrarian Structure: 1765-1865," The Americas XXVII (July 1971), 86-88. Also see Haring, 178.

[154]Bauer, The Americas, 86-88.

[155]Ibid., 79.

[156]D. A. Brading, Miners and Merchants in Bourbon Mexico 1763-1810 (Cambridge: Cambridge University Press, 1971), 340-341; and Ibid., 88-90.

[157]Haring, 297-300.

[158]Ibid., 303.

[159]Stein and Stein, 48; and Sarfatti, 41.

[160]Stein and Stein, 51.

[161]Góngora, 111.

[162]Ibid., 164.

[163]John Leddy Phelan, "Authority and Flexibility in the Spanish Imperial Bureaucracy," Administrative Science Quarterly V (1960), 47-65.

[164]Sarfatti, 23-28.

[165]Ibid., 23-24.

166Ibid., 24-25.

167Haring, 113.

168Ibid., 131.

169Gibson, 98-99.

170Stein and Stein, 73.

171 Ibid., 44-53; Vicens Vives, 427; and Davis, 146.

172Góngora, 156.

173Fernando Henrique Cardoso, "The City and Politics," in Urbanization and Latin America, ed. Jorge E. Hardoy (New York: Doubleday, 1975), 163-167.

174Mörner, 75-77.

175Góngora, 156.

176Haring, 112-113.

177Gibson, 108-109.

178Phelan, 59.

179Cecil Jane, Liberty and Despotism in Spanish America (Oxford at the Clarendon Press, 1929), 63; and O. Carlos Stoetzer, The Scholastic Roots of the Spanish American Revolution (New York: Fordham University Press, 1979), 11-13.

180Stoetzer, 13.

181 Stein and Stein, 14.

182Ibid., 14-15.

183Anderson, 71.

184Ibid. Marx similarly commented that, ". . . while the absolute monarchy found in Spain material in its very nature repulsive to centralization it did all in its power to prevent the growth of common interests arising out of a national division of labor and the multiplicity of internal exchanges--the very basis on which alone a uniform system of administration and the general rule of law can be created. Thus the absolute monarchy in Spain, bearing but a superficial resemblance to the absolute monarchies of Europe in general, is rather to be arranged in a class with Asiatic forms of government. Spain, like Turkey, remained an agglomeration of mismanaged republics with a nominal sovereign at their head." Karl Marx, Revolution in Spain (New York: International Publishers, 1939), 25-26.

185Richard M. Morse, "A Framework for Latin American Urban History," in Urbanization in Latin America, ed. Jorge E. Hardoy (New York: Doubleday, 1975), 57-100.

65

[186]Ibid., 80-89.

[187]Lang, 28.

[188]Stoetzer, 8.

[189]Lang, 43-44.

[190]Stoetzer, 10.

[191]Lynch, 184-228.

[192]Ibid., 68-86. Also see Wallerstein, 115-125.

[193]Anderson, 70-72.

[194]Frederick Stirton Weaver, "American Underdevelopment: An Interpretive Essay on Historical Change," Latin American Perspectives III, Issue 11, Number 4 (Fall 1976), 23.

3
The Bourbon Reform Era:
The Modern Absolutist State
in Colonial Spanish America

The Bourbon reforms of the latter half of the eighteenth century, and the Wars of Independence are crucial to any understanding of the origin of the underdevelopment in nineteenth century Spanish America. A re-invigorated Spanish State, under the direction of a modernizing Bourbon dynasty, attempted to readjust the relationship between Spain and America on a basis of "trade imperialism."[1] In doing so they intensified old tensions and conflicts held in check by the Hapsburg bureaucracy and, at the same time, introduced new tensions and conflicts. The new policies of the Bourbons not only called for a readjustment of the economic relationship between Spain and America, but more importantly, a political readjustment. In order to give the State administration greater extractive capability, the balance between central State bureaucracy and local interests had to be done away with. Bourbon re-centralization, in the form of the intendancies, destroyed that balance and led to a crisis of legitimacy that only worsened with the fall of the royal government in Spain during the Napoleonic Wars. This crisis of legitimacy, characterized as it was by tensions and conflicts between elements of the old Hapsburg bureaucracy and the new Bourbon bureaucracy, and compounded by tensions and conflicts caused by economic reforms (particularly trade and taxation), could not be contained once the basis of the regime, the monarchy, was eliminated with the abdications of Charles IV and Ferdinand VII.

The Wars of Independence were less liberation struggles against Spain than civil wars between the elites in Spanish America. With the legitimacy the crown conferred upon the colonial bureaucracy removed, the administration itself became a battleground for contending economic and political interests. This explains the more confusing aspects of the "liberation" struggle in Spanish America. On the one hand, it has been seen as progressive, an attempt to go further in the direction of the Enlightenment both politically and economically. According to this view, the Bourbon reforms only spurred on the Americans to seek greater economic[2] and political freedom, ultimately moving them in the direction of political independence.[3] On the other hand, the struggle has also been viewed as reactionary, a revolt against the "new absolutism" of the Bourbons which destroyed the symbiotic relationship between the colonial bureaucracy and local interests. This, of course, included economic interests which sought a return to the previous restricted system of trade and labor control by which they had profited.[4]

The conflict and instability of nineteenth century Spanish America had its origin in the breakdown of the legitimacy of the State during the Bourbon reform period and Wars of Independence. Nineteenth century conflict and instability were indications that the civil war had not ended with the winning of independence. Rather, it was exacerbated by the fact that the State itself was the prize of political conflict. Neither the Hapsburgs nor the Bourbons left to the Spanish American elite any workable formula for the creation of the class solidarity necessary to create a legitimate State. How these conflicts were worked out and the State rebuilt in the various Spanish American countries bears more on the origin of underdevelopment in Spanish America than any recourse to explanations emphasizing international trade. A brief analysis of the Bourbon reforms here, and the Wars of Independence in the following Chapter, will lay the foundation for a discussion of the nineteenth century origins of Spanish American underdevelopment.

THE BOURBON REFORMS IN SPAIN

The seventeenth century decline of Spain reached its nadir by the turn of the century. The decadence and infertility of the Hapsburgs mirrored the similar fate of Spain as its more powerful neighbors, principally France and England, stripped it of its European Empire and imposed a new dynasty upon the State. The new Bourbon monarchy, however, began a process of reform which it hoped would reverse the decline. This reform program closely followed the experience of French Bourbon absolutism by centralizing political power in a unitary bureaucratic system and stimulating trade and production within and between Spain and Spanish America.[5] Although a discussion of the Bourbon reforms in Spain itself is beyond the scope of this study, some mention of them is in order as their seeming success in Spain led to some of them being transferred to America.

Most important were the political reforms. The administrative and political confusion caused by early unification was rectified. Local autonomy, which had been an important aspect of Hapsburg absolutism, was obliterated by the incorporation of all the kingdoms of Spain (except for the Basque Provinces) into one centralized bureaucracy. Separate administrations were suppressed in Valencia in 1707, Aragon in 1711, Catalonia in 1716, and Majorca in 1715. Bureaucratic direction was centralized in the Council of Castile in 1707 and, at the local level, in regional intendants in 1749.[6] The intendants were armed with broad fiscal and military authority

68

and, it was hoped, would stimulate trade and production by reducing internal trade barriers.[7]

During the reign of Charles III (1759-1788), the pace of reform in Spain quickened and in America was begun in earnest. As Spain suffered military and strategic reverses in its alliance with France against Great Britain, the need for economic reform with the aim of generating greater revenues for the State became crucial. In Spain, the State encouraged greater agricultural and manufacturing production while loosening the bindings that held trade in the hands of the Cádiz monopolists. During the latter half of the eighteenth century, Spain's long moribund textile industry was revived and began organizing production on a truly capitalist basis.[9] Other manufacturing was encouraged,[10] while agricultural commodities, principally grains and Mediterranean crops such as olive oil, wine, and fruits, were given impetus.[11] Both internal and external trade were encouraged, particularly with the American colonies, yet in neither case was a nineteenth century type "free trade" practiced. Trade was highly protectionist, geared towards the economic and industrial development of Spain.[12]

As with all early capitalist development, the role of the State was extremely important in Spain during this period. Though hardly an example of a successful State induced transformation,[13] it was, nevertheless, a genuine effort within the context of the aims of the State. The Bourbon reforms in America and Spain, it should be emphasized, were aimed at shoring up the State in the face of internal and external challenges, not economic development in itself or the greater will-being of the incipient bourgeosie. In fact, the Spanish State under the Bourbons was invariably an aristocratic State. Although the economic reforms encouraged the formation and growth of the bourgeoisie, and increased the administrative and fiscal powers of the bureaucracy, the aristocracy was not ignored. Between 1768 and 1797 the number who could claim nobility was reduced by 43%, lending greater prestige and exclusivity to the higher nobility.[14] Its dominance in landownership, social prestige, and high bureaucratic position was never challenged.[15]

Although Bourbon political and economic reforms in Spain may be interpreted as an effort to encourage capitalist development in the interest of the State a la the French Bourbons, the reforms as applied to Spanish America must be seen in a different light. Only Spain was to form the basis for a capitalist core nation--Spanish America was to be its colony and fuel its growth. The Bourbon reforms were not Spanish America's capitalist revolution--they were its introduction to capitalist colonialism.

The keystone of the whole Bourbon reform program was the policy to readjust the political and economic relationship of Spain to her American possessions. The Bourbons sought to impose a capitalist colonial policy on the Americans. Spain's economy would be stimulated by a trade in which the Americans produced raw materials for "factory" Spain and provided her industries with a protected market. Production and trade thus stimulated,

69

the State's revenues, through taxation, monopoly, and investment, would expand. But, in order to achieve this result economic reform alone was not enough. Given the enormous role played by the bureaucratic machinery in the economy, political administrative reform was imperative. Below, I shall examine these reforms in broad outline, not to evaluate their success or failure, as this does not affect the thesis presented here, but rather to indicate the nature and degree of the tensions and conflicts they produced which, as we will see, were carried over into the early national period and exacerbated the formation of new States in Spanish America.

THE BOURBON REFORMS AND THE SPANISH AMERICAN RESPONSE

Given the close connection between the State and the economy in eighteenth century Spanish America, it is impossible to separate political and economic reforms--all political reforms had an economic content and all economic reforms had a political content. Chief among the reforms in South America proper was the geo-administrative reorganization of the empire. Out of the Viceroyalty of Peru was carved two additional major administrative centers-- the Viceroyalty of New Granada in 1739, and the Viceroyalty of the Río de la Plata in 1776. Of the two, the establishment of the latter was more important both from the crown's point of view and in the effect it had in creating conflict. Peru not only lost administrative and economic hegemony over the la Plata region (modern day Argentina, Uruguay and Paraguay) which was virtually worthless, but also the valuable region called Upper Peru (modern day Bolivia) which held the rich silver producing mines at Potosí.[16] Not only was the silver of Upper Peru redirected towards Buenos Aires, but long established trade networks for the provisioning of the mines, and interregional trade between Lower Peru and western Argentina were disrupted. In addition, bureaucratic posts, particularly lucrative spots in Upper Peru, were then closed to the scores of office seekers in the once supreme viceregal center at Lima. In John Fisher's words, "The double blow of commercial and territorial reorganization threatened the interests of the powerful merchant and office holding groups as well as the general prosperity of the Viceroyalty."[17]

The crown's purpose in elevating the la Plata region to viceregal status was military-defensive as well as administrative-economic. Fearing a Portuguese (Great Britain's ally) attack on the rich interior provinces through the back door of the Río de la Plata, Charles III sent a large military expedition with Pedro de Cevallos, the first Viceroy of the Río de la Plata, to dislodge the Portuguese from their stronghold at Colonia del Sacramento, directly across the river from Buenos Aires.[18] The viceroyalty was designed to include the rich provinces of Upper Peru because it obviously would not have been viable otherwise. Even as a small pre-viceregal colony, Buenos Aires required a subsidy from the Lima treasury. With the increased expense of becoming a viceregal center, some tributary area had to be attached. Herbert Klein has shown that fiscally, even with the increased taxes imposed by the Bourbons and the greater prosperity created by the quickening of economic activity induced by comercio libre, the province of Buenos Aires would never have been able to support a Viceregal administration without the revenues provided by Potosí.[19] But, although not fiscally profitable, a large amount of trade was funneled through Buenos Aires which, presumably, stimulated the Spanish economy and thus provided increased revenue to the Spanish State.[20]

Regardless of what other results they produced, the Bourbon reforms in America were designed to increase revenue for the Spanish State. Fiscal and economic-trade reforms were crucial and will be discussed presently, but more important, if this goal was to be met, were the administrative-political reforms. The crown perceived that to be successful in harnessing the wealth of America for the benefit of the Spanish State, the close relationship between local interests and its bureaucracy in America had to be broken. The new forms of surplus extraction required administrators who were less tied to local interests than the Hapsburg type bureaucrats and therefore a bureaucratic reorganization of both hierarchy and personnel was necessary.

The creation of intendancies throughout Spanish America by 1786,[21] was designed to root out the corruption in the bureaucracy which the Bourbon reformers believed stood in the way of the Spanish State's fuller exploitation of the colonies. Juan de Ulloa, an early reform minded bureaucrat found, in the Peru of the 1750s, that from the corregidores on up to the viceroy there was a trail of corruption in which administrators were paid off for favors.[22] Similar charges of corruption can be found, especially with regard to the corregidores and alcaldes mayores, in the visitas of José de Gálvez to New Spain and Antonio de Areche to Peru.[23] Though modern historians have generally agreed with the Bourbon reformers' characterizations of the Hapsburg bureaucracy as being corrupt, it is hardly a fair evaluation and gives the impression that there was something "wrong" with the system. For the Spanish Americans and colonial bureaucracy it was functional and did not constitute a corruption of the system - it was the system.[24] James Scott has observed this apparent paradox and has argued that such "recurring acts of violence and corruption are thus more successfully analyzed as normal channels of political activity than as cases of deviant pathology . . ."[25] What the crown produced by attempting to close off this channel of political expression and reduce the creoles to the status of subservient colonials was grumbling, resistence, and the sabotaging of its policies.

The major "evil" the intendants were supposed to rectify was the corregimiento. They were also to tighten up on the collection of taxes and to stimulate production and trade in their provinces. The corregidores (alcaldes mayores in New Spain) were royal officials who supplemented their meager salaries (when they were paid at all) through repartimiento (the forced sale of goods) to Indians in their districts.[26] In

71

order to pay for these goods the Indians were forced to either work the lands of local hacendados (to whom the corregidor would distribute such labor) or grow cash crops on their own land to be sold in Spanish markets (these products were of course not sold in the market by the Indians themselves but by the corregidor who made additional profits for himself).[27] The repartimiento served two important functions in the colonial economy. First, it connected the Indians to the Spanish economy and provided merchants with a ready market for their goods. Second, it forced the Indians to produce for the Spanish economy at below subsistence renumeration thus assuring Spaniards and creoles any Indian produced surplus. Connected to this system were merchants, landowners, and bureaucrats who may have had money tied up in the trade or who profited by looking the other way. It was, in fact, one of the major surplus-appropriation tools of the colonial era.

Corregidores also collected Indian tribute due the crown. Corregidores tended, though, to "cheat" both the crown and the Indians by preparing double tribute lists--one for themselves, and one for the crown. The corregidor's list was much longer than the crown's, and thus the corregidor could skim off a good portion of what was owed to the crown.[28] In fact, in New Spain, Gálvez estimated that 50% of the Indian tribute was pocketed by alcaldes mayores.[29]

The intendancies, which were designed to end these abuses and provide greater revenue for the crown, have been characterized by Stanley Stein as "internal free trade."[30] Through the elimination of the corregidores and their repartimiento, trade with the Indians would be opened to many small traders, reducing prices for the Indians and stimulating greater production on their part. With the monopoly of the corregidores broken, the Indians would be attached to the colonial economy directly through the market.[31] The tribute tax would be collected for the benefit of the crown, not the corregidor and his cohorts. In addition, all other taxes, principally the royal fifth and alcabala (sales tax), would fall under the supervision of the intendants with the aim of eliminating fraud.[32]

The creation of the intendancies in America was resisted in both Spain and America. In Spain, the reform was blocked at every step by those whose interests (both political and economic) would be adversely affected by it.[33] Although Gálvez first proposed intendancies for New Spain in 1768, it was not until 1782 that the reform was brought to America, and then only in the new Viceroyalty of Río de la Plata. It was not until 1786 that the reform was established where Gálvez had originally proposed it--New Spain, the richest and most populous colony.[34]

More important though, was the opposition the intendancies engendered, and the tensions and conflicts they created, in Spanish America. Resentment against this new and powerful layer of bureaucracy was immediate within the old Hapsburg bureaucracy. Viceroys and audencias did not take the reduction of their powers and status gracefully.[35] Disputes and conflicts arose immediately between viceroys and the

72

superintendants who were to take over the fiscal administration of the viceroyalties.[36] However, the reduction of the fiscal authority of the viceroys was recinded, and the superintendancies abolished, when the intransigence of the viceroys made the new system unworkable.[37] Conflicts between viceroys and intendants over jurisdiction were endemic, with Viceroy Croix of Peru recommending, in 1789, the abolition of the intendancy and the restoration of the corregimiento.[38] The audencias, royal law courts whose role included administrative and consultative functions, similarly resisted and subverted the reform. John Lynch argues that, "The introduction of the Intendants into Upper Peru provoked a reaction on the part of the Audencia (of Charcas) which completely shattered the united front of Spanish Government in this part of the Empire, and created a tension which contributed in no small way to the undermining of the colonial regime in Upper Peru."[39] Since the intendants had judicial jurisdiction at the local level, it was inevitable that a clash between these institutions would develop, especially when one saw in the establishment of the other a diminution of its jurisdiction and status.[40]

If the establishment of the intendancies distressed the older elements of the Spanish American bureaucracy, it distressed merchants and large landowners even more. With the abolition of the corregimiento, these important elements of colonial society could see only ruin. Unable to legally compel them to buy their goods, merchants withdrew credit from their trade with the Indians; and landowners lost an important source of free labor.[41] In New Spain, for example, cochineal and cotton production and trade declined dramatically with the aboliton of the repartimiento.[42]

The crux of the problem was that the Indians would not work for the Spaniards or creoles without some compulsion being exerted by the authorities. True, tributes were raised and better collected, but repartimiento directed Indian labor into projects and production the Spaniards and creoles desired--abolition made this all the more difficult. In the colonies, there was sustained protest throughout the last quarter of the eighteenth century against the abolition of repartimiento.[43] However, it never really died out in the colonial era. Subdelegates, subordinates of the intendants who often were creoles (and many times former corregidores), continued the practice of repartimiento, although in a less formalized and more imtermitent way.[44] These subdelegates, due to their very low salaries (5% of tribute collected), continued repartimiento but, at least in the Peruvian sierra, used it simply as a means of supplementing their meager wages, not as a means of forcing Indian labor into the colonial economy.[45] They therefore, in John Fisher's words, ". . . contented themselves with making them (the Indians) pay for goods without bothering about how they obtained the money. As a result, many communities which had been relatively prosperous were now stripped of their wealth and property."[46] In the end, the formal abolition of repartimiento satisfied very few in Spanish

73

America. Rather, it only worsened old tensions and conflicts and created new ones. Merchants, landowners, intendants, subdelegates, Indians and reformers found in the new situation only chaos.

The relationship between the intendants and the cabildos is more problematic. According to most observers, the cabildos were in a state of decline and decadence when the intendancies were instituted.[47] The intendants are generally given credit for reviving the cabildos and, by inference, giving them the strength to perform a very important and leading role in the independence struggles. Intendants did have much to do with the revival of the cabildos as important administrative and political institutions. Where town governments had disappeared, intendants re-established them. Where interest in serving on them was weak, intendants forced service upon the citizens. Where town revenues were sparse and inadequate, intendants found new sources of income.[48]

In the early years of the intendancies, evaluations of intendants by these newly revived cabildos were generally favorable. Town life had greatly improved with the greater civic activity and revenues of municipal government.[49] After about the first 15 years of the intendancies though, the relationship between the intendants and the cabildos deteriorated and became highly conflictual.[50] The most common explanations of this phenomena have been, on the one hand, the poorer quality of intendants under the administration of Charles IV and Godoy,[51] and on the other hand, the rising aspirations of the cabildos once they had been revived by the intendants.[52] In both these explanations there is some truth, but there was more to the revival of the cabildos than this. Magali Sarfatti and O. Carlos have argued that the revival of the cabildos had a great deal to do with the reduced creole presence and influence in the Spanish colonial bureaucracy proper. As creoles lost influence and position there, the cabildos once again became important as representatives of creole interests.[53] In fact, Stoetzer sees a direct relationship between creole exclusion from viceregal office and the revival of the cabildos.[54] No doubt, crown officials directed creole influence and energies into the cabildos in order to better control them.

While creole influence increased within the authority-weak cabildos, it decreased in other, more powerful institutions. In Lima, for example, after having dominated the viceregal administration through an overwhelming majority on the audencia and in other offices, the creole share of offices decreased throughout the Bourbon period.[55] The crown, its other reforms apparently threatened by such creole dominance, began a policy to exclude them from bureaucratic office in America. The newly formed Audencias of Buenos Aires and Cuzco were almost exclusively made up of peninsulares,[56] and creole representaton on the Audencias of Lima[57] and Mexico City[58] was systematically reduced. As the Bourbons tightened the screws on creole placemen, it became more and more difficult to secure a bureaucratic position. Few creoles were appointed intendants, and even access to lower bureaucratic positions was denied them although, as Jacques Barbier has shown, at least in Chile, creole influence could survive and even thrive in such an atmosphere given the peninsular and creole tendency to create family alliances.[59] Though creoles still held a preponderance of bureaucratic offices in the lower ranks towards the end of the colonial era, the perception that the tide had turned against them and that promotion into the higher bureaucracy would be closed, caused deep resentment against peninsulares. The introduction of the intendancies only hardened opposition to the reforms as creoles saw a new wave of peninsulares take posts which they felt they should have by right.[60] Creoles, in fact, were demanding they get all the bureaucratic positions in America[61] and Juan Egaña, a contemporary, claimed that exclusion from high office was one of the major reasons for the Wars of Independence.[62]

Administrative reforms under the Bourbons began a shift away from the church as a major prop of the colonial system in favor of the military.[63] The first attack on the church was the expulsion of the Jesuits in 1767. The Jesuits, who disputed the "divine rights" doctrine of absolutist kings, supported the universal monarchy concept of the Pope and resisted the secularizing of political power in Spain.[64] Their overwhelming influence in the Spanish American society, economy, and educational system made them formidable competitiors to Charles III's drive for complete control of the colonies.[65] Their expulsion not only removed this threat, it also freed up a great deal of Jesuit owned land which the crown sold for its own profit.[66]

Most Spanish Americans were outraged by the expulsion (although in Paraguay, because the Jesuits so dominated the economy, the creoles supported the expulsion). Of the 650 Jesuits expelled from New Spain, 450 were native creoles[67] and riots immediately broke out in Guanajuato, San Luis Potosí and San Luis de la Paz,[68] while resentment was widespread.[69] In New Spain, D. A. Brading writes, ". . . the Visitation (of Gálvez) and the Expulsion marked a turning-point in relations between the Spanish monarchy and that small colonial establishment which had hitherto governed Mexico."[70]

The reduction of church influence and power did not end there. Throughout the latter half of the eighteenth century, the church saw itself subjected to greater ignomies. In 1753, the religious clergy lost the right to occupy parishes in Indian villages,[71] while in 1774, tithe collection in the colonies was taken away from the church and given to the royal bureaucracy.[72] The establishment of the intendancies also diminished the status of the church by subjecting it locally to the patronato of the intendants.[73] Intendants, directly responsible for the constructon and maintenance of churches and cemetaries, the conduct of the clergy, and the collection of tithes, created conflicts not only between themselves and the clergy, but also within the clergy between the lower clergy, directly supervised by the intendants, and the upper clergy supervised only by the viceroys.[74]

In addition to these affronts, a conscious policy of reducing clerical fueros (special privileges which prevented their being brought before secular courts) was undertaken. For many of the lower clergy who suffered on meager pay, the loss of the fuero was an outright attack on the only social distinction they held.[75]

The reduction of the clergy's status affected both upper and lower clergymen but, for later developments, an understanding of the feelings of the lower clergy is more important. Recruited predominantly from creole families in economic adversity, the lower clergy was filled with creoles who seethed at their misfortune. Victims of downward social mobility, many creoles found in the church the last bulwark between them and social oblivion.[76] New attacks on the church and its status only alienated them further from the system and ripened them for oppositional action.[77]

The Bourbon administrative reforms were a necessary part of the crown's attempt to create "real colonies" which would benefit Spain. The administrative reforms worked together with commercial and fiscal reforms designed to extract greater surpluses from the colonies. These commercial and fiscal reforms have been viewed by historians as the most important aspects of the Bourbon reforms. They were seen by contemporaries to have, on the one hand, disrupted a perfectly well run system and, on the other, not gone far enough, and thus caused the Wars of Independence.[78] This apparent paradox only indicates the very real tensions and conflicts they created in Spanish colonial society and points to the origin of conflicts within the elite that continued into the national period.[79]

The commercial reform--"comercio libre" was designed to abolish restriction and monopoly in the Spanish trade with the American colonies. Between 1765 and 1776, tariffs were lowered, the monopoly of Cádiz and Seville abolished, and other Spanish ports allowed to trade with the Caribbean. When, in 1778, "comercio libre" was extended to the mainland and formalized, Buenos Aires, Peru, and Chile were added. In 1789, Venezuela, whose trade had hitherto been the exclusive monopoly of the Caracas Company, and New Spain, the wealthiest colony in America, were integrated into the system.[80]

By 1789, "comercio libre" was geographically unlimited within the Spanish Empire, but trade between Spanish America and foreign ports was strictly prohibited. Although a wide range of foreign goods were sold in Spanish America by Spanish merchants, these were subject to high duties both on arrival in Spain and then again in the colonies.[81] These restrictions were, of course, little different from those of other colonial powers.[82] As John Fisher argues, ". . . it was typical of the general European pattern of the period . . ."[83]

With "comercio libre," Spanish merchants and creole producers were no longer bound to the inefficient fleet system. Goods could be shipped to and from America at any time and a larger number of ports could send and receive goods. Trade between

Spain and America expanded dramatically, though not as dramatically as Haring's estimate of a 700% increase.[84] In fact, Spanish goods, which at the end of the seventeenth century made up only 15% of the goods exported to America, rose to more than 50% of the goods sold by 1792.[85] The system, however, did not change overnight and, up till the end of the colonial era, the traditional pattern of trade continued to survive. In Spain, Cádiz continued to dominate the export trade,[86] while in America, although Buenos Aires did become a major port, Vera Cruz (Mexico City) and Callao (Lima) still remained the major import and export centers.[87]

In America, "comercio libre" had differing effects geographically and on the various fractions of the colonial elite, but in all cases it caused controversy, tension, and conflict. In Peru and New Spain, both chief beneficiaries of the old monopoly system, the Consulados of Mexico City and Lima were loud in their denunciation of the new system of trade.[88] Few were, however, ruined by "comercio libre" because the bulk of trade still passed through the large merchant houses in Cádiz where the Mexico City and Lima merchants had superior contacts.[89] Nevertheless, these merchants who had once monopolized all of the American trade now had to put up with competition from new men who geared their operations to the new market conditions.[90]

In New Spain, the crown established new Consuldados in Vera Cruz and Guadalajara, and Vera Cruz became a new major center of trade.[91] As the New Spain trade fell more and more into the hands of Vera Cruz merchants who expected a smaller return on capital, the larger Mexico City merchants accelerated their transformation into landowners and miners.[92] The enormous increase of silver production in New Spain at this time can, in large part, be attributed to the dramatic rise of investment capital made available by merchants getting out of commerce.[93] In Peru, competition came principally from the merchant communities in Chile and Buenos Aires as merchants in these colonies, granted their own Consulados, captured a good deal of the trade that would have been funneled through Lima.

Obviously, the new conditions of trade tended to serve the interests of some while hurting those of others. The new men of commerce, principally Basques and Montaneses, saw the opening up of commerce as a great opportunity, while the monopoly merchants found markets now constantly flooded with cheap goods that undercut their previous practices and high profits.[94] "Commercio libre" though, had other, perhaps more serious effects. Many local industries which had grown up in the colonies during the sixteenth and seventeenth century period of mercantile neglect by Spain saw themselves ruined by competition from goods imported from Spain. In New Spain and Peru, the textile industry was hit hard by the influx of Spanish textiles. In Peru, the number of textile obrajes was reduced by half by the end of the eighteenth century, victims of Spanish textiles brought overland from Buenos Aires.[95] Textile production in Quito and Tucumán similarly suffered.[96] In New Spain, the textile industry in Querétaro and Puebla was "suffering crippling competition from exports from Europe."[97] Wine production in western Argentina was all but eliminated with the influx of Spanish aguardiente. Any internal producton which directly competed with goods from Spain declined.[98]

Other industries, particularly agricultural cash crops-- cacao, indigo, tobacco, coffee, cotton, and hides--saw a dramatic rise in their fortunes. Yet, none was more important, as always, than silver mining. Both of the principal mining centers, Peru (also Upper Peru now in the Viceroyalty of Río de la Plata) and New Spain, increased their silver production in the last half of the eighteenth. In fact, "comercio libre" and colonial silver production fed off one another. The main export of the colonies--used to pay for the enormous rise in imports--was silver.[99] Even Buenos Aires, whose economy some argue rose on the basis of the export of hides,[100] really lived off the silver it extracted from Upper Peru through its monopoly of trade.[101]

If commercial reforms were not enough to disrupt the colonial economies, the crown increased the number, rate, and classes of people subject to imperial taxes. Not only did the Spanish State seek to reap the bounty of mercantilist trade, it also sought the benefits of direct taxation. While many of the taxes and imposts that had held back trade between Spain and America were lowered or abolished,[102] sales taxes and tribute were increased and better collected. Indian tribute rolls were reformed by adding many more tributees and thus increasing total revenues.[103] In Peru, tribute collections jumped 1,000,000 pesos in a year by 1778 to about 4,000,000 pesos, and to 5,838,852 pesos in 1779.[104] In addition, capitation taxes were extended, although unsuccessfully, to free Blacks on the coast.[105] In New Spain, the tribute, which had averaged about 596,220 pesos a year during the 1760s, jumped to 955,813 pesos in 1779.[106]

By 1776, the alcabala (sales tax), which had hitherto been farmed out to private individuals, was collected by an army of paid royal officials.[107] Once the intendancies were established, these officials were supervised exclusively by peninsular Spaniards and customs houses collected dramatically increased sales tax revenues.[108] In New Spain alone, total receipts rose from 1,488,690 pesos in 1775, to 2,360,252 pesos in 1779, and later to about 3,000,000 pesos.[109] In Peru, the alcabala was increased from four to six per cent and, with the increasing efficiency of the fiscal system, many merchants, landowners and miners who had once escaped taxation found themselves forced to pay.[110]

The commercial reforms and taxation policy of the Bourbons clearly agitated social, economic, and political life in the Spanish American colonies. Greater taxaton touched off tax revolts throughout the colonies, and a commercial system through which the colonies were drained of their surpluses only exacerbated social relations between all groups. In societies primarily based upon subsistence production, where no fundamental change in the mode of production had occurred but more surplus was extracted, it is not surprising that fairly violent revolts by all classes would ensue.

Revolts, particularly of the lower classes, were certainly not unknown in the period before 1750. In fact, they were quite common and understandable given the rigid class system of the colonial era.[111] But, after 1700, and particularly after 1750, the number of revolts grew, with 32% of all the revolts in the colonies occurring after 1750.[112] After 1750, tax revolts were endemic throughout the colonies. In 1776, riots broke out in Santiago de Chile with the publication of decrees reforming the tax system. These protests ultimately led to the recinding of the decrees and the removal of the Contador, González Blanco.[113] In 1779, free Pardos in Lambayeque, Peru, resisted the "military contribution" imposed upon them by Visitor Areche.[114] Anti-tax revolts also broke out in New Spain,[115] but were generally low pressure affairs compared with those in the poorer colonies of South America.[116]

The most serious of the revolts occurred in the Viceroyalties of Peru and New Granada. The more important of the two revolts, the Tupac Amaru revolt in Peru, clearly indicated the pressures put upon the system of production by Bourbon commercial and tax reforms. The revolt burst out on November 4, 1780, when José Gabriel Condorcanqui (Tupac Amaru II), a curaca of Tinta, seized the Corregidor, Antonio de Arriaga, charging him with extorting excess repartimiento from the Indians and, ten days later, had him executed.[117] The revolt spread rapidly throughout the sierra and melded with other revolts which were going on contemporaneously. On January 1, 1780, revolt broke out in Arequipa, and conspiricies were discovered in Cuzco, Moquegua, Huancavelica, Huaraz, Pasco and La Plata.[118] In December 1780, Oruro, in Upper Peru, was taken over by Indians and half-castes led by Jacincto Rodríguez, a wealthy Spanish miner, while by January 1781, the Puno area was also in revolt. In the La Paz region, an Aymará Indian, Julian Apaza who took the name Tupac Catari, initiated a seige of La Paz in the middle of March 1781. To the North, Tupac Amaru's nephew, Andres, led a revolt in the corregimiento of Larecaja.[119] Revolt spread elsewhere in the viceroyalty, from Cuzco to Tucumán and, by the end of 1781, it seemed that the whole sierra was in revolt. Though the Tupac Amaru revolt had specific grievances against the system which included the repartimiento, the corregidores, the mita, and the alcabala, its extent and social make-up makes it more complex and indicates the wide dissatisfaction caused by the commercial and fiscal measures taken by the Bourbons.[120]

The Tupac Amaru revolt was not just a tax rebellion.[121] The economy of the whole area of revolt had been hit particularly hard by administrative, commercial and fiscal reforms. By separating Upper Peru and Lower Peru which had constituted, up until the creation of the Viceroyalty of Río de la Plata in 1776, one economic/commercial region, hardships were created for all classes.[122] Commercial reforms coupled with higher taxation siphoned the life blood out of the productive heart of Peru. As tribute and taxes rose and were sent to Lima, less and less of the surplus produced remained in the sierra which must have caused merchants, landowners, miners and corregidores to extract a greater surplus from the laboring classes. This explains the vacillation of creoles and Spaniards within and without the Tupac Amaru rebellion. While the revolt addressed the grievances of all those adversely affected by the bourbon reforms--the owning classes, poor mestizos of some property, and Indians--the movement impossibly tried to hold that contentious alliance together. As the revolt strengthened and moved from success to success, those who relied upon the State to insure their superior economic and/or social position over the Indians, including Indian curacas, very quickly moved from support or neutrality to open opposition to the movement.[123]

The Spanish State did not respond to the rebellion by adjusting the system in favor of Indian or creole grievances. Although repartimiento and mita were abolished, tribute collections and taxes rose. The intendant system was imposed on the sierra while the creoles, now considered unreliable and potentially rebellious, were watched over by garrisons of regular Spanish troops.[124] In the crown's opinion, the creoles could no longer be trusted to administer or protect its interests in the colonies.

The reaction of the crown to the Tupac Amaru revolt was in sharp contrast to its reaction to the Comunero Revolt which broke out in Socorro, New Granada.[125] The initial impetus for this revolt, which brought an army of 20,000 creoles, mestizos and Indians to threaten the capital of the viceroyalty at Bogotá, was very similar to that of the Tupac Amaru revolt--taxes. The grievances of the comuneros revolved around the higher taxes, higher prices for tobacco and aguardiente (which had become crown monopolies), and restrictions on the growing of tobacco imposed by Visitor Gutíerrez de Piñeres. The alcabala was raised from four to six percent with the addition of a sales tax for the Armada de Barlovento (Windward Island Fleet), and was better collected by royal officials. For the comuneros though, the reform of the tobacco and aguardiente monopolies were a greater source of discontent. The tobacco monopoly not only raised the price of the good outraging consumers, it also restricted its growing throughout the colony. Many small property owners (who made up the bulk of the comuneros), therefore, lost the only cash crop they had. Although the restriction on the production of aguardiente was not an issue, its price rise, coupled with that of tobacco, was a main focus of popular rage.

The Comunero Revolt began in March 1781 with tax riots by the lower class people of Soccoro. By April, a good portion of the elite of Soccoro had joined the rebellion and had become its leadership. The participation of the elite tempered the riotous activities of the lower orders and made the rebellion, in terms of property damage and loss of life, a low gauge affair. Under elite leadership, the Comunero Movement became a coalition of upper class creoles, mestizos and Indians (although the Indian component was infinitesimally less important than in the Tupac Amaru revolt). By uniting the towns and villages along the road to Bogotá, the comunero leadership was able to force the viceregal authorities to capitulate to all their demands--fundamentally, the dismantling of the Bourbon reforms.

Once back in control though, the new viceregal authorities, principally the new Viceroy, Archbishop Antonio Caballero y Góngora (who had negotiated the capitulation as Archbishop of Bogotá), began a process of pacification that was in sharp contrast to the draconian measures taken by the authorities in Lima in the wake of the Tupac Amaru rebellion. The capitulations were annuled and the ringleaders either exiled or made politically impotent, but tax relief was granted in a reduction of the price of tobacco and aguardiente and the suppression of the sales tax for the Armada de Barlovento. Because the elite of Socorro was so heavily involved in the rebellion, the new viceroy's policy was aimed at separating the elite from the lower classes so that such a dangerous coalition never form again. Harsh in its treatment of lower class leaders (the only leader executed was José Antonío Galán, a lower class leader), the viceregal authorities attempted to shepherd the creole elite back into the Spanish fold through conciliation and compromise.

The Spanish State's distrust of American creoles led it to seek a de facto alliance with groups it felt could countervail their pretentiousness. Mestizos and pardos, who under the "society of castas" found themselves locked into subordinate social positions, were favored by a new State policy.[126] Though one had to be wealthy enough, and few were, a cedula de gracias al sacar which conferred legal "whiteness" on the bearer could be purchased.[127] In 1795, pardos who were granted cedulas de gracias al sacar were authorized to receive an education, hold public office and enter the church.[128] Creole reacton to this policy, especially in Venezuela where the Black population clearly overwhelmed the white, was predictably hostile.[129] Even though the "society of castas" had been breaking down because large numbers of mestizos and pardos were "passing," legalizing and encouraging the social mobility of these groups was a threat to creole domination of the laboring classes.[130]

Bourbon alienation of Spanish American creoles continued unabated into the beginning of the nineteenth century when, in 1804, pressed for revenues with which to fight his war against Great Britain, Charles IV decreed the amortization of church held mortgages in the colonies. Known as the Consolidacion de Vales Reales, this policy sought to appropriate the funds of pious foundations and chantries, paying these funds 5% interest for the money "borrowed."[131] The calling in of these loans had disastrous effects on creole landowners, merchants, and miners, and had a depressing effect on the whole colonial economy.[132] Because the church was the major creditor for the colonials, few owners of property were not affected.[133] Although the crown did attempt to soften the blow by requiring only 40-50% of the loan immediately, with the rest in installments over a 10 year period,[134] many landowners found it impossible to pay back their loans on such short notice and many lost their property.

To make matters worse, there were so many selling property in search of hard cash that most properties were sold for only a fraction of their real worth, and a good deal of property could find no buyers at all.[135] In New Spain, the richest colony, 12,000,000 pesos were siphoned out, with smaller amounts from the other colonies.[136] The levy was so onerous that while other colonies were beginning to revolt against Spain, the most loyal colony, Peru, asked only that the amortization decree be recinded.[137]

Creoles were dissatisfied not only with the Bourbon reforms per se, but also with the style of rule that the new Bourbon administrators brought with them. Throughout the Hapsburg period, and up to the reign of Charles III, Spanish rule had always been mediated through a bureaucracy in which the creoles had some input. As John Leddy Phelan has argued in the case of New Granada, "Until the arrival of the regent visitor general, Gutíerrez de Piñeres, the creoles were accustomed to a government of compromise, conciliation and accomodation in which some creoles actively participated in the decision making process."[138] The, what Phelan calls, "Hapsburg system with its complex blending of centralizaton and decentralization . . ."[139] was abrogated by the Bourbon State's uncompromising demeanor.

This change was indicative of the change in the philosophy of government under the Bourbon rulers. The Hapsburg absolutist State's political philosophy, true to its medieval origins, mirrored the later medieval thinkers, principally Francisco Suarez who, following St. Thomas, stressed the limitations on political power, the popular origin of sovereignty, a kind of "social contract" between the people and their king, resistance to unjust rule and government by consent under the rule of Natural Law.[140] Thus, the king sought to be just to all of his subjects and if his policies were unjust, it was because they were badly administered or the king did not understand local conditions. If any of these conditions held, the king, intent only on ruling justly, would adjust these policies. During the Hapsburg era, if colonial bureaucrats found great opposition to decrees or policies of the crown they would suspend them by "obeying but not executing" them--acknowledging the legitimacy of the king but recommending against the rules--and informing the king as to the proper adjustments necessary to make them just.[141] Bourbon rule, on the other hand, reflected the idea of the "divine right of kings." According to this idea, of which the regime of Louis XIV of France was the consciously emulated example for the Spanish Bourbons, the king's authority was derived from God, absolute, devoid of compromise or consent. All the orders of the king or his ministers required unquestioning obedience, resistance to "unjust" policies was forbidden. The aim of justice was secondary to the achievement of order, peace and stability.[142]

More than any other aspect of the Bourbon reforms, this constitutional innovation conditioned the crisis brought about by the Napoleonic invasion of Spain and the abdication of the king.

For, in the midst of an ongoing constitutional crisis in the American colonies, the only thing that held together all of the contentious factions, the king, disappeared.

NOTES

[1] John Lynch, The Spanish American Revolutions: 1808-1826 (New York: W. W. Norton, 1973), 2.

[2] For example see Hernán Ramírez Necochea, "The Economic Origins of Independence," in The Origins of the Latin American Revolutions, 1808-1826, eds. R. A. Humphreys and John Lynch (New York: Knopf, 1975), 169-183; and José Carlos Mariategui, Seven Interpretive Essays on Peruvian Reality, trans. Marjory Urquidi (Austin: University of Texas Press, 1971), 6-8.

[3] For a discussion and critique of this position see Charles C. Griffin, "The Enlightenment and Latin American Independence," in Latin America and the Enlightenment, ed. Arthur P. Whitaker (Ithica: Cornell University Press, 1961), 119-143.

[4] O. Carlos Stoetzer, The Scholastic Roots of the Spanish American Revolution (New York: Fordham University Press, 1979), 258-263.

[5] For this period see Richard Herr, The Eighteenth Century Revolution in Spain (Princeton: Princeton University Press, 1958). The Steins have characterized these policies as "defensive modernization" see Stanley Stein and Barbara Stein, The Colonial Heritage of Latin America (New York: Oxford University Press, 1970), 88.

[6] Jaime Vicens Vives, An Economic History of Spain, trans. Frances López-Morillas (Princeton: Princeton University Press, 1969), 476-477; and Stein and Stein, 91-92.

[7] Stein and Stein, 92.

[8] The greatest blow to the Spaniards, at least in terms of the security of their American possessions, was the loss of Havana to the British in 1762. Ibid., 97.

[9] Vicens Vives, 524-526.

[10] Ibid., 526-539.

[11] Ibid., 511-513.

[12] Ibid., 552-571.

[13] See the evaluation in Stein and Stein, 103-104.

[14] Vicens Vives, 492.

[15]Stein and Stein, 91.

[16]John R. Fisher, Government and Society in Colonial Peru. The Intendant System 1784-1814 (London: Athlone Press, 1970), 4-5.

[17]Ibid., 5. Also see Timothy Anna, The Fall of the Royal Government in Peru (Lincoln: University of Nebraska Press, 1979), 5.

[18]Fisher, 4. Also see Charles Haring, The Spanish Empire in America (New York: Harcourt, 1947), 92.

[19]Herbert S. Klein, "Structure and Profitability of Royal Finances in the Viceroyalty of Río de la Plata in 1790," Hispanic American Historical Review LIII (August 1973), 440-469; and Fisher, 5.

[20]Klein, 456-457.

[21]Fisher, 4. The Intendancies were the creation of José de Gálvez who determined that such an administrative change was necessary after his Visita General to New Spain in 1765. For an account of the trials and tribulations of his program see Stanley Stein, "Bureaucracy and Business in the Spanish Empire, 1759-1804: Failure of a Bourbon Reform in Mexico and Peru," Hispanic American Historical Review LXI, Number 1 (February 1981), 2-28.

[22]Fisher, 10-11.

[23]Ibid.; and D. A. Brading, Miners and Merchants in Bourbon Mexico, 1763-1810 (Cambridge at the University Press, 1971), 34-80.

[24]For example, Stoetzer argues that the report of Juan Jorge and Antonio Ulloa, "Noticias Secretas de America," which claimed such great corruption in America and was instrumental in forming a negative attitude within the Spanish bureaucracy towards the Americans, was intended to create that attitude rather than give an accurate picture of the American reality. For Stoetzer, the enlightened Bourbons turned the world upside down, defining as corrupt what were acceptable practices during the Hapsburg era. Stoetzer, 113-114.

[25]James C. Scott, Comparative Political Corruption (Engelwood Cliffs, New Jersey: Prentice Hall, 1972), viii.

[26]Stein, Hispanic American Historical Review, 6-7; and Fisher, 14.

[27]Stein, Hispanic American Historical Review, 6-7.

[28]Fisher, 17.

[29]Stein, Hispanic American Historical Review, 10.

[30]Ibid., 4.

[31] Ibid.

[32]John Lynch, Spanish Colonial Administration, 1762-1810: The Intendant System in the Viceroyalty of the Rio de la Plata (London: Athlone Press, 1953), 128-130.

[33]Ibid., 54-58; and Stein, Hispanic American Historical Review, 11-12.

[34]Stein, Hispanic American Historical Review, 12-13.

[35]James Lang, Conquest and Commerce: Spain and England in the Americas (New York: Academic Press, 1975), 90.

[36]Fisher, 54-61; and Lynch, Colonial Administration, 68, 92-104.

[37]Lynch, Colonial Administration, 104-105.

[38]Fisher, 62-64, 65-76.

[39]Lynch, Colonial Administration, 241.

[40]Ibid., 239-260; and Fisher, 47-48.

[41] Fisher, 63, 89, 127-131.

[42]Brading, 85-86; and Brian Hamnett, Politics and Trade in Southern Mexico, 1750-1821 (Cambridge: Cambridge at the University Press, 1971), 92-129, 130, 143.

[43]Fisher, 198; and Stein, Hispanic American Historical Review, 27.

[44]Fisher, 91.

[45]Most who have studied the Intendant reform then and now agree that the lack of salaries for subdelegates was the weakest link in the whole reform. See the discussions in Stein, Hispanic American Historical Review, 15-18; Fisher, 95-96; and Hamnett, 84-93.

[46]Fisher, 98.

[47]Both Fisher and Lynch agree here. Fisher, 174-176; and Lynch, Colonial Administration, 204-209

[48]Fisher, 177-183.

[49]Ibid., 184-190; and Lynch, Colonial Administration, 228-230.

[50]Fisher, 190-200; and Lynch, Colonial Administration, 230-236.

[51] Lynch, Colonial Administration, 230-231.

[52]Fisher, 237.

[53]Stoetzer, 10; and Magali Sarfatti, Spanish Bureaucratic-Patrimonialism in America (Berkeley: Institute of International Studes, University of California Press, 1966), 76

[54]Stoetzer, 10.

[55]Leon G. Campbell, "A Colonial Establishment: Creole Domination of the Audencia of Lima During the Late 18th Century," Hispanic American Historical Review LII (February 1972), 3-21. For a full account of the decline of creole participation in the audencia see Mark Burkholder and D. S. Chandler, From Impotence to Authority: The Spanish Crown and the American Audencia 1767-1808 (Columbus and London: University of Missouri Press, 1977).

[56]Mark Burkholder, "From Creole to Peninsular: The Transformation of the Audencia of Lima," Hispanic American Historical Review LII (August 1972), 413.

[57]Campbell, 16-18.

[58]Brading, 39-44.

[59]Jacques A. Barbier, "Elite and Cadres in Bourbon Chile," Hispanic American Historical Review LII (August 1972), 416-435.

[60]Lynch, Colonial Administration, 77.

[61]Sergio Villalobos R., "The Creole Desire for Office," in The Origins of the Latin American Revolutions, 1808-1826, eds. R. A. Humphreys and John Lynch (New York: Knopf, 1965), 260.

[62]Jaime Eyzaguirre, "Promise and Prejudice in Spanish America," in The Origins of the Latin American Revolutions, 1808-1826, eds. R. A. Humphreys and John Lynch (New York: Knopf, 1965), 254.

[63]Brading, 27.

[64]Claudio Véliz, The Centralist Tradition of Latin America (Princeton: Princeton University Press, 1980), 83-84.

[65]John Johnson, Simon Bolívar and Spanish American Independence, 1783-1830 (Princeton: Van Nostrand, 1968), 20-21; and Lynch, Revolutions, 9-10.

[66]J. Lloyd Mecham, Church and State in Latin America (Chapel Hill, North Carolina: University of North Carolina Press, 1934, 1966), 40.

[67]Lynch, Revolutions, 10.

[68]Brading, 234-235.

[69]Ibid., 34-35.

[70]Ibid., 34.

[71]A. Tibesar, "The Peruvian Church at the Time of Independence in the Light of Vatican II," The Americas XXVI (April 1970), 359.

[72]Johnson, 21.

[73]Fisher, 62, 68.

[74]Ibid.

[75]Lynch, Revolutions, 10.

[76]Brading, 211-215. Many creole sons of Buenos Aires merchants found careers in the church, see Susan Midgen Socolow, The Merchants of Buenos Aires, 1778-1810 (Cambridge: Cambridge University Press, 1978), 25-26.

[77]For example see Nancy Farriss, Crown and Clergy in Colonial Mexico, 1759-1821: The Crisis of Ecclesiastical Privilege (London: Athlone Press, 1968). Also see Brian Hamnett, "The Counter Revolution of Morillo and the Insurgent Clerics of New Granada, 1815-1820," The Americas XXXII, Number 4 (April 1976), 597-617; and Véliz, 86.

[78]These views are expressed in Humphreys and Lynch, 21.

[79]Lynch, Revolutions, 15.

[80]Ibid., 12.

[81]John Fisher, "Imperial 'Free Trade' and the Hispanic Economy, 1778-1796," Journal of Latin American Studies XIII, Part 1 (May 1981), 23.

[82]Ships had to be owned by Spaniards and carry a 2/3 Spanish crew, Ibid., 23.

[83]Ibid.

[84]Haring, 342. This figure is disputed by Fisher, but he gives none of his own, Fisher, Journal of Latin American Studies, 24-25.

[85]Fisher, Journal of Latin American Studies, 27 Table I.

[86]Ibid., 42 Table II.

[87]Ibid., 44 Table III.

[88]For New Spain see Brading, 116; and Hamnett, Politics and Trade, 97-98. For Peru see Fisher, Government and Society, 131; and Anna, 5.

[89]According to Shane Hunt, few large merchants in Lima were hurt by the change, Shane Hunt, Growth and Guano in Nineteenth Century Peru. Research Program in Economic Development. Woodrow

Wilson School. Discussion Paper #34. (Princeton: Woodrow Wilson School of Public and International affairs at Princeton University, February 1973), 19. Even in Buenos Aires, the wealthier merchants were those who still had monopoly contacts in Spain, Socolow, 54-55, 58.

[90]Hamnett, Politics and Trade, 117-118.

[91]Ibid., 99, 105; and Brading, 115.

[92]Brading, 115-116. Surviving generationally as merchants in the colonies was always difficult. Due to the laws of inheritance and the non-existence of joint stock companies, merchant fortunes could not be passed along undivided to one child, or even one's wife. Merchants, therefore, encouraged their sons to find other careers - particularly in the civil bureaucracy or church while, at the same time, they brought in young peninsular Spaniards to become their partners in the business and marry their daughters. Many also bought land and attempted to create mayorazgos which would enable them to pass along their wealth undivided, see Brading, 104-105, 112-113. This last solution was absent in areas like the Río de la Plata where land was of little value and thus, merchant families there often found their wealth dissipated with the death of the patriarch, see Socolow, 21-23.

[93]Brading, 158.

[94]Lynch, Revolutions, 13.

[95]Hunt, 21-22. A large part of the decline must be laid to the abolition of repartimiento since a goodly amount of textiles were distributed to the Indians in this manner.

[96]Lynch, Revolutions, 13; and Lang, 82.

[97]Lynch, Revolutions, 14.

[98]Ibid.

[99]Ibid., 12-15; and Anna, 5-6.

[100]Lynch, Revolutions, 15; and Miron Burgin, The Economic Aspects of Argentine Federalism 1820-1852 (New York: Russell and Russell, 1946, 1971), 11-12.

[101]Tulio Halperin-Donghi, Politics, Economics and Society in Argentina in the Revolutionary Period (Cambridge: Cambridge University Press, 1975), 36-37.

[102]Haring, 263.

[103]Fisher, Government and Society, 20. Karen Spalding claims that in the eighteenth century, Spanish officials began to enforce laws calling for a periodic re-distribution of Indian lands in order to increase the tribute rolls. This re-distribution halted the process of economic differentiation which was proceeding in many areas of the Peruvian highlands and

thus, halted the rise of an Indian yeomanry. See Karen Spalding, "Hacienda-Village Relations in Andean Society to 1830," Latin American Perspectives II, Issue 4, Number 1 (Spring 1975), 117-118.

[104]Lillian Estelle Fisher, The Last Inca Revolt, 1780-1783 (Norman: University of Oklahoma Press, 1966), 19.

[105]Leon G. Campbell, "Black Power in Colonial Peru: The 1779 Tax Rebellion in Lamayque," Phylon XXXIII (Summer 1972), 144-145.

[106]Brading, 53.

[107]Ibid., 29.

[108]Oscar Cornblit, "Society and Mass Rebellion in Eighteenth Century Peru and Bolivia," in Latin American Affairs. St. Antony's Papers #22., ed. Raymond Carr (London: Oxford University Press, 1970), 38.

[109]Brading, 52.

[110]Cornblit, 37-39 & note 83, p. 36.

[111]Ibid., 10-11.

[112]Leon G. Campbell, "Recent Research on Andean Peasant Revolts, 1750-1820," Latin American Research Review XIV, Number 1 (1979), 4.

[113]Sergio villalobos R., "Opposition to Imperial Taxation," in The Origins of the Latin American Revolutions, 1808-1826, eds. R. A. Humphreys and John Lynch (New York: Knopf, 1965), 128-131.

[114]Campbell, Phylon, 140-152.

[115]Ralph Lee Woodward, Central America: A Nation Divided (New York: Oxford University Press, 1976), 73.

[116]Lang, 92.

[117]Campbell, Latin American Research Review, 6.

[118]Cornblit, 12.

[119]Ibid., 12-14.

[120]Spaniards, mestizos, pardos and Indians all participated to varying degrees although it became very quickly an exclusively Indian revolt, see Leon G. Cambell, The Military and Society in Colonial Peru 1750-1810 (Philadelphia: American Philosophical Society, 1978), 153.

[121]This is the view of John Fisher and Campbell, see John Fisher, Government and Society, 23; and Leon G. Campbell, "Social Structure of the Tupac Amaru Army in Cuzco, 1780-1781,"

Hispanic American Historical Review LX, Number 4 (November 1981), 677.

122John Fisher, Government and Society, 5; Anna, 5; and Hunt, 18.

123For general accounts see Lillian Fisher, Tupac Amaru; Campbell, Latin American Research Review 3-49; and Cornblit, 9-44. On creole participation in the Tupac Amaru high command see Campbell, Hispanic American Historical Review, 675-693. On the war itself, within the context of the Bourbon military reforms, see Campbell, Military and Society, 106-153.

124Anna, 29. Creole militia in the sierra were demobilized and creoles discriminated against in the Spanish Army, see Campbell, Military and Society, 158-177; and Leon G. Campbell, "Changing Racial and Administrative Structure of the Peruvian Military Under the Later Bourbons," The Americas XXXII (July 1975), 132.

125The following is based on John Leddy Phelan, The People and the King: The Comunero Revolution in Colombia, 1781 (Madison: University of Wisconsin Press, 1978).

126Coastal pardos in both New Spain and Peru (particularly after the poor performance of creole militia in the Tupac Amaru revolt) were seen by the crown as the more reliable military forces the colonies had to offer against Indian revolts, see Campbell, The Americas, 128 & 131; and Criston Archer, "Pardos, Indians and the Army of New Spain: Interrelationships and Conflicts 1780-1810," Journal of Latin American Studies VI, Part 2 (November 1974), 246-255.

127Leslie B. Rout, The African Experience in Spanish America: 1502 to the Present (Cambridge University Press, 1976), 156-159.

128Magnus Mörner, Race Mixture in the History of Latin America (Boston: Little, Brown, 1967), 45; and Lynch, Revolutions, 20.

129Lynch, Revolutions, 22.

130Ibid., 22-23.

131Arnold J. Bauer, "The Church and Spanish American Agrarian Structure, 1765-1865," The Americas XXVII (July 1971), 88-89.

132Brading, 340.

133Bauer, 86-88.

134Bauer, 89.

135Brading, 340-341.

[136]Bauer, 89.

[137]Anna, 40.

[138]Phelan, 81-84.

[139]Ibid., 84.

[140]Richard M. Morse, "The Heritage of Latin America," in The Founding of New Societies, ed. Louis Hartz (New York: Harcourt, 1964), 153-159.

[141]Phelan, 83.

[142]Ibid., 213-217.

4
The Crisis of the Colonial State:
The Spanish American Wars
of Independence

For dependency writers, the Wars of Independence expressed the economic maturity of Spanish America. Accordingly, they view the independence movements primarily as movements for economic freedom. Andre Gunder Frank argues that,

The driving force of the 1810 revolution was the complex of demands by abourgeoisie determined to seize power, to achieve self determination and to control both economic power and the political power vested in the state apparatus . . . . The creole bourgeoisie was aware that the colonial system barred them from access to the political power that was the key to a new economic policy designed exclusively for their benefit.[1]

while Juan E. Corradi believes that,

The growing disparity in the rate of economic development between the various parts of the Spanish empire was accompanied by a weakening of the bonds that held them together. The political and social unity of the metropolis and the colonies . . . became increasingly tenuous on account of that uneven development.[2]

and Fernando Henrique Cardoso and Enzo Faletto claim that,

The advances of modern capitalism had placed Spain in the role of intermediary between the colonies and the new industrial Europe. As a result of these political vicissitudes, merchants and especially producers in Latin America came to view colonial relations as an obstacle to be surmounted. They wanted to establish direct links with Great Britain . . .[3]

In other words, "The Wars of Independence were waged to achieve a political order and a different "pact" with the new metropolis."[4] That this was the ultimate result of independence is not in doubt. However, as Stanley and Barbara Stein argue, ". . . it would be a gross simplification to state that this was the principal goal of the early insurgents."[5] In fact, they justifiably fault the popularity of this interpretation for "clouded" versions of the post-independence era.[6]

The economic grievances of the Spanish Americans, discussed in the previous Chapter, did not <u>cause</u> the final break with Spain. The movements for independence, rather, evolved out of the conjunction of two crises: the crisis of the American bureaucracy which began with the implementation of the Bourbon reforms; and the crisis of the Spanish State with the Napoleonic usurpation of the Spanish crown. It was only once the king, the connective tissue of the empire, had disappeared that the bureaucratic crisis in America allowed Spanish American grievances with the Bourbon reforms to clearly affect the outcome of events.

The independence movement in each colony had its own specific character even though the origin and outcome of the movements was essentially the same. The different characteristics themselves were a result of the particular grievances each sector of the colonial elite had against the Bourbons (and amongst themselves) and how these and the actual movements were worked out. Although it is impossible to give a full account of the independence movements throughout Spanish America here, what follows will analyze the nature of the movements in general with special attention given to a few specific examples.

The movements for independence in Spanish America were not, in their origin, independence movements at all. When the crisis of 1808--the abdications of Charles IV and Ferdinand VII, the overrunning of the Peninsula by Napoleon's armies, and the imposition of a new dynasty with the accession of Joseph Bonaparte to the throne--unfolded, there were few among the "revolutionaries" in America who would have envisioned an outcome that included a permanent break with the Spanish Crown.[7]

With the news from Spain, the Americans immediately rejected the French usurpation and declared their loyalty to the Bourbon dynasty.[8] The question the French invasion raised then, was not the colonists' loyalty to the monarch, but rather where sovereignty lay in his absence. The question was answered in Spain when the various town cabildos set up juntas to lead the resistance against the French. They ultimately joined together to form a Junta Central which gave some semblance of central authority.[9] A solution was not so easily found in Spanish America though. First, the authorities who represented the king had not been unseated by the invasion, but the legal basis for their authority, the king, had been. Second, the Spanish Americans were concerned about the actual loyalty of these officials to the "legitimate" king, Ferdinand VII, because they had been appointed by the administration that handed the crown over to the French.[10] Third, the conflicts within the Spanish American colonial bureaucracy caused by Bourbon administrative reorganization rose to the surface without the mediating hand of the crown. Each sector of the bureaucracy (now including the cabildos) scrambled for the support of creoles, Spaniards, and the other elements of colonial society in order to gain the upper hand in their jurisdictional disputes. Finally, the Spanish Americans were outraged when the Junta Central took up where the Bourbons had left off and demanded their obedience, not the basis of its representation of the king, but rather its being the legitimate authority of the Spanish nation. The Americans rejected this formula, opting rather for the old Hapsburg formula which defined their relationship to the other parts of the empire, including Spain, through the king and only the king. The movements thus sought, and generally accomplished, the unseating of the top Spanish administrators. They ultimately declared autonomy from the Junta Central (and later the Regency), but generally declared in favor of Ferdinand VII. The movements became genuinely independentist only after the return of Ferdinand VII to the throne in 1814. His uncompromising absolutism and repression of the American movements made an accomodation with the crown impossible.

THE MOVEMENT IN THE RÍO DE LA PLATA

The Viceroyalty of the Río de la Plata was the only Spanish American colony in which the crisis of the colonial bureaucracy came to the surface before the loss of legitimate authority in Spain. An unauthorized invasion of Buenos Aires by the English General William C. Beresford in 1806 (and a second invasion by General John Whitelocke in 1807) threw all the viceregal authorities into disarray and fundamentally changed the balance of forces in the viceroyalty before the crisis in Spain.

With the first invasion and occupation of Buenos Aires by Beresford, Viceroy Sobremonte and his administration fled the city while the city's main corporations, including the cabildo and consulado, swore their loyalty to the English King.[11] Buenos Aires was reconquered, not by the viceroy who bided time in Córdoba collecting a force he felt sufficient to expel the British, but by a Frenchman in the service of the Spanish crown, Santiago Liniers, who defeated the British with a force of about 1,000 given to him by Governor Ruiz Huidobro of Montevideo.[12] With the British defeated and the viceragal administration in disarray, the cabildo with the other city corporations-- civil, ecclesiastic, and military--organized a Council of War which forced the viceroy to give military command of the colony to Liniers. Such a formula was preferable to the viceragal authorities--viceroy and audencia--to the full removal of the viceroy from office and a further crisis of the administration.[13] It was at this point that the political balance in Buenos Aires began to turn in favor of the creoles.

The threat of further invation led to a great expansion of military forces dominated by creoles. Although the Spanish dominated cabildo was apprehensive over this development and attempted to get control of this force through the appointment of Spanish born officers, there was general agreement in the colony as to the need for a defense force.[14] When the British attacked again in 1807 and captured Montevideo from the hapless Viceroy Sobremonte, he was deposed by the Council of War and viceregal authority was transferred to the reluctant audencia.[15] The subsequent British invasion of Buenos Aires by General Whitelocke was then ultimately defeated at the hands of the creole and Spanish military forces led by Liniers and Martín Alzaga, alcalde and Spanish born leader of the cabildo.[16]

Liniers soon became provisional viceroy,[17] but very quickly fell out of favor with the Spanish dominated cabildo because he allied himself with the viceregal bureaucrats and the new military force created to repel the British. With the turn of events in Spain in 1808, suspicions of disloyalty arose on both sides. Liniers' French birth, his admiration for Napoleon, and his attachment to the viceregal officials of Charles IV made him suspect to both Spaniards and creoles. His acceptance of the Seville Junta Central did not allay these suspicions. Both Spaniards and creoles began to suspect the loyalty of the Junta Central as, rather than dismissing discredited viceregal officials, it clung to them as the surest way to maintain the continuity of the empire.[18] Into this mix of suspicions was thrown the intrigues of Ferdinand's sister, Princess Carlota Joaquina of Portugal, who took up residence in Río de Janeiro to escape the French. Princess Carlota represented a solution to the crisis for viceregal officials because her royal mantle might again legitimize their rule. In a similar fashion, some creoles supported the cause of Carlota because they feared the autonomist leanings of the Spanish dominated cabildo. Recognition of Carlota, they felt, would check the designs of the cabildo. In any case, many on both sides opposed Carlota on traditional grounds, the fear of Portuguese expansionisn in the River Plate.[19]

The Spanish dominated cabildo brought matters to a head in October 1808, when it attempted to depose Viceroy Liniers and, in imitation of Montevideo, set up a local junta controlled by Spaniards and loyal to the Seville Junta Central. The successful Spanish coup of Montevideo, however, was not repeated in Buenos Aires. The forces of the cabildo, led by Alzaga, were outmaneuvered by the creole military force under the command of Cornelio Saavedra who threw his support to Viceroy Liniers.[20] The leaders of the coup attempt were exiled to Patagonia, but tensions between those who had supported the cabildo and those who had supported Liniers did not ease. The Junta Central sought to solve the crisis by appointing Baltasar Hidalgo de Cisneros the new viceroy in August 1809.

Cisneros very briefly united the warring parties in the viceroyalty, disbanding some of the creole military units, ressurecting some Spanish units defeated in the coup as militia, and readmitting Alzaga and his compatriots into Buenos Aires.[21] Events in Spain, however, undid all of Cisneros' peacemaking. By May 1910, news arrived that French armies had overrun Seville, the Junta Central was no more, and the prospects looked awfully dismal for Spanish resistance. The viceroy attempted to suppress the news for as long as he could, fearing the worst, but was forced to relent when events in Spain became common knowledge. On May 18, he officially published the sad news from Spain.[22]

The creole military force created for the defense of the viceroyalty now became the arbiter of its future. The creole elite officers forced the viceroy and cabildo to hold a cabildo abierto (open town meeting) which, with the reluctance of the cabildo, deposed the viceroy and set up a local junta, loyal to Ferdinand VII, to take over the administration of the viceroyalty.[23] With the Spaniards cowed by their defeat at the hands of Liniers, afraid of the military superiority of the creole elite, and having no love for Cisneros (he had opposed their interests by opening up the port to British trade in order to fill his depleted treasury with the resulting import taxes), the field was left open to the creoles.[24]

Similar justifications for creole accession to power were heard in every part of Spanish America where a junta movement appeared. It was argued that once the legitimate government of Spain had fallen, sovereignty reverted back to the people who could then confer it upon anyone they chose. Since the Junta Central had argued the equality of Spanish America with Spain, the Spanish Americans had the right to set up their own juntas for their defense in the absence of the king. Although in light of later events such views became revolutionary, they did not break with traditional Spanish political and legal thought.[25] With the legitimacy of the State in question, both creoles and Spaniards sought to fill the vacuum in Spanish America--in the case of Buenos Aires, the creoles won.[26]

THE MOVEMENT IN CHILE

With the loss of the legitimizing hand of the crown in Chile, conflicts and tensions based on creole grievances against the Bourbon reforms surfaced very quickly. As in Buenos Aires, once the authority of royal officials began to be questioned, the various bureaucratic institutions and creole and Spanish factions vied for control over the colony.

The two chief grievances of the Chilean creoles were first, the increased difficulty in obtaining positions and advancement in the colonial bureaucracy upon which many less fortunate creole families depended,[27] and second, Chile's colonial status vis-à-vis the viceregal capital at Lima (since the decline of the agricultural regions in the vicinity of Lima in the late seventeenth century, Chile became the major source of wheat for Lima--the Lima merchants controlled this trade, manipulated the price of Chilean wheat, keeping prices artifically low to the detriment of Chilean producers). In fact, the Chilean Independence movement was always more directed at Lima then it was at Spain.[28]

As in Buenos Aires, loyalty to the monarchy was unquestioned. There were no indications of disloyalty even after the news of the abdications reached Chile.[29] What was

97

unfortunate for the royal bureaucracy in Chile though, was that in the same year the colony lost its king, its popular governor, Luis Muñoz de Guzman, died and was replaced by the less competent Francisco Antonio García Carrasco. García Carrasco was either easily manipulated or understood too well the tenuous position of Spanish authority in America with the loss of the king. He first fell under the influence of elements of the creole elite and, when it seemed his administration was tottering, then gravitated towards the Spaniards.[30] In his two years in office, García Carrasco managed to alienate the audencia, the cabildo of Santiago, and the creole aristocracy.[31]

García Carrasco alienated the spaniards in Chile when he came under the influence of Juan Martínez de Rozas, a creole tied to the wealthy Mendiburo family of Concepcion. Martinez de Rozas convinced Garcia Carrasco that, given the crisis in Spain, the cabildo of Santiago was best suited to direct the defenses of the colony. He argued that its membership should be increased by 12 regidores, including himself and a disproportionate number of creoles.[32] Spaniards were further alienated when a representative of the Seville Junta arrived in Santiago with a request for 100,000 pesos and García Carrasco, instead of honoring the request, had him sent to head the garrison at the Chilean-Indian frontier.[33]

García Carrasco's fortunes truly declined when he alienated all in the colony by his involvement in the Scorpion Affair. It seems that either García Carrasco was a partner with, or had been duped by, Martínez de Rozas in a scheme to seize a British merchant ship, the Scorpion, in October 1808, under a letter of Marque rather than under the contraband law. The difference was important. Taken under a letter of Marque, the cargo of the Scorpion was considered spoils of war and the treasury was deprived of the 300,000 peso cargo which went to Martínez de Rozas and his cohorts.[34] This incident upset every sector of opinion in the colony and severely damaged the credibility and authority of García Carrasco's administration. Creoles and Spaniards began agitating for his replacement, creoles though, for a junta.[35]

These agitations led García Carrasco to interfere with cabildo elections in Santiago and, when this tactic failed, he arrested three prominent Chilean creoles who he thought were conspiring against his administration. The protests of the cabildo and ecclesiatic cabildo against this move, and the audencia's fear of revolt, convinced García Carrasco not to send the three to Lima for trial but rather to hold them in Valpraiso. News, which later turned out to be false, that Spain had fallen to the French led García Carrasco, on July 12, 1810, to send two of the alleged conspirators to Lima for trial. The uproar over this act led to his fall and the events which were to lead to the formation of a local junta.[36] As the creole cabildo plotted to overthrow García Carrasco, the Spanish audencia diffused the situation by deposing him itself and designating the prominent creole, Mateo de Toro Zambrano, Conde de la Conquista, as captain general.[37]

The audencia's move had a generally calming effect on the agitated colony, but this was not to last. Pressure was almost immediately brought to bear on Toro Zambrano by two opposing groups. One group, centered in the cabildo, was made up of creoles who agitated for a local junta because they distrusted the royal officials (as in Buenos Aires, fear that royal officials would turn the colony over to the French or Portuguese was prevalent). The other centered around the audencia and included the clergy, top royal officials, and some creole aristocrats who sought to maintain royal officials in power.[38]

Toro Zambrano was finally convinced to call for a cabildo abierto after the agitation of the cabildo group reached a high pitch with the impending arrival of the new governor, Francisco Javier Elío, who was noted for his anti-creole feelings (Elío had led the Spanish coup in Montevideo against the creole supported Viceroy Liniers).[39] In addition, news from Spain added to the high level of suspicion and tension. First, news arrived of the fall of the Seville Junta Central and its replacement by a Regency at Cádiz. This Regency denounced past Spanish discrimination against the colonials, asked for their recognition, and suggested that they might set up their own local juntas on the model of Cádiz. Further news informed the Chileans of Ferdinand's denunciation of Godoy (Charles IV's favorite) and his appointments in the royal bureaucracy for "whoremongering, French sympathies and disloyalty." Since many royal officials received their appointments from that administration, practically the whole colonial bureaucracy was suspect.[40]

The cabildo abierto installed a creole dominated junta, with Toro Zambrano as its life president, to take over the administration of the colony. It called for a congress made up of representatives from the whole colony and retained the cabildo and the audencia. All of this was done with expressions of genuine loyalty to Ferdinand VII and was ultimately recognized by the Regency in Cádiz and Viceroy Abascal of Peru[41] (it seems that Abascal was suspicious of these developments and would have liked to have ended them, but Lima was too dependent on Chilean wheat and he was otherwise occupied putting down junta movements in Upper Peru and Buenos Aires).[42] The justification for the movement was, as in Buenos Aires, not revolutionary but traditional -- sovereignty fell back to the people once the monarch could no longer exercise it and they had a right to confer it on another for their own well being.[43]

THE JUNTA MOVEMENT ELSEWHERE IN SPANISH AMERICA

Elsewhere in Spanish America, similar movements broke out. In Upper Peru, junta movements arose, one in Chuquisaca led by the audencia and another in La Paz led by the cabildo, but were suppressed; the former by Viceroy Cisneros, the latter by Viceroy Abascal.[44]

In New Granada, the first junta appeared in Quito on August 10, 1809, when creoles deposed the president of the audencia and placed the Marquis de Selva Alegre and the Bishop of Quito at the head of the government.[45] The Quiteños acted out of a fear that the Napoleonic conquest of Spain would bring the French to America and that the only defense was for the Americans to declare their independence. The Quiteños also feared the Spaniards of the city who, they believed, planned to assassinate the creole nobility on August 19.[46] The movement was smashed, not by the authorities of the viceregal capital at Bogotá where the Quiteños had sympathy among many creoles, but by the viceroy of Peru who unleashed a violent repression that only confirmed the Quiteños worst fears.[47]

In Caracas, creoles reacted with dread to Napoleon's occupation of Spain, fearing a French invasion of America would unleash the forces which overturned the slave system in Haiti. The creoles of Venezuela already suspected the viceregal authorities of trying to undermine white creole supremacy by their administration of Bourbon reforms favorable to pardos and slaves. Creole attempts to set up a junta, which they felt would assure their security and predominance, were met by repression and the incitement of the pardos and slaves against them by the royal administration. When news of the fall of the Seville Junta Central arrived, the creoles acted, deposing the captain general and instituting a creole junta loyal to Ferdinand VII.[48] By the end of 1810, most of the Viceroyalty of New Granada was lost to the Spanish administration.

All junta movements, however, were not as successful. In New Spain, the audencia and consulado short-circuited a move by Viceroy José de Iturrigaray and his creole supporters in the cabildo to install a junta in 1808. The Spanish audencia deposed Iturrigaray, put in their own viceroy, repressed the creole challengers, organized its own military force, and encouraged Spaniards in the provinces to seize power.[49] The reaction to the Spanish coup led directly, by 1810, to the movements of Hidalgo and Morelos. The success of these movements reflected the weakness and vaccilation of provincial royal officials even though they were ultimately put down by the forces of the capital.[50]

LIMA: BULWARK OF SPANISH ADMINISTRATION IN AMERICA

The movement for local juntas arose in Peru also, but only at the provincial level and, it seems, never infected the viceregal center at Lima.[51] Few areas in Spanish America suffered the Bourbon reforms to the extent of Lima--loss of territory and thus control over bureaucratic appointments, loss of its trade monopoly in South America, the imposition of higher taxes, discrimination against creoles for high office, Indian revolts and agricultural decay--yet no other major center remained as loyal to the Spanish administration.[52] Lima joined the general movement for independence in Spanish America only when San Martín's Army entered the city in 1821.[53]

100

Several factors contributed to the relative stability of Lima when the balance of the royal administration on the continent was crumbling. The Peruvian elite, both creole and Spanish, was inordinately privileged in a veritable sea of under-privilege. On the coast, and particularly in Lima, this elite was far outnumbered by Blacks, morenos, mestizos and Indians. Out of a total population of 63,809 in 1813, whites comprised only 32% in Lima and, out of a population which reached 1,115,207 for the entire viceroyalty, they comprised a meager 12%.[54] Indian and slave revolts bred insecurity that tended to attach this elite to the viceregal administration which, it felt, would maintain the social hierarchy.[55]

Even with the loss of a great deal of the old viceregal territory, Lima's position as the capital of the viceroyalty enabled it to drain resources from, and control the trade of, the productive highland provinces. Bureaucratic control of the provinces from Lima made this all possible and few who benefited were in favor of innovations in government that might have threatened the system.[56] Further, the vast majority of the Lima elite depended upon bureaucratic appointment, not agriculture or even commerce, for their incomes. Lima was a consumer/administrative center par excellence. Timothy Anna has estimated that only 26.3% of the elite could be considered producers (not of course that they themselves produced, but that their income and wealth were derived from the ownership of productive establishments), while 41.7% were regular or secular clergy, 18.2% were in the royal service and the balance were escribanos, lawyers, doctors or titled nobles, bringing the occupational elite dependent upon the viceroyal treasury to 67.2%.[57] An elite so tied to the royal administration would have to have been very sure that it was in its interest to revolt, as Anna remarks, "The Peruvians would not revolt until the Royal regime lost authority."[58]

Maintenance of the Spanish administration in Lima also had a good deal to do with the capable and politic hand of Viceroy Abascal. Abascal navigated the administration through stormy periods of creole discontent and regional highland revolt against the hegemony of Lima. Though Lima and the viceroyalty were riven by the same sort of inter-bureaucratic rivalries and creole discontent with the Bourbon reforms as the rest of Spanish America, a strong determined hand at the helm could hold things together.[59] This was even more remarkable in that on top of provincial revolts, Chilean insurgency, the challenge from the Río de la Plata, bureaucratic infighting, and creole agitation for relief from Bourbon commercial and fiscal reforms, Abascal had to maintain his authority and calm in the colony with his position weakened by the authorities in Spain who announced to the Americans that "your destinies no longer depend upon Viceroys, Governors and ministers."[60] The colonists were also invited to send representatives to the Spanish Cortes which drew up the Constitution of 1812. Under this constitution, the viceroy's authority was further undermined by the institution of elective cabildos, freedom of the press, the abolition of Indian tribute and royal monopolies, and the creation of a minicortes in the colony within which the viceroy would be only the "superior political chief" sharing power with local elected representatives.[61]

THE WARS OF INDEPENDENCE AND THE CRISIS OF THE STATE IN AMERICA

Although the economic and social grievances of the colonists were undoubtedly important conditioning factors in the junta movements, the success of Abascal in holding together the Viceroyalty of Peru underscores the essentially political nature of those movements. Bourbon administrative reorganization not only destabilized internal relations within the bureaucracy, it closed off traditional Hapsburg avenues of redress that had inured the creole elite to the system at a time when creoles had mounting grievances with Bourbon commercial and fiscal reforms. As Jorge Domínguez argues,

> Traditional elite political participation, which was neopatrimonial, had also been accommodated within the empire. The elite sought access to governmental jobs, military privileges or economic advantage; it opposed governmental efforts to set it free. Even under conditions of economic growth, traditional elites sought to increase access to government in traditional ways . . . Goals were typically adjustive or backward looking. Many sought to restore lost rights or circumstances. Others resisted change or sought to adjust their position within the system.[62]

Thus, it is not surprising that once the Bourbon regime had proved its incompetence to the creoles by not only mishandling colonial affairs, but also Spanish international affairs--in being instrumental in the loss of Spanish Independence--they reacted in a very traditional manner to protect their interests and what they felt were the interests of the crown. Rather than seeking change, the creoles who took control of the colonies through the junta movements attempted to maintain traditional patterns and policies of Spanish rule. This attempt, however, could not reproduce the order and harmony of the Hapsburg era that the creoles sought. As discussed earlier,[63] the Hapsburg system made possible the existence of conflicting forms of social relations of production and land tenure (as well as trade) by mediating the conflicts between (and within) them through the colonial bureaucracy. Not only did the legitimacy of the crown, and the adjustive practices of the "relatively autonomous" State make these various interests harmonious, they were major aspects of their maintenance. Thus, what was considered by some creoles to be their traditional legitimate rights and interests conflicted with what other felt to be theirs. As Frederick Stirton Weaver argues,

The differences in the local forms in which production was organized and surplus appropriated created a regional diversity far more important than the superficial uniformity that standardized colonial administrative organization and selective aspects of the Spanish culture lent to diverse places.[64]

Not only did fledgling creole States have to contend with, and try to harmonize such interests, they found it almost impossible to assert the interest of the State over the interests of provincial governments which, for all intents and purposes acted as States with their own State interests. The junta movements lifted the lid from a boiling pot of conflict which boiled over and engulfed Spanish America until a new formula for elite harmony was worked out.

The conflicts which engulfed Spanish America from 1810 into the national period were not the result of innovations introduced by the creoles into the political, economic, and social systems of the colonies. They were, rather, the result of the clash of competing elites who sought to impose their traditional rights and interests against one another, and the attempts of fledgling States to assert the traditional rights and interests of the State in societies where the State had lost its legitimacy.

The events in the Viceroyalty of Río de la Plata subsequent to the installation of the junta on May 25, 1810, best illustrate how this complex of forces worked to create the anarchy that plagued much of Spanish America in the first half of the nineteenth century. Upon its accession, the Junta of Buenos Aires attempted to assert its authority throughout the viceroyalty by assuming the authority of the Spanish administration. The junta expected change neither in the political nor in the economic hegemony of Buenos Aires--but the provinces were not very cooperative.

Paraguay, which had been an unwilling tributary of the viceroyalty, sought to maintain its own autonomy in the face of the rapid political changes in Buenos Aires.[65] Under Governor-Intendent Colonel Bernardo de Velazco, Paraguay met the call of the Buenos Aires junta for submission and the sending of delegates to a general congress with a careful and cautious response. It swore obedience to the Regency in Spain, declared fraternal solidarity with Buenos Aires (but did not recognize its superiority) and formed a Junta of War to defend itself.[66]

The Junta of Buenos Aires responded by sending a military force, under the command of Manuel Belgrano, to force the Paraguayan authorities to submit. He was unsuccessful, being defeated twice by a Paraguayan creole militia which, though deposing Velazco for his incompetence in meeting the military challenge from Buenos Aires, nevertheless maintained the policy of autonomy. The Paraguayans, under the leadership of José Gaspar Rodríguez de Francia, thus began the process of creating a Paraguayan State.[67]

The junta was more successful, at least initially, in asserting its authority in the interior and littoral provinces, yet these too ultimately revolted against it. By 1820, the State thrown up by the junta movement of 1810 precariously controlled only the province of Buenos Aires. This disastrous disintergration of the authority of the State, which ended in its complete collapse after the Battle of Cepeda, was the direct outcome of its attempt to re-establish its hegemony in Upper Peru. The assertion of its authority in Upper Peru was crucial to Buenos Aires because, as we have seen,[68] Buenos Aires could not maintain its large bureaucracy, nor finance its external trade, except with great difficulty, without the silver from Upper Peru. More than in any other viceregal center (except perhaps Lima) the elite of Buenos Aires depended on bureaucratic position and trade.[69]

The problem of the loss of Upper Peru (Buenos Aires' military expedition was defeated by Abascal's troops) was made immediately apparent when, in order to continue the war against the royalists in Upper Peru and Western Argentina, urban wealth, acquired by the State through draconian forced loans and "contributions," was quickly exhausted.[70] The exhaustion of urban sources of revenue led the State to shift its support, at least in the provinces, to those whose wealth was generated directly by the land. The State needed men, horses, and food to continue the war and thus, production finally asserted itself in a system where it had always been subservient to trade and political administration.[71] Perhaps the best example of this was State support for the regime of Martin de Güemes in Salta.[72]

This policy proved to have disastrous consequences for the State when it was applied to the Banda Oriental (Uruguay). First supporting the rural forces of José Artigas against an intransigent and royalist Montevideo, Buenos Aires created a formidable enemy in Artigas and his littoral allies when it abandoned his movement to liberate the Banda Oriental. The rationale for supporting the Artigas movement and its eventual abandonment conformed to the interests of the Buenos Aires State at each specific moment, yet both positions were to set the stage for its ultimate collapse. Certainly the royalist challenge just across the river was one good reason for supporting Artigas. But more important was the need of the State at Buenos Aires to eliminate the autonomy of Montevideo which had presented itself as a direct threat to the hegemony of Buenos Aires throughtout the viceregal era.[73] Buenos Aires' preeminence in the region was assured by its control of internal and external trade, a function of its political position as the viceregal capital. The better harbor at Montevideo was a constant source of dismay (during the colonial era a good deal of contraband trade--not subject to control or taxation by Buenos Aires--was funneled through Montevideo) during viceregal days. Montevideo represented an even more serious challenge with its self proclaimed independence from the Junta of Buenos Aires in 1810.[74] Buenos Aires only jettisoned Artigas and his movement when an even greater threat than the royalists in Montevideo appeared--a Portuguese army in Montevideo threatening Buenos Aires.[75]

While the State at Buenos Aires encouraged the rise of rural elite influence in the urban administrations of the provinces, it demanded greater resources from them and did not protect their economic interests any better than did the Bourbons. In order to raise further revenue for the war, the State opened up the port to British and American ships that flooded interior markets with cheap goods and stole the Buenos Aires market away from interior producers.[76] After 1815, the provinces began opting out of their union with the State at Buenos Aires.[77] The response of Buenos Aires was to attempt to impose a centralist form of State on the provinces through the Constitution of 1819. The State tried to enforce it and the provinces reacted in kind. The now almost nonexistent authority of the State at Buenos Aires collapsed when confronted with the defeat of its military forces at Cepeda on January 20, 1820 at the hands of the combined forces of the littoral provinces.[78]

The ruralization of the bases of political power fomented by the policies of the State at Buenos Aires affected Buenos Aires itself after 1820. Forced back upon the resources of the province of Buenos Aires alone, the political elite of Buenos Aires, who reconstituted the political system on a provincial basis, made it possible for rural based elites to rise in influence. First, in order to reduce the cost of the military (which had been the major drain on the revenues of the State) the provincial authorities disbanded much of the army and based the security of the Province on rural militia under the control of the estancieros (ranchers).[79] Second, they proceeded with a policy of reconstructing the provincial economy on the only basis now possible--the export of hides and other cattle based products.[80] This ruralization of the bases of political support for the State was a process that continued throughout the crisis of the 1820s, and culminated in the rise of Juan Manuel de Rosas in 1829.[81]

Similar processes and forces were at work elsewhere during the Spanish American Wars of Independence. Lima, which was reluctantly liberated by Argentine and Chilean troops, became a quagmire for San Martín. The Lima elite lent only lackluster support, funds were extremely scarce and his army fell apart while the royalist army threatened from its highland retreat.[82] San Martín failed to liberate Peru because he based himself in Lima which not only had been exhausted financially by its support of the royalist cause, but was now cut off from the source of its wealth--the Andean highlands.[83]

With San Martín's withdrawal in favor of Simon Bolívar (who did not make the same mistakes and instead based his forces in the northern province of Trujillo) Peru was finally "liberated" and the Spanish Army in America destroyed.[84] But, as in Argentina, the war ruralized the political bases of power. The State administration organized at Lima suffered a lack of legitimacy and authority, and constant invasions from provincial/military caudillos. It was not until Ramón Castilla became President in the middle of the nineteenth century that the state, financed by an independent source of revenue (guano), was

105

able to subdue the provinces.[85]

The independence movement in New Granada was wracked from the begining with regionalist sentiments that led to the collapse of the movement in Colombia and royalist resurgence and invasions.[86] In Venezuela, royalists fomented a race war against the creole insurgents and then crushed their movement with Murillo's invasion in 1815.[87] Although New Granada was finally liberated under the leadership of Simon Bolívar, and the various provinces united into the State of Gran Colombia, the centrifugal forces which plagued the other former colonies asserted themselves there too. Gran Colombia disintegrated into Colombia, Venezuela, and Ecuador, and even this did not end the political strife.[88]

The Spanish army in America was not immune from the disintegration caused by political factionalism. In both New Spain and Peru, the last bastions of imperial power in America, the viceroys were deposed by military revolts as a result of political conflict. In both colonies, animosity between officers who supported the absolutism of Ferdinand VII and those who supported the Constitution of 1812 "burst into the open."[89] In New Spain, Viceroy Juan Ruiz de Apodaca was deposed and replaced by Field Marshall Francisco Novella when he resisted the re-promulagation of the Constitution of 1812.[90] The Constitution was implemented in earnest by the liberals, but conservative creoles and Spaniards led by Colonel Augustín Iturbide revolted, destroying the Spanish regime in New Spain forever.[91]

In Peru, Viceroy Jocquín de la Pezuela was deposed under very similar circumstances. According to Margaret Woodward, liberal constitutionalist officers in Pezuela's army revolted against him in 1821 when he delayed promulagating, and showed little support for, the Constitution of 1812.[92] Pezuela was replaced by General La Serna who was more accepable to the liberal officers. However, in 1823 the Constitution was again overthrown in Spain and the absolutists regained power. Genereal Pedro Antonio Olañeta, a creole who commanded the royal army in Upper Peru, received the news of the overthrow of the Constitution before La Serna. He revolted against the viceroy, overturned the constitutionalist authorities in Upper Peru, and declared to the king that he had been the only truly loyal officer in Spanish America for the past three years.[93] Confusion and demoralization pervaded La Serna's army when the king supported Olañeta, even appointing him Viceroy of the Río de la Plata (a very hopeful appointment) over the objections of La Serna.[94] Olañeta's revolt drove the last nail into the coffin of Spanish military power in America because, with a demoralized and under strength army, La Serna was forced to meet the insurgent armies at Ayacucho and was defeated.[95]

The upheavals in Spanish America did not abate with the defeat of Spanish power in America. According to Richard Morse,

The collapse of the supreme authority activated the latent forces of local oligarchies, municipalities, and extended

106

family systems in a struggle for power and prestige in the new, arbitrarily defined Republics . . . . In the absence of developed and interacting economic interest groups having a stake in constitutional process, the new countries were plunged into alternating regimes of anarchy and personalist tyranny. The contest to seize a patrimonial state apparatus, fragmented from the original imperial one, became the driving force of public life in each new country.[96]

In Part II, the continuing crisis of the State in Spanish America and its effects on the new nations' integration into the international economy will be discussed and analyzed.

NOTES

[1]Andre Gunder Frank, Lumpenbourgeoisie - Lumpendevelopment (New York: Monthly Review Press, 1972), 48.

[2]Juan E. Corradi, "Argentina," in Latin America: The Struggle with Dependency and Beyond, eds. Ronald Chilcote and Joel Edelstein (New York: Wiley, 1974), 320.

[3]Fernando Henrique Cardoso and Enzo Faletto, Dependency and Development in Latin America (Berkeley: University of California Press, 1979). 31.

[4]Ibid., 35.

[5]Stanley Stein and Barbara Stein, The Colonial Heritage of Latin America (New York: Oxford University Press, 1970), 131.

[6]Ibid.

[7]O. Carlos Stoetzer, The Scholastic Roots of the Spanish America Revolution (New York: Fordham University Press, 1979), 152

[8]Ibid., 162-163.

[9]Ibid., 156-158; and John Lynch, The Spanish American Revolutions: 1808-1826 (New York: W. W. Norton, 1973), 35.

[10]Charles IV's ministers, especially Manuel Godoy the king's favorite, were suspected of being afrancesados owing to their reliance on the French model of development, administration, and foreign affairs.

[11]Tulio Halperin-Donghi, Politics, Economics and Society in Argentina in the Revolutionary Period (Cambridge: University Press, 1975), 125.

[12]Ricardo Levene, A History of Argentina, trans. William Spence Robertson (Chapel Hill, North Carolina: University of North Carolina Press, 1957), 195.

[13]Halperin-Donghi, 127.

[14]Ibid., 131.

[15]Levene, 198.

[16]Ibid., 199-200.

[17]Ordinarily, the president of the audencia would have become the new viceroy, but under wartime conditions the crown decreed that the office go to the highest ranking military man in the colony. This was Ruiz Huidobro but he had been taken prisoner by the British and sent to England--the next in line was Lineirs, see Halperin-Donghi, 133.

[18]Ibid., 136-138.

[19]Ibid., 137-139.

[20]Ibid., 140-143.

[21]Montevideo also recognized his authority and dissolved its separate pro-Sevilla junta, see Ibid., 149.

[22]Levene, 218.

[23]Stoetzer claims that the real reason Cisneros was deposed was because of his close relationship with Manuel Godoy who had been denounced by Ferdinand VII. The implication is that if he had not been so disgraced, he would have been satisfactory to the creoles to lead the junta, see Stoetzer, 197.

[24]Claudio Véliz, The Centralist Tradition of Latin America (Princeton: Princeton University Press, 1980), 130-132.

[25]Perhaps the best work that argues this position is Stoetzer. Also see Richard M. Morse, "The Heritage of Latin America," in The Founding of New Societies, ed. Louis Hartz (New York: Harcourt, 1964), 123-177; Richard M. Morse, "Toward a Theory of Spanish American government," Journal of the History of Ideas XV (1964), 71-93; Glen Dealy, "The Tradition of Monistic Democracy in Latin America," in Politics and Social Change in Latin America: The Distinct Tradition, ed. Howard J. Wiarda (Amherst: University of Massachusetts Press, 1974), 71-103; and Howard J. Wiarda, "Corporatism and Development in the Iberic-Latin World: Persistent Strains and New Variations," in The New Corporatism, eds. Frederick B. Pike and Thomas Stritch (South Bend, Indiana: University of Notre Dame Press, 1974) 3-33.

[26]Jorge I. Domínquez, Insurrection or Loyalty: The Breakdown of the Spanish American Empire (Cambridge: Cambridge University Press, 1980), 250.

[27]Mary Felstiner, "Kinship Politics in the Chilean Independence Movement," Hispanic American Historical Review LVI. Number 1 (February 1976), 63-67.

[28]Simon Collier, Ideas and Politics of Chilean Independence: 1808-1833 (Cambridge: Cambridge University Press, 1967), 31.

[29]Ibid, 12-13.

[30]Roger Haigh, The Formation of the Chilean Oligarchy, 1810-1821 (Salt Lake City: Historical S & D Research Foundation, 1972), 14-22.

[31]Collier, 46.

[32]Haigh, 15.

[33]Ibid., 19.

[34]Ibid., 16-17

[35]Ibid., 19.

[36]Ibid., 19-22; and Collier, 46-47.

[37]Collier, 47.

[38]Haigh, 23.

[39]Ibid.; and Collier, 48. For the Elío led revolt against Buenos Aires see Halperin-Donghi, 139-141.

[40]Haigh, 23-28.

[41]Ibid., 28-30; and Collier, 93.

[42]Haigh, 30.

[43]Collier, 69-70.

[44]Lynch, 49-51; Stoetzer, 214-216; and Halperin-Donghi, 148.

[45]Stoetzer, 225.

[46]Robert Gilmore, "The Imperial Crisis, Rebellion and the Viceroy: Nueva Granada in 1809," Hispanic American Historical Review XL, Number 1 (February 1960), 8-10.

[47]Stoetzer, 226. A second movement succeeded there in October 1810, but lasted only to November 1812, when Quito was overrun by the royalists.

[48]Lynch, 191-195.

[49]Ibid., 303; and D. A. Brading, Miners and Merchants in Bourbon, Mexico, 1763-1810 (Cambridge: Cambridge at the University Press, 1971), 341-342.

[50]Lynch, 305-318.

[51]John Fisher has convincingly argues that the provincial revolts in highland Peru were more revolts against Lima than against Spain. It was Lima, in the first instance at least, that exploited the highlands through its political supremacy. These movements attempted to tie the various highland towns to Cuzco rather than Lima, or when the opportunity presented itself with the success of the armies of Buenos Aires in Upper Peru, to re-unite highland southern Peru with Upper Peru. The desire for reunification held into the National period in both southern Peru and Bolivia and was to become a major source of conflict in both, see John Fisher, "Royalism, Regionalism and Rebellion in Colonial Peru 1808-1815," Hispanic American Historical Review LVIX, Number 2 (May 1979), 232-257.

[52]The Captaincy General of Guatemala saw instability, as in Peru, but experienced no breakdown of royal administration, see Ralph Lee Woodward, Central America: A Nation Divided (New York: Oxford University Press, 1976), 82-89.

[53]Timothy Anna, "The Peruvian Declaration of Independence: Freedom by Coercion," Journal of Latin American Studies VII, Part 2 (November 1975), 121.

[54]Timothy Anna, The Fall of the Royal Government in Peru (Lincoln: University of Nebraska Press, 1979), 16.

[55]Lynch, 158.

[56]Ibid., 158-160.

[57]Anna, Royal Government, 19-22.

[58]Ibid., 25.

[59]Ibid. Also see David Werlich, Peru: A Short History (Carbondale: University of Southern Illinois Press, 1978), 59.

[60]John R. Fisher, Government and Society in Colonial Peru: The Intendent System 1784-1814 (London: Athlone Press, 1970), 213-214.

[61]Anna, Royal Government, 43-91.

[62]Domínquez, 247.

[63]See above, Chapter 1.

[64]Frederick Stirton Weaver, "American Underdevelopment: An Interpretive Essay on Historical Change," Latin American Perspectives III, Issue 11, Number 4 (Fall 1976), 24.

[65]Lynch, 106.

[66]Ibid., 107; and Levene, 249.

[67]Lynch, 107-109. Also see Stoetzer, 184-185.

110

[68]See above, p.

[69]Land ownership (farming and ranching) was not considered a prestigious occupation in Buenos Aires. The more prestigious combination was Merchant-Bureaucrat. See Susan Migden Socolow, The Merchants of Buenos Aires, 1778-1810 (Cambridge: Cambridge University Press, 1978), 60-61 and 65.

[70]Halperin-Donghi, 72-81, 159-160, 235-236; and Levene, 348-349.

[71]Halperin-donghi, 812-108, 260-269.

[72]Roger Haigh, "Martin Güemes: A Study of the Power Structure of the Province of Salta, 1810-1821" (Ph.D. disertation, University of Florida, 1963); and Halperin-Donghi, 260-269.

[73]Halperin-Donghi, 272-274.

[74]Lynch, 88-92; and Levene, 252-254.

[75]Levene, 330-333.

[76]Lynch, 65-66.

[77]Ibid., 68.

[78]Halperin-Donghi, 239-334.

[79]Ibid., 353-355.

[80]Ibid., 346, 351-353.

[81]Ibid., 364-372; and Levene, 396-405.

[82]Timothy Anna has shown that the claim of overwhelming support for the Declaration of Independence was, in fact, a sham. Most of the signers did so not out of a burning conviction for independence, but rather out of a good sense of what was required to save their skins or innure themselves to the new regime, see Anna, Journal of Latin American Studies, 221-228.

[83]Anna, Royal Government, 192-213; and Timothy Anna, "The Economic Causes of San Martín's Failure in Lima," Hispanic American Historical Review LIV, Number 4 (November 1974), 657-681.

[84]Anna, Royal Government, 229-234.

[85]Ronald Berg and Frederick Strirton Weaver, "Toward a Reinterpretation of Political Change in Peru During the First Century of Independence," Journal of Latin American Studies XX, Number 1 (February 1978), 69-79.

[86]Lynch, 238-242.

[87]Brian Hamnett, "The Counter Revolution of Morillo and the Insurgent Clerics of a New Granada, 1815-1820," The Americas

XXXII, Number 4 (April 1976), 598-599.

[88]Lynch, 248-257.

[89]Margaret L. Woodward, "The Spanish Army and the Loss of America, 1810-1824," Hispanic American Historical Review XLVIII, Number 4 (November 1968), 601.

[90]It was, in fact, a revolt of the Spanish Army being sent to recover the Río de la Plata in 1820 that sparked the constitutionalist reaction that forced Ferdinand VII to re-proclaim the liberal Constitution of 1812, see Margaret L. Woodward, 595-598, 601-602.

[91]Lynch, 318-321.

[92]Margaret L. Woodward, 603.

[93]Ibid., 603-604; and Anna, Royal Government, 230-231.

[94]Anna, Royal Government, 231.

[95]Ibid., 231-233; and Margaret L. Woodward, 604-605.

[96]Morse, 162.

Part Two

The State Origins of Dependency in Nineteenth Century Peru and Argentina

Introduction

The aftermath of the Wars of Independence is generally presented by dependency writers as a crucial period in the histories of the Spanish American countries. For dependentistas, modern Spanish American underdevelopment really begins with its incorporation into the world capitalist economy after independence.[1] Although they often lay a great deal of emphasis on the creation of "structures of dependency" during the colonial era, independence is presented as a critical historical break in which the opportunity for autonomous economic development was lost.[2] Indeed, independence did offer the Spanish American countries the opportunity for relatively autonomous economic development, but the dependentistas have essentially misread the process and the struggle by which it was lost.

Following their insistence upon a purely economic interpretation of the Wars of Independence, dependency writers have carried this type of interpretation into the first half of the nineteenth century insisting that the political instability and civil warfare of that era revolved around the consolidation of power of an export oriented class. Andre Gunder Frank, whose interpretation is most emphatic on this count, has argued that the civil wars of the first half of the nineteenth century were essentially fought over the issues of "nationalism" and "free trade."[3] Frank contends that,

> For half a century the two parties struggled for control of the state and for the decision as to which of the two policies would prevail. The "European" party, which favored the closest possible relations of dependence on the European metropolis, and which therefore had the firm political and military support from that quarter . . .[4]

while the other, or "American" party's,

> . . . roots were in the interests of the provinces, which sought protection for local industries struggling against the ruinous competition imposed upon them by the "European"

policy of the cattle raising exporters (in Argentina) . . .[5]

While Fernando Henrique Cardoso and Enzo Faletto are more realistic in arguing that political and social factors had important effects on the struggles that wracked Spanish America in the first half of the nineteenth century,[6] they essentially agree with Frank in arguing that,

> After independence, the problem of national organization in Latin America consisted in keeping local control of an export-oriented production system while creating a system of internal political alliance that would permit the group that maintained relations with the outside (the world market and national states of the central countries) a minimum of internal power to preserve stability and represent the economic domination of the export-oriented production sector.[7]

While this was certainly the result, the struggle was not expressed in these purely economic terms. Rather, the crisis of the post-colonial era in Spanish America was essentially political and it was not a foregone conclusion that Spanish American countries would turn to the international economy to solve it.

Although Cardoso and Faletto may argue that ". . . one of the principal motives of the Independence movement was to find a new link with the outside . . ."[8], according to D. C. M. Platt, independence did not immediately transform Spanish America into a major market for importers.[9] Although a period of intensive exporting to Spanish America did ensue (principally by the British whose export production was bottled up by Napoleon's control of the continent) with the opening up of the ports upon independence, it was short lived and highly speculative. British traders came to Spanish America to sell their wares, not to buy Spanish American products. They were interested in specie, and only when that was unavailable did they search for something else to return to Britain.[10] The market for European goods was, in any case, extremely limited. For the most part, the population was involved in subsistance production, and even those who were involved in the money economy had little excess income to spend on imported manufacturers. The needs of most people were still met by local household and handicraft production.[11] According to Platt, even native textile production, often assumed to have been destroyed by the importation of cheap British goods, hardly disappeared from local consumption.

British traders had very little interest in the products of Spanish America and, in fact, Spanish America had very little to sell. Most countries paid for the bulk of their imports with specie or funds acquired through loans.[13] In Argentina, specie made up almost 28% of the value of its exports in 1825,[14] while most Peruvian imports were still being paid for in silver in 1840.[15] Those lucky few countries that did have an export

116

commodity with which to trade for foreign goods found that the bonanza of dramatically increased markets was either short lived, or subject to severe slowdown once peace was restored in Europe. Argentina, for example, found that after a dramatic rise in demand for cattle hides and tallow in Britain, the market slowed for one, and almost disappeared for the other when traditional Russian exports of these products reappeared.[16] Even though Argentina was relatively successful in cementing a link to the international market, it was a weak one as exports in 1848 remained at 1820s levels.[17]

The fact is, Western Europe and its colonies, with the addition of Southern and Eastern Europe and the United States, could supply themselves with food and most industrial raw materials without Spanish America.[18] Though Spanish American trade did shift its direction from Spain to Northwestern Europe and the United States, and some new products were traded, Spanish American external trade remained fundamentally unchanged from the late colonial era into the national period.[19] For British trade, Platt notes,

No reliable comparison can be made between the volume of British manufacturers reaching Latin America before or after emancipation. But what does emerge from such random estimates is that the pattern and constitutes of the trade between Britain and Latin America were well established long before the breakaway from Spain. Once the excitement was over and the needs created by a decade of interrupted trade were satisfied, trade settled back into a familiar pattern, expanded for British cottons by their success in displacing Spanish cottons and German linens, swollen by new fashions and needs, supplemented by the demand of resident foreign communities, but not, in the final analysis so very different in volume or content from the trade with the Spanish Colonies.[20]

The claim that merchants were a driving force behind Spanish America's opening up to the international economy[21] is difficult to sustain. The majority of merchants in the Spanish American colonies had been peninsulares who, if they had not fled with their lives and what part of their wealth they could carry, were mercilessly taxed by penurious independence governments in need of cash with which to carry on the war against Spain.[22] Creole merchants often did not fare much better and, of course, had much less wealth. In international trade, both were displaced by foreign merchants who had vital connections with the centers of export in Europe and the United States. Domestic trade, however, remained in creole hands for the most part, although these were not the super wealthy merchants of colonial days.[23] In Argentina, domestic trade became speculative--the antithesis of the rigidly controlled mercantilism which dominated the colonial era--and therefore fraught with risk. Although one could become very rich, many were ruined.[24] The more powerful merchants of the colonial consulados were against the opening of trade with foreigners and were willing to give the governments--rebel or royalist--grants or loans to compensate for the loss of revenue raised through import taxes on foreign trade.[25] Though merchants remained an important part of the elite in Spanish America, their influence was never decisive.

Producers of export crops were never very important in the Spanish colonial regime, given its principal reliance on the export of specie rather than bulk agricultural produce. They suffered even further as the Wars of Independence decimated vast agricultural areas that had been agro-export oriented. The slave based agricultures of Colombia and Venezuela were severely disrupted by the wars, as was the coastal agricultural zone of Peru.[26] Slaves were freed and inducted into the various contending armies. These armies fed off of the plantations and haciendas leaving them in a state of ruin.[27] The large cattle raising areas of Venezuela and Uruguay were destroyed and the combination of the Wars of Independence and civil war created such a shortage of cattle in Buenos Aires province that Director Pueyrredon ordered the closing of the saladeros (salting plants) in 1817.[28] Indeed, agro-exporters became powerful and influential in the nineteenth century, but not by their efforts alone. As I will show later, export interests were often brought to predominance by Spanish American States or by the conditions of political crisis itself.

In reality, the effects of Spanish America's initial contact with the international economic system were less profound than dependency writers would have us believe. Granted, some domestic production was adversely affected by competition from foreign goods, but on the whole, much of it remained untouched by this new trade.[29] If commerce and production suffered, it suffered from the effects of Bourbon economic and political reforms, the closure of traditional markets due to new political boundaries, and the devastation of the independence and civil wars.[30] Nevertheless, economic disputes centering around the progress of export sectors and their effect on domestic manufacturing and agriculture did have salience in some areas, as Miron Burgin's work on Argentina clearly shows.[31] However, one has to question whether these disputes were determinative in the creation of the export economies in most Spanish America, including Argentina.

The evidence, as I will show, supports a rather different interpretation of the origins of nineteenth century dependency and underdevelopment in Spanish America. This interpretation holds that while having a decidedly economic basis, the forces which created the export economies in Spanish America were essentially political--conflicts over the creation of new States and the form they would take.

The following chapters will explore the political conflicts between the various sectors of the owning classes, their ultimate economic basis, and the policies of the States that led to the creation of the export economies as a solution to political conflict. The analysis will focus primarily on Peru and Argentina.

NOTES

[1] See Andre Gunder Frank, Lumpenbourgeoisie - Lumpendevelopment (New York: Monthly Review Press, 1972), 46-66; and Fernando Henrique Cardoso and Enzo Faletto, Dependency and Development in Latin America (Berkeley: University of California Press, 1979), 30-35.

[2] Ibid.

[3] Frank, 51-62.

[4] Ibid., 51.

[5] Ibid., 52.

[6] Cardoso and Faletto, 36-73.

[7] Ibid., 35.

[8] Ibid., 34.

[9] D. C. M. Platt, "Dependency in Nineteenth Century Latin America: An Historian Objects," Latin American Research Review XV, Number 1 (1980), 115.

[10] Tulio Halperin-Donghi, Politics, Economics and Society in Argentina in the Revolutionary Period (Cambridge: Cambridge University Press, 1975), 58.

[11] D.C.M. Platt, Latin America and British Trade, 1806-1914 (New York: Barnes and Noble Books, 1973), 13-22.

[12] Platt, British Trade, 15-16. For Argentina see Halperin-Donghi, 91.

[13] Platt, British Trade, 34-38.

[14] Jonathan C. Brown, A Socio-Economic History of Argentina, 1776-1860 (Cambridge: Cambridge University Press, 1979), 81 Table 6.

[15] Platt, British Trade, 38.

[16] Ibid., 36.

[17] Roberto Cortés Conde, The First Stages of Modernization in Spanish America (New York: Harper, 1974), 120-121.

[18] Platt, Latin America Research Review, 115.

[19] Ibid., 117; and Platt, British Trade, 31.

[20] Platt, British Trade, 33.

[21] Frank, 60-61.

119

[22]Even Cardoso and Faletto cite this, Cardoso and Faletto, 39.

[23]For Argentina see Jonathan C. Brown, "The Dynamics and Autonomy of a Traditional Marketing System: Buenos Aires, 1810-1860," Hispanic American Historical Review LVI, Number 4 (November 1976), 605-629; and Jonathan C. Brown, Socio-Economic History, 86-87, 117-120.

[24]See Halperin-Donghi, 92-99; and Platt, British Trade, 39-61.

[25]Arnold J. Bauer, "The Church and Spanish American Agrarian Structure, 1965-1865," The Americas XXVII (July 1971), 94-95; and Claudio Véliz, The Centralist Tradition of Latin America (Princeton: Princeton University Press, 1980), 139-140.

[26]William Bollinger, "The Bourgeois Revolution in Peru: A Conception of Peruvian History," Latin America Perspectives IV, Issue 14, Number 3 (Summer 1977), 28; Shane Hunt, Growth and Guano in Nineteenth Century Peru. Research Program in Economic Development. Woodrow Wilson School. Discussion paper #34. (Princeton: Woodrow Wilson School of Public and International Affairs at Princeton University, February 1973), 33; and Charles Griffin, "Economic and Social Aspects of the Era of Spanish American Independence," Hispanic American Historical Review XXIX, Number 2 (May 1949), 174-177.

[27]Griffin, 174-177.

[28]F. A. Kirkpatrick, A History of the Argentine Republic (Cambridge: Cambridge at the University Press, 1931), 126-127; and Ricardo Levene, A History of Argentina, trans. William Spence Robertson (Chapel Hill, North Carolina: University of North Carolina Press, 1957), 350.

[29]Platt, British Trade, 18-22.

[30]Any trade that depended on Peruvian and Bolivian silver mining, as did that of western Argentina and highland Peru, saw a marked decline, see Aldo Ferrer, The Argentine Economy, trans. Marjory Urquidi (Berkeley: University of California Press, 1967), 65-73.

[31]Miron Burgin, The Economic Aspects of Argentine Federalism 1820-1852 (New York: Russell and Russell, 1946, 1971).

5
Economic Class Conflict in Peru and Argentina: The Economic Basis of Political Class Conflict

Although the conflicts that wracked the Spanish American countries in the first half of the nineteenth century had an essentially political nature, they also had an economic basis. The social relations of production within Spanish America set the context within which the political battles of the era would be fought. That these conflicts emerged in a political form only indicates the non-capitalist nature of these economies. Had they been capitalist economies we would expect the conflicts to be expressed, as Frank would have them, economically.[1] But Spanish America's heritage from the colonial period did not bestow upon it capitalist social relations of production, nor did the nineteenth century bring with it much progress in that direction. Commercialization did make substantial inroads, but not capitalist social relations of production.

For the same reason that the War of Independence was essentially a political struggle, so too were the conflicts between the owning classes in the nineteenth century. The Spanish colonial State's regulation of access to, and use of, the factors of production--land, labor, and commerce--politicized the economy and gave economic issues and conflicts a decided political character. This did not change with the independence of the former colonies. In fact, political independence served to channel conflicts, with a vengeance, towards the nascent Spanish American States. However, at this juncture these states were extremely weak and unable to regulate and harmonize the conflicting interests that had been contained by the Spanish colonial State.

Yet, without firmly tying them to a material basis, the political conflicts of the first half of the nineteenth century appear as battles exclusively over ideas, constitutions, beliefs, and principles. Of course the protagonists of the conflicts perceived them as such, but they also reflected conflicts at the economic level which conditioned their political attitudes.

This Chapter will survey the economies and social relations of production of Peru and Argentina in the first half of the nineteenth century, emphasizing how inter- and intra- economic class conflicts shaped the political attitudes of various sectors

121

of the owning classes. Chapter 6 will analyze the political conflicts between these sectors of the owning classes.

PERU

Peru emerged from the War of Independence with a severely damaged system of labor control and surplus extraction. The role of the Spanish colonial State in the economy of Peru had been decisive and its collapse placed the Peruvian elite--both those involved in production and those not (bureaucrats, merchants, and soldiers)--in dire straits.

In the sierra, which had been a major theater of the war, the decline of the commercial economy moved apace as the independence war destroyed the mines, and thus the markets they provided sierra agriculture.[2] Production then, for the most part, fell back to the local and subsistence levels--except for one bright spot, wool production and export.[3]

The commercial and economic decline of the sierra, coupled with the disappearance of the Spanish colonial State, had serious consequences for most landowners, miners, and merchants in the sierra. Sierra landowners were never allowed to completely dominate the socio-economy of the highlands owing to the Spanish State's fear of creating a landed aristocracy and its need for Indian labor in the mines that filled the imperial treasury. Indian communidades were protected (however poorly) by the church and State[4] and, even with the decline of mining in the eighteenth century, only a few hacendados were able to expand their holdings and control of Indian labor given the reduced markets for their production. As Karen Spalding argues,

The activity of the Indian villages limited the possibilities of accumulation open to the European landholder, forced to compete with the village producers who had to unload their produce in order to obtain money to meet their debts. The available market was limited, and in the 18th century, since the mines were in decline, it was actually shrinking. There was space for the emergence of a relatively few wealthy landowners, whose wealth depended as much upon their relation to the colonial bureaucracy as it did upon the production of their estates.[5]

In fact, Spalding claims that in the early nineteenth century, at least in the southern Peruvian highlands, landholding did not become very concentrated and society was made up of large to small landowners, petty merchants and traders, and a growing landless labor force made up of Indians and mestizos.[6]

The foregoing gives a picture of the Peruvian sierra as a relatively fluid society in which, given the large number of small and medium producers and the survival of Indian communidades, a system of purely economic domination would have been difficult. It was. Up until the close of the colonial era, the hacendado elite maintained a predominant position in, and

122

control over the Indian labor of the sierra through its close relationship with the State bureaucratic apparatus. With the State's disappearance in the wake of the Wars of Independence, some alternative means had to be devised.

The process of re-establishing landowner domination in the highlands was further complicated by the policies of early independence governments which, with the idea of winning ths support of the Indian masses for the new regime, attempted to transform the Indians into a class of yeoman farmers who would form a major class support for the new republican States.[7] In 1825 Bolívar decreed that,

> (1) the state could not require personal service, direct or indirect, without drafting a contract which established the wages of the Indians; (2) provincial officials, judges, church officials at all levels, hacendados, and mine owners were prohibited from employing Indians against their will; (3) labor drafts for public works had to affect all citizens equally; (4) the supplying of the army could not be confined to the Indian but had to fall on all citizens equally; (5) all work in the mines, haciendas, and other jobs had to be paid for in money unless the employee desired otherwise; (6) article 5 was to be enforced by local and provincial officials; (7) the church could not charge the Indian more for services than it charged others; (8) the civil authorities were to insure that the church did not take advantage of the Indian.[8]

Bolívar further decreed that the communidades be disolved and that their lands be distributed to their members as freeholds. The curacas (Indian headmen), who Bolívar believed oppressed the communidad Indians, were to be stripped of their role as hereditary political leaders of the Indians and lose much of their inflated landholdings.[9]

Had these decrees been promulaged in a vacuum, they might have produced their intended results. But in the context of the Peruvian sierra, where the power of the State to enforce these decrees was almost non-existent, and the landowning class was fearful of additional competition from free Indian farmers, the reforms were doomed to failure. However, Bolívar was not so wrong to think that if hacendado control over Indian labor was broken, and the stifling effects of the Indian communidades removed, the stagnant sierra economy could be revived. Indeed, in the case of the Indian communidades, the interest of the crown in the survival of these archaic social forms had been the preventing of the rise of a class of independent Indian farmers. The crown made sure that any tendency towards economic differentiation among the Indians would be eliminated by enforcing regulations requiring periodic redistributions of community lands. Rich Indians, it seems, did not make up for the loss of tribute from Indians who became too poor to pay it.[10]

That these reforms were not successful is not surprising. Although according to the original Bolivarian decree, Indians were not allowed to sell their lands until 1850, a good deal was sold or, more often, stolen by virtue of hacendado control of the highland politico-legal apparatus, well before that date.[11] The Constitution of 1828, in fact, made it possible for literate Indians to sell their lands before 1850.[12] This usurption of Indian lands, however, did not occur wholesale and continued throughout the nineteenth and twentieth centuries. Landgrabbing in the first half of the nineteenth century in any case indicated the weakness, rather than the strength, of the highland landowning elite. Lands were taken not because the hacendados could use them for expanded production, but rather so that the Indians could not use them free of their control and thus become an economic challenge. In any case, very little changed except that more Indians and communidades became tenants of the haciendas. The hacendados by no means sought to proletarianize the Indians. They had neither the markets nor the capital for such a project. Rather, they assured themselves a cheap labor force which had at its disposal its own means of subsistence. Rents, labor, and personal services came fee of charge if only the hacendados could maintain their local political predominance.

Hacendados had little advantage over the Indians in the market place without political control of the provinces, and therefore preferred a decentralized national political system. Though the hacendados owned the land upon which the Indians lived and toiled, it was left in the Indians' possession. In some areas, particularly the wool producing areas of the southern highlands, communidad and hacienda Indians competed directly with the hacendados for markets. Given that pastures were open, and Indian sheepherders tended both their own and hacienda sheep together, the hacendados could not gain any advantage over the Indians in the marketplace through greater efficiency or more advanced technology.[13] However, through their control of the local political system, hacendados could prevent this equality in the marketplace from creating a competing Indian elite. It is here that political control was indispensable to keep the Indian population on and off the hacienda subservient. Drafts of gang labor, or faenas, called by local officials for "public projects" (which often included the maintenance of hacienda gristmills or canal systems), requirements of personal service to local officials, fines, imprisonment, tribute collection, and use of the legal system against the persons and/or property of the Indians maintained the dominance of the elite. That such elaborate political-legal mechanisms were necessary to maintain the sierra landowning elite is evidence of their still relatively weak economic control over the land during the first half of the nineteenth century.

The dominant impression of the regime in the Andean highlands, at least from the time of independence to the present, has been of a harsh system of unrelenting social, political, and economic oppression directed against the Indian;[15] this view may be somewhat exaggeraged. Granted, some descriptions, such as that of Henri Favre who found that in Moya and Cuenca during the

124

"good old days," ". . . it was sufficient to throw a ten centavo piece at the feet of the first Indian to come along to obtain all the labor needed to work the fields. [and] If the Indian refused to work, he was thrown in prison and kept there until he agreed to carry out the task for which he had been "paid,"[16] starkly reveal the subservient position of the Indians in the sierra--but this was not a completely one sided affair. Although they were generally able to move the Indians off of the fertile valley lands and onto less agriculturally viable lands in the mountains, the hacendados employed very little of the sierra labor force.[17] Where Indians did work on hacienda lands, they often controlled production to the detriment of the hacendados: "In some cases, "tied" peasants were able to build up considerable amounts of livestock and commercialize them on their own account; likewise, on arable haciendas, peasant colonos often had effective control over their production that could equal that of the hacienda itself."[18] Even in the early twentieth century, as Juan Martínez Alier has found, hacienda owners had a great deal of difficulty getting the Indians to use the land as they wished, and in removing the Indians from the land at all.[19] Indeed, as the resistance of the highland Indians to becoming coastal wage workers in the latter half of the nineteenth century indicates, the conditions of "unfree" labor were often found to be more desirable than "free" wage labor.[20]

If landowners were in a precarious position in their struggle with the highland laboring classes, mine owners were all but ruined. Mining in the sierra, although it did see a boom in the late colonial era, was moribund by the end of the Wars of Independence. Generally, miners had never been particularly wealthy given the crown's close control and interest in this industry. The problems of inadequate financing, technological backwardness, flooding of the mines, exhaustion of ore bodies, and inadequate labor supply also plagued the industry throughout much of the eighteenth century.[21] The infusion of British technology and capital in the early nineteenth century breathed some life into the industry but failed, principally, at least in the estimation of Shane Hunt, because of the small scale of production which required that miners join together in a guild for large scale projects (such as drainage), and the perpetual lack of credit which forced miners to pay their workers in ore rather than wages.[22] In fact, it was perhaps because mine owners did better when poor grades of ore were mined, given that they had to pay their workers in ore, that mining remained at so low a level of production and efficiency.[23]

The major problem for miners was in attracting a work force. With the mita abolished once in the eighteenth century,[24] and then again by Bolívar in the nineteenth,[25] they competed for labor in an environment where most labor was either tied to haciendas and communidades or not highly mobile. The haciendas could offer the Indians security and subsistence whereas the mines, given their condition of continual failure and penury, could only be of marginal interest to the Indians. The association of mine work with the hated mita, and the fact that

125

many mines were far from major areas of Indian domicile, condemned the mine owners to chronic labor shortages. In comparison to hacienda owners, mine owners remained chronically weak politically, apparently unable to attain the local power necessary to tip the scales of labor distribution in their favor.

Coastal haciendas, in decline since the late colonial period, continued to decline during most of the first half of the nineteenth century. Mostly sugar and cotton plantations based upon slave labor, they suffered directly from the policy of liberation governments offering slaves their freedom in return for service in the armies of independence.[26] In addition, a great deal of the hacienda slave labor force simply disappeared in the confusion of the social and political instability that ensued after the Wars of Independence.[27] The abolition of the slave trade in 1823 (slaves were again legally imported only between 1835 and 1839) dealt another blow to the coastal slavocracy which found that it could not replace its losses through massive re-importation.[28] It is unclear though, given the sorry state of their enterprises, whether they could have afforded large slave imports in any case.

While slavery survived, it could not provide the amount of cheap labor necessary to revive the industry.[29] Sugar and cotton production remained at low levels and coastal hacendados erected a precarious system of tenant farming based on sharecropping, preferring the surety which dependable small rents provided.[30] This system of tenancy, called yanaconaje, according to José Matos Mar, ". . . represents an unequal union between a capitalist system of exploitation which provides land, water and capital, and a pattern of agricultural labor operating within a pre-capitalist system of land tenure."[31] In essence, the yanacona performed as a sharecropper, reducing the risks of cultivation to the landowner, purchasing his own seed and tools while handing over to the hacienda owner a large portion of his production.[32]

In 1854, President Ramón Castilla formally abolished slavery and thereby set the stage for the re-invigoration of coastal commercial agriculture. Castilla's government, flush with massive revenues from the guano trade,[33] re-capitalized coastal agriculture by compensating slave owners 300 pesos per slave. The State paid slaveowners for those slaves still in their possession, and for many who had already left. By 1850, 25,505 slaves were compensated for at a cost of 7,651,500 pesos.[34] Most of the former slaves moved out of the coastal agricultural regions to Lima, or became brigands roaming the countryside. A few also remained, becoming yanacona or overseers of Chinese coolies.[35]

From the 1850s onwards, Chinese coolies filled the perceived labor shortage on the coast.[36] Coastal hacienda owners with new wealth acquired in the guano trade or through slave compensations began, in the 1850s, importing large numbers of Chinese coolies who, although they came as indentured servants, suffered in conditions of servitude not unlike, though sometimes

worse than, the slaves they replaced.[37] Paid in depreciated
paper money which made it almost impossible to pay back their
debts and thus free themselves, the Chinese labor force rebelled
in a series of bloody uprisings in the 1870s.[38] The Chinese
trade was finally abolished in 1874, chiefly because of pressure
from the British who literally closed off this human traffic at
its source.[39] At least part of the coastal agricultural
depression of the late 1870s can be ascribed to the ensuing
shortage of cheap labor.[40]

Since no manufacturing industry proper arose in Peru during
the whole of the nineteenth century, no industrial proletariat
developed in the urban centers. Manufactured goods were either
acquired through foreign trade or produced in shops which had yet
to develop the production process much beyond the handicraft
stage.[41] In the first half of the nineteenth century, Lima,
the capital and largest city, actually lost people. Between 1820
and 1836, Lima lost about 15% of its population.[42] Pardos,
mestizos, and Indians carried the burden of what manual labor
there was in the urban areas.[43] As in the coastal agricultural
regions, in Lima it was believed that a severe labor shortage
existed and so explained the relatively high cost of labor.[44]

Peruvian social relations of production in the nineteenth
century remained, as we have seen, fundamentally non-capitalist.
This fact was both a cause and effect of the perceived labor
shortage which, in conditioning the views of the Peruvian owning
classes, formed the economic basis of their political conflicts.
Peru, of course, was not labor short, rather it lacked a free
labor market.[45] In the highlands, the hacendados could not
(and did not) want to proletarianize the Indians. Thus, they
sought to immobilize them by controlling the land on which they
worked and the socio-political enviroment in which they lived.
The Indians, preferring to remain if not the owners, at least the
possessors of the land, were accommodated by the strategy of the
hacendados. Where land was seen as the only sure means of
subsistence, the Indians fought to remain attached to it. In any
event, the strategy of the hacendados required direct political
control of the sierra and thus they grew to prefer the type of
State and State policies that would assure them of that control.

Coastal hacendados, who bore the brunt of the restrictive
colonial labor distribution system and had to rely on relatively
expensive imported slave labor, did not fare any better during
the early post colonial era. The Wars of Independence only
exacerbated their chronic labor shortages, and early republican
legislation which sought to remove the restrictions on labor
mobility between the sierra and the coast was ineffective against
the dam erected by the confluence of interest of sierra
hacendados and Indians. Since a cheap labor force was not
available to them internally, the coastal hacendados were forced
to rely on a dying slave system, sharecropping and later,
imported indentured servants. Real prosperity always eluded
them. Given these conditions, coastal hacendados developed an
ambivalent position towards the type of State they perferred. On
the one hand, they sought policies which would weaken the archaic

social and economic system of the sierra, hoping to tap into the sierra labor force, and thus tended to support State political centralization. On the other hand, given that they too relied on non-capitalist social relations of production which required local political control, they favored a weak decentralized State.

ARGENTINA

Perhaps more than any other former Spanish American colony, Argentina suffered the severe dislocations of both the break with the colonial system and the Wars of Independence. Certainly more than any other Spanish American country its economy, society, and polity were restructured by the events that gave it independence. As we saw in Chapter 4, the sources of urban wealth that sustained the bureaucrat-merchant elite of Buenos Aires dried up when the new State could not maintain the viceregal system of political and economic domination. With the traditional sources of urban wealth lost, the basis of political power became ruralized. A similar process of ruralization affected the interior provinces but was more profound. Rather than discovering new sources of wealth in the countryside, as did the elite of Buenos Aires, the disappearance of its traditional markets in Peru and Bolivia (Upper Peru) left the interior elite with little to fall back on. In an effort to maintain their position, the elites of the interior were forced to turn their economies inward in an attempt to isolate their provinces from the effects of foreign trade. The task which occupied the elites in both areas, given the crisis, was the same--to institute or maintain control over the available sources of wealth, principally land and labor. However, though their aims were similar, the political requisites for the success of each threw them into a conflict that was to take most of the nineteenth century to sort out.

In Buenos Aires province, the bureaucrat-merchant elite began its conversion into a landholding elite in the 1820s when it became clear that the old viceregal pattern of domination and trade could not be reconstructed after the fall of the Directory in 1820. As John Lynch argues,

. . . the decline of trade with the interior, the wartime destruction of the littoral cattle industry, and above all the irresistable competition of British merchants dislocated the traditional economy and curtailed the opportunities of local enterpreneurs. The increase in exports provoked by the British and the failure of the export sector to respond caused an outflow of precious metals, which was accompanied by an increase in local demand for currency. The time arrived when the traditional economy of Buenos Aires could no longer sustain the merchant elite. From about 1820 many of them began to seek other outlets and, without abandoning commerce, to invest in land, cattle and meat salting plants. [47]

It was in this ruralization of a portion of the Buenos Aires elite that the origin of the Federalist-Unitarian conflict lies. Those who remained faithful to the traditional power structure--principally professionals, politicians, intellectuals, and some merchants--became Unitarians, dedicated to the erection of a powerful centralized State centered in Buenos Aires. Those who turned their attention to the countryside and cattle raising--merchant-landowners--became Federalists, opposed to the nationalizing and centralizing tendencies of the Unitarians, which they felt neglected or harmed the cattle raising industry.[48] Though the political position of the Unitarians was conditioned by the economic class struggles on the land, they themselves had very little of an economic or social base, their fortunes were tied to those of the state.[49] They will be examined more closely in Chapter 6. It is rather to the Federalists, those who went out to conquer the land and the people, and whose political attitudes were most conditioned by the economic class struggle, that we turn here.

Although cattle raising had advanced in Buenos Aires province prior to 1820, its development had always been constrained by lack of markets, competition with the cattle areas of Uruguay, insecurity arising from Indian attack, and the low social status accorded to land ownership in the Río de la Plata.[50] As a frontier area in the Spanish colonial system, Buenos Aires province became a haven for those displaced or discriminated against by the caste system in the colonies.[51] Large expanses of unclaimed land, where the authority of the State was weak and a living could be made off of the thousands of cattle roaming the pampa, nurtured a population of gauchos (cowboys) who were relatively independent and dangerous because of their equestrian and military-like skills.[52] This relatively nomadic rural population had always been of concern to the Spanish colonial authorities who identified them as "vagos (vagrants) y mal entretenidos (n'eer do wells)" because they were thought to have stirred up and/or led Indian attacks on rural estancias (ranches), and because this large rural population operated, on the whole, outside of the colonial economy creating a labor shortage.[53]

As land under the legal ownership of estancieros increased in the early nineteenth century, problem of controlling this rural population became more and more acute. According to Silvio R. Duncan Baretta and John Markoff, ". . . as the value of cattle rose and the former colonies were threatened with political disintegration, the need to settle and discipline populations became more pressing than ever before."[54] The Wars of Independence, the Indian wars, and the interminable civil wars only exacerbated the problem of controlling the rural population. Deserters from the armies swelled the nomadic rural population. At the same time, civil war made it difficult to settle the people on the land since the gaucho was needed as cannon fodder in the political conflicts of the era.[55] Further, land expansion directed against both the Indians and the rural population only made the gaucho more determined to elude peonization. "In short, wars, forced recruitment, the continuous expansion of the great estates and the judicial repression of vagabonds continually created new wanderers and kept the old ones in movement."[56]

Prominent in the first half of the nineteenth century were legal efforts to control the rural population of the province. Legislation of this type was supported by all elites, whether Unitarian or Federal, but not for the same reasons. The Unitarian Bernardino Rivadavia, ". . . gave Argentine vagrancy statutes their enduring force and form during the 1820's."[57] The legislation of Rivadavia required that rural workers have a passport for travel within and without the province, have the written permission of an estanciero to leave his ranch, and expanded the definition of "vagos y mal entretenidos" to include any rural male so defined by the testimony of a justice of the peace. Anyone who broke these laws or was defined as a vagrant was subject to several years of forced military service.[58] The rural inhabitants found no relief under the Federalist Juan Manuel de Rosas who, while giving the impression that he "understood the gaucho and was concerned with his welfare," enforced the vagrancy laws against the gaucho with increased vigor.[59] According to Richard Slatta, "Rosas blamed the backwardness of the pampa on the "throngs of idlers, vagrants and delinquents" that afflicted the countryside. He expended much of his administrative energies on converting those he considered idlers into sedentary, contractual ranch workers or cavalrymen for his army."[60] During the Rosas era, the repression of the rural population was carried out, for the most part, by rural justices of the peace who patrolled the countryside keeping order at the behest of the estancieros.[61]

Although Unitarian and Federal policies against the rural population were the same, the intent seems to have been dissimilar. While the Unitarians were interested in the health of the cattle raising industry, they were more interested in creating the conditions for a stable farming sector in which the "vagrant" population of the pampa would have no place. For Rivadavia, the rural population of Buenos Aires was "an unproductive class, a deadweight, harmful to public morals and a cause of social disorder."[62] His prescription was conscription into the army for the mass of them, harsh rural labor laws, and European colonization to create an honest and hard working rural laboring population.[63] The Federalists' apparent reason for desiring such legislation was the lack of available labor to work and expand their ranches.[64] As Slatta argues, the vagrancy laws had the effect of ". . . curtailing worker mobility, it functioned much as the colonial labor systems of encomienda and yanaconaje in controlling the Indians in New Spain and Peru . . ."[65] However, although testimonies of labor shortage by landowners abound,[66] the primary reason for their desire of such harsh legislation ". . . was to impose law and order in the countryside . . ."[67]

Not only did the estanciero seek to force the gaucho to work on his estancia, he sought to prevent the roaming gaucho from becoming his competitor in the market and a danger to his herds. The gaucho, who ". . . maintained his custom of free grazing on the open range and appropriating unmarked animals even after "terratenientes" (landowners) had gained title to most of the better lands . . ."[68] became a rustler by definition and thus a threat to the estanciero. The low labor requirement of cattle raising indicates, in fact, that the estanciero's objective in controlling the rural population was not primarily his need for workers,[69] but rather to monopolize the resources of the countryside--land and cattle.[70] The only advantage he held over the gaucho in the raising of cattle was his legal ownership of the land and control of the local political-legal system with which he could prosecute the gaucho for being an "independent enterpreneur." What in fact often necessitated the need for more workers than cattle raising required was the fear of raids by gauchos and other landowners. Because wealth--the cattle-- was so mobile, large bodies of armed men were needed to protect that wealth from neighboring estancieros and gauchos alike. These bodies of armed men formed the basis for elite armed struggle during the civil wars. In fact, the landgrabbing of many estancieros who had no actual need for more land can only be explained by their attempt to deny the gauchos free possession of the land and cattle and turn them into dependent cowboy-soldiers.[71]

Control of the rural population necessitated a State that would promote the export of cattle products, enforce vagrancy laws, assure protection from the Indians, and provide cheap, if not free, land to the landowners. In the absence of such a State the estancieros preferred local political control.

The elite of the interior tended to favor local political control too, for not so wholly different reasons. The economies of the interior had received a shock equal to, if not greater than, that of Buenos Aires from the Wars of Independence and civil wars. The interior provinces held a strategic place within the viceregal economy, selling their produce in the mining areas of the Peruvian and Bolivian highlands in return for silver with which they purchased imports coming through Buenos Aires. The interior also dominated the transport of both trades.

The definitive shutting down of this trade with the loss of Bolivia (Upper Peru), ushered in the political and economic disintegration of the interior.[72] The Wars of Independence also took a heavy toll on the interior provinces. In La Rioja, for example, in 1819, the scarcity of cattle due to confiscations for the armies of independence became so severe that slaughtering for commercial purposes had to be reduced by half. In Córdoba, in that same year, the province could no longer provide horses for San Martín's army.[73] Civil war too took a heavy toll in the interior as the march of armies across the provinces destroyed production and commerce and both national and provincial governments scoured the countryside for funds to

131

support their causes.[74]

The same processes that ruralized the bases of political power in Buenos Aires affected the interior provinces, but the economic base which the interior elite was forced to fall back upon was contracting, not expanding as in Buenos Aires. Because the State in Buenos Aires monopolized the funds collected from foreign trade, and trade in the interior was in a state of ruin, public office and commerce, the two pillars of the interior urban elite, crumbled. Treasuries everywhere in the interior provinces were empty, the public debt went unfunded, and the civil bureaucracy and military often went unpaid.[75] Nowhere could sufficient revenues be found as even Córdoba, the most populous (60,000) and prosperous of the interior provinces, could barely raise 70,000 pesos in 1824.[76]

In the absence of a national policy favoring their trade over foreign imported goods, the elites of the interior provinces could only try to protect themselves against the total ruination of their economies through protectionism.[77] Yet, as Miron Burgin clearly argues, protectionism against Buenos Aires was not what they really desired, rather they sought to monopolize the Buenos Aires market for their own goods.[78]

Protectionism did not, however, stem the decline of the interior economies. Aldo Ferrer notes,

Given the factors conditioning its development, the economy of the interior did not change . . . . The output of each region went to the local market and a large part of the working population continued in subsistence activities. In the Northwest, where exports actually declined, . . . it is likely that the economy regressed from the levels it had reached in the eighteenth century and that the proportion of the labor force occupied in subsistence activities even increased.[79]

In the interior provinces, production everywhere suffered primarily from the loss of markets and was sustained at low levels only by inter-provincial trade.[80]

To a large degree, the disintegration of the interior economies reproduced the labor control problems found in Buenos Aires province. Of the interior James Scobie writes,

Among the lower classes, the constant insecurity and lack of employment resulted in the disintegration of the family unit and the disappearance of trained, disciplined laborers. Landless, nomadic masses increasingly replaced the industrious peons and skilled artisans. Many formerly prosperous areas now fell back on the rudimentary economy which had existed in seventeenth century Buenos Aires. The gaucho and the colonial estancia invaded the Andean region . . .[81]

In addition, the interior provinces lost men, not only through conscription into the independence and civil war armies, but also through migration to the coast and other provinces in search of work.[82] As Donna Guy shows, economic activities associated with men declined in many areas of the interior leaving womens' household handicrafts the mainstay of provincial economies.[83]

As in Buenos Aires province, draconian vagrancy laws were used against the laboring poor not only to create a cheap labor force, but to immobilize the rural population. In Tucumán, for example, anti-vagrancy laws were enacted in 1823 and a ley de conchabo, or forced labor law, was put into force in 1832.[84] Given the severe crisis prevailing with regard to labor control in the interior, the vagrancy laws there contained many more provisions for worker registration and the capture of vagrants, and they lasted much longer than in the coastal provinces.[85]

The need for such harsh legal control of the rural working classes in the interior, as in Buenos Aires, indicated an extraordinary lack of economic control by the owning classes. It is perhaps for this reason that they clung to local political and administrative control, and thus became Federalists. However, if Unitarianism would have sustained the interior elites by them a share of the revenues collected by the port of Buenos Aires, they might have been satisfied with a centralized national State. Unitarianism, though, denied them both the revenues and political and economic autonomy, and thus they rejected it for Federalism.[86] Federalism, however, turned out to be a double edged sword for the interior provinces. The political and economic autonomy they gained only prevented their complete ruin--Federalist Buenos Aires province remained in control of the port, the import-export revenues, and the future of the interior.

In both Peru and Argentina, political conflicts between sectors of the dominant classes arose on the basis of economic conflicts between them and their laboring classes. Already conflict ridden during the colonial era, relations between the dominant and dominated classes deteriorated further with the ruinous economic effects of the Wars of Independence and the disappearance of the colonial administrative apparatus that had managed those conflicts.

Inter- and intra-economic class conflicts always had the potential of breaking out into open warfare during the colonial period but were held in check by the colonial State bureaucracy. This was possible as long as the bureaucracy was viewed by all as the legitimate arbiter of such conflicts. Its delegitimation in the wake of the Bourbon reforms and independence struggles meant not only that these conflicts might break out into the open, but that they would affect the manner in which political power was exercised and constituted.

The economic systems of both Peru and Argentina were made up of a hodge-podge of non-capitalist forms of production, each which required definite political requisites for its maintenance and reproduction. Although these political requisites were often contradictory, the "relative autonomy" and flexibility of the colonial bureaucracy provided each sector of the elite with what it required and thus prevented open conflict on either an

133

economic or political level. Independence, however, transformed the context of the struggles between elites whose dominance was based on conflicting social relations of production. Without the independent hand of the colonial political-administrative apparatus, they were thrown into face to face competition at both the economic and political levels. Their conflicts though, did not take an economic form--this would have required a transformation to capitalist forms of production. Rather, their conflicts took political form as each sector of the dominant class sought a State apparatus that would provide it with the political requisites necessary to exploit its working class.

Thus, in both Peru and Argentina, inter- and intra-economic class conflict formed the basis for the political instability of the first half of the nineteenth century. Because political power and the State were crucial in providing the requisites of elite domination, how political power would be exercised, and what form the State would take, became the focus of elite conflict. In Chapter 6, the political conflicts that shaped the policies and form of the State in Peru and Argentina will be examined.

NOTES

[1] See Karl Marx, Capital, 3 Vols., (New York: International Publishers, 1967) I:81-82 note 1, where Marx argues that each historical epoch exposes the dominant material base of society in a different manner, ". . . it is the mode in which they gained a livelihood that explains why here politics and there Catholicism played a chief part." In the capitalist epoch the chief part is played by the economy--business.

[2] Shane Hunt, Growth and Guano in Nineteenth Century Peru. Research Program in Economic Development. Woodrow Wilson School. Discussion Paper1#34. (Princeton: Princeton University, February 1973), 52.

[3] Jean Piel, "The Place of the Peasantry in the National Life of Peru in the Nineteenth Century," Past and Present XLVI (February 1970), 120.

[4] Ibid., 117; and Karen Spalding, "Hacienda-Village Relations in Andean Society to 1830," Latin America Perspectives II, Issue 4, Number 1 (Spring 1975), 116-119.

[5] Karen Spalding, "Class Structure in the Southern Peruvian Highlands 1750-1820," Radical History Review III (Fall-Winter 1975), 11.

[6] Ibid., 11-13.

[7] Thomas M. Davies, Indian Intergration in Peru: A Half

Century of Experience, 1900-1948 (Lincoln: University of Nebraska Press, 1970, 1974), 20; and Thomas M. Davies, "Indian Integration in Peru, 1820-1948: An Overview," The Americas XXX (October 1973), 184-208. Also see Piel, 118.

[8]Davies, Indian Integration, 20-21.

[9]Ibid., 21-22.

[10]Spalding, Latin American Perspectives, 116-118.

[11]Davies, Indian Integration, 23.

[12]Ibid.

[13]Spalding, Radical History Review, 13.

[14]Benjamin S. Orlove, Alpacas, Sheep and Men: The Wool Export Economy and Regional Society in Southern Peru (New York: Academic Press, 1977), 156-159. Spalding acknowledges the political control of hacendados but sees it as less effective, see Spalding, Radical History Review, 14.

[15]For example see Richard Stephens, Wealth and Power in Peru (Metuchen, New Jersey: Scarecrow Press, 1971).

[16]Henri Favre, "The Dynamics of Indian Peasant Society and Migration to Coastal Plantations in Southern Peru," in Land and Labour in Latin America, eds. Kenneth Duncan and Ian Rutledge (Cambridge: Cambridge University Press, 1977), 257-258.

[17]Norman Long and Bryan R. Roberts, eds., Peasant Cooperation and Capitalist Expansion in Central Peru (Austin: University of Texas Press, 1978), 11-12.

[18]Ibid., 13.

[19]Juan Martínez Alier, "Relations of Production in Andean Haciendas: Peru," in Land and Labour in Latin America eds. Kenneth Duncan and Ian Rutledge (Cambridge: Cambridge University Press, 1977), 141-162.

[20]Ibid., 154-155.

[21]Hunt, 43.

[22]Ibid., 47-48.

[23]Archibald Smith, Peru As It Is, 2 Vols. (London: Richard Bentley, 1839), I:13-15.

[24]Hunt, 22.

[25]Davies, Indian Integration, 20-22.

[26]Laura Randall, A Comparative Economic History of Latin America 1500-1914. Vol. 4 Peru (Published for the Institute of Latin American Studies, Columbia University, by University

Microfilms International. Ann Arbor, Michigan, 1977), 71.

[27]Ibid.; Piel, 122; and Hunt, 33.

[28]Randall, 71. On the emancipation struggle see Leslie B. Rout, The African Experience in Spanish America: 1502 to the Present (Cambridge: Cambridge University Press, 1976), 218-220.

[29]Hunt, 54.

[30]Piel, 122-123.

[31]José Matos Mar, "Sharecropping on the Peruvian Coast," in Haciendas and Plantations in Latin American History, ed. Robert G. Keith (New York: Holmes and Meier, 1977), 164.

[32]Ibid.

[33]Guano, a fertilizer formed by the concentration of bird feces became, in the second half of the nineteenth century, the major export commodity of Peru. It not only created most of the revenues for the national budget, but formed the basis for the creation of a ruling class, see Chapter 7 below.

[34]Randall, 87.

[35]See Watt Stewart, Chinese Bondage in Peru (Durham, North Carolina: Duke University Press, 1951), 101; Piel, 125; and Rout, 220-221.

[36]Stewart, 101.

[37]Hunt, 55.

[38]Stewart, 121.

[39]David Chaplin, The Peruvian Labor Force (Princeton: Princeton University Press, 1967), 61-62.

[40]Ibid., 63.

[41]John Miller, The Memoirs of General Miller in the Service of the Republic of Peru, 2 Vols. (London: Longmann, Rees, Orne Brown and Green, 1828-1829), II:9-11.

[42]Hunt, 32.

[43]See the description of the Lima working force in Manuel A. Fuentes, Lima or Sketches of the Capital of Peru (London: Trubner & Company, 1866), 180-205.

[44]Ibid., 66.

[45]Randall, 87.

[46]This is the main theme of Miron Burgin, The Economic Aspects of Argentine Federalism 1820-1852 (New York: Russell and Russell, 1946, 1977); and Tulio Halperin-Donghi, Politics

Economics and Society in Argentina in the Revolutionary Period (Cambridge: Cambridge University Press, 1975).

[47]John Lynch, Argentine Dictator, Juan Manuel de Rosas 1829-1852 (London: Oxford University Press, 1981), 43-44.

[48]Ibid., 44-45.

[49]Ibid., 37, 43, 45; and Burgin, 83-88.

[50]Halperin-Donghi, 22-23.

[51]Silvio R. Duncan Baretta and John Markoff, "Civilization and Barbarism: Cattle Frontiers in Latin America," Comparative Studies in Society and History XX Number 4 (October 1978), 595-597.

[52]See the description in Lynch, 102-103. Also see Richard W. Slatta, "Rural Criminality and Social Conflict in Nineteenth Century Buenos Aires Province," Hispanic American Historical Review LX, Number 3 (August 1980), 454.

[53]Duncan Baretta and Markoff, 592-597, in particular note 11, p. 592. Also see Slatta, 453-454.

[54]Duncan Baretta and Markoff, 598.

[55]Lynch, 105-106; and Slatta, 462-463.

[56]Duncan Baretta and Markoff, 603. Also see Slatta, 461.

[57]Slatta, 455.

[58]Ibid., and Lynch, 115.

[59]Lynch, 113-117.

[60]Slatta, 456.

[61]Ibid., 458-460; and Lynch, 116-117.

[62]Quoted in Lynch, 106.

[63]Burgin, 91-92.

[64]Slatta, 457.

[65]Ibid., 460.

[66]Lynch, 118.

[67]Ibid., 104.

[68]Slatta, 465.

[69]The claim that wages were high in the countryside and thus necessitated these draconian labor laws in questionable. Workers were most often paid in depreciated currency making wages seem high, see Burgin, p. 28 note 24; and Laura Randall, A

Comparative Economic History of Latin America 1500-1914. Vol. 2
Argentina: (Published for the Institute of Latin America Studies,
Columbia University, by University Microfilms International. Ann
Arbor, Michigan: 1977), 50. If James Scobie were correct, and
immigrants could earn enough in three weeks to start their own
sheep farms, Argentina would hardly have become a land of large
landowners and landless peons, see James Scobie, Revolution on
the Pampas (Austin: University of Texas Press, 1964), 14.

[70]Duncan Baretta and Markoff, 599-601; and Halperin-Donghi,
24.

[71]A. F. Zimmerman, "The Land Policy of Argentina with
Particular Reference to the Conquest of the Southern Pampas,"
Hispanic America Historical Review XXV (February 1945), 12; and
Jose Ferrer, "The Armed Forces in Argentina Politics to 1830"
(Ph.D. dissertation, University of New Mexico, 1966), 18-20.

[72]Halperin-Donghi, 67-68.

[73]Ibid., 76.

[74]Ibid., 77-81.

[75]Burgin, 125.

[76]For a complete examination of the finances of the
interior provinces see Ibid., 125-134. Also see Aldo Ferrer, The
Argentine Economy, trans. Marjory Urquidi (Berkeley: University
of California Press, 1967), 68-71.

[77]Burgin, 136-138.

[78]Ibid., 139-140.

[79]Aldo Ferrer, 69.

[80]Lynch, 134-136.

[81]James Scobie, Argentina, 2nd ed. (New York: Oxford
University Press, 1971), 93.

[82]Donna Guy, "Women, Peonage and Industrialization:
Argentina, 1810-1914," Latin American Research Review XVI, Number
3 (1981), 67.

[83]Ibid., 67-69.

[84]Ibid., 69-70.

[85]Ibid., 71. In Tucumán, new, more stringent vagrancy laws
went into effect in 1888 with the rise of the sugar industry, see
Donna Guy, "The Rural Working Class in Nineteenth Century
Argentina: Forced Plantation Labor in Tucumán," Latin American
Research Review XIII, Number 1 (1978), 135-145.

[86]Burgin, 82, 139-144.

6
Political Conflict in Nineteenth Century Peru and Argentina: Political Crisis and the State

In the first half of the nineteenth century, most Spanish American countries were the scene of intense and often bloody political conflicts. Though having a basis in inter- and intra-economic class conflict, these conflicts essentially dealt with how political authority would be reconstituted in the wake of the colonial State's collapse. At issue was which groups would be privileged by the new States and under what State forms and policies these privileges would be alloted, as well as what would constitute the nation itself.

Although the Spanish colonial administration had been losing legitimacy throughout the Bourbon period, its final destruction hardly solved the problems its loss of legitimacy created. However inefficient or discriminatory the Spanish State in America had been, it managed, even in the late Bourbon era, to mediate disputes between sectors of the creole elite. Though there may have been opposition under the surface, "All of these social factions were bound together during the colonial period by a common denominator, their loyalty to the crown."[1] Independence governments, most of which were based upon town cabildos, the only institutions capable at the time of exercising authority outside of the Spanish bureaucratic administration, were hardly credible replacements.[2] The crisis of legitimacy infected them too, and it became difficult for any authority to claim the kind of legitimate power represented by the king once it was discovered that the system could be overturned. In fact, the popularity of monarchism with many exhausted independence regimes can be explained by their search for some unifying force, above the fray, that could impose order.[3]

Spanish colonialism did not prepare the Americans for independence, though this is not meant in the conventional sense that it did not give develop in the creoles an aptitude for government or that those who directed the new States were without political experience.[4] Indeed, those in charge had varied experience within the Spanish colonial bureaucracy as lawyers, bureaucrats, churchmen, and soldiers.[5] Rather, as Charles Anderson argues, the nationalizing tendencies of absolutism and mercantilism did not touch Spanish America because the Spanish

State deemed it in its interest that the economy, society, and polity of Spanish America remain fragmented, with the Spanish State as the only unifying principle.[6] The result was that,

> Independence became not a process of mitosis, in which prior interaction had led to the emergence of more or less self sufficient organisms which could now go their separate ways, but a rending and tearing apart of the systemic substance about which social and economic life was organized . . . The separation from Spain did not serve to disentangle a network of economic and social systems from the strict regulation of absolute monarchy. Rather, it severed the web of these relations and left a ragged edge of broken strands.[7]

Fragmented socially and economically, the break with Spain only served to fragment Spanish America politically. The competition within the elite for privileges, wealth, honors, and status that had been constrained within the Spanish colonial administration became, in its absence, a naked struggle for political power.[8] Those who had been favored by the colonial system tenaciously clung to those institutions and arrangements which assured their domination, while those not favored attempted to destroy the old system and erect a new regime more in concert with their interests. As William Breezley succinctly states, "Spanish America, at the beginning of the national period, was characterized by a society in which there were numerous factions lacking a common ground for compromise because there was no agreed-upon loyalty or shared conception of a state idea."[9]

Political conflict and State formation in early nineteenth century Spanish America were intergrally linked. At just the point when the elites required the intervention of the State to ameliorate or reconcile their differences it lost the requisite strength and legitimacy to perform that role. The weakness of the State made elite conflict that much more serious because the State was seen as a tool that could be captured and used against one's opponents. The relative autonomy of the Spanish colonial State was replaced with administrations that were not only subject to bribery and influence (as admittedly was the Spanish colonial State), but more importantly, outright manipulation and control.

Political conflict was therefore directed at the State, particularly with regard to how the country would be structured socially and economically. The role of the State was crucial to all interests because of its central role in maintaining and reproducing the social and economic domination of Spanish American owning classes. As we have seen in Chapter 3, the reforms introduced by the Bourbon State led to discontent and protest. With the disappearance of the Spanish colonial State after the Wars of Independence, discontent and protest was transformed into direct action.

Below, the four major political conflicts--liberalism vs conservatism, centralism vs federalism (regionalism), church vs State, and the issue of caudillism--that emerged in Spanish

America during the first half of the nineteenth century will be examined in the national contexts of Peru and Argentina.

LIBERALISM VS CONSERVATISM

Although the conflict between liberals and conservatives dominated other political conflicts in Spanish America in the first half of the nineteenth century (in fact the centralism vs federalism and church vs State conflicts were subsumed within it), there is a great deal of confusion as to who and what constituted these political tendencies. Excessive concentration on an economic interpretation of these tendencies has reduced them, as Charles Hale has noted, to the positions of for or against free trade.[10] Hard and fast delineations of these two groups tend to dissolve upon closer inspection. Liberals in Peru, according to Fredrick Pike, were opposed to monarchism, urged the establishment of democratic institutions, backed federalism, opposed a large standing army, sought legislative supremacy over the executive, and favored religious toleration and church-State separation. Conservatives favored a strong centralist State, hierarchic aristocratic government, a large standing army, executive predominance, and a State church.[11] However, as John Lynch points out,

> In theory liberals favored federalism, supposedly a decentralized and democratic form of government, while conservatives demanded a strong executive and central control. But when the opportunity occurred liberals would impose liberalism by central institutions in a unitary regime, such as that formed by Rivadavia and Sarmiento in Argentina. And to preserve their control in particular provinces, or if they happened to be the "outs," conservatives might well be federalists.[12]

Nor did conservative politics mean conservative economics as Frank Safford's examples of the "liberal" economic ideology of Mariano Ospina Rodríguez in Colombia and Lucas Alamán and Esteban de Antuñano in Mexico clearly show.[13] The confusion over the definition of these tendencies is furthered, in the opinion of Safford, by giving them an occupational determination.[14] Robert Schwartz, for example, argues the traditional identification of conservatives as landowners and liberals as wealthy merchants.[15] This delineation, according to Safford, cannot be sustained because landowners and merchants, as well as bureaucrats, lawyers, military officers, and intellectuals can be found on both sides.[16] For Safford, "There may have been a functional reason for this--to survive, each party needed the various contributions that could be made by landowners, merchant-capitalists, lawyer-ideologists and, certainly, military men."[17] Safford is perhaps exaggerating the occupational equality between liberals and conservatives, but he nonetheless has indicated the pitfalls of such static analysis. More promising is his suggestion of defining these groups and their supports in terms of social location. Accordingly, it is the relationship of various individuals or groups to the centers of institutional power which determines whether the individual or group leans towards liberalism or conservatism. In Safford's words, "Those in the elite whose close early relationship to the structures of power gave them strategic advantages at the beginning of the republican epoch were likely to end up being termed "conservative," those who stood at a greater distance were likely to become "liberal."[18] This should not be at all surprising, liberalism in the nineteenth century was an ideology of protest, particularly against privileges derived from close association with the State.[19] It was only natural that elements of the creole elite who were not favored by the colonial compact would find in this European bourgeois ideology an echo of their own dissatisfaction.

Although creole liberals in Spanish America may have generally accepted the liberal credo intellectually, the evident selectivity they exhibited in its application indicates only the lack of the appropriate conditions for its application in their countries, not opportunism.[20] Indeed, it was also that their liberalism was tainted with a large dose of Spanish medieval scholasticism, as we have seen in Chapter 4, which leads many commentators to interpret the independence movements as "liberal." The creole ideologists of independence could appropriate some aspects of liberalism because on the issue of absolute power it mirrored their own scholastic thinking.[21]

A distinction should also be made between liberal and conservative politicians, bureaucrats, and intellectuals and the elements of the elite which they were representing.[22] Particularly in the old viceregal centers of administration like Lima and Buenos Aires,[23] there were large numbers of lawyers, bureaucrats, and clerics who made their livings off of the administration, and hundreds more who wanted to. These administrators and potential administrators became conservative or liberal in much the same way the economic elite did. However, they became the ideologists of the others and fought the political battles in the capitals. The ideological disputes received particular clarity and venom precisely because of competition within this group of office seekers for political and administrative positions. Nevertheless, this should not be construed to mean that the disputes had no social or economic content. As we have seen in Chapter 5, the economic conflicts of the owning classes led them to connect themselves with either the preservers of the status quo or the reformers in the capital.

The roots of liberalism and conservatism in Spanish America during the first half of the nineteenth century are clearly linked to Spanish Bourbon reformism. Although there was general dissatisfaction with the reforms in America, the issue for many creoles was not the reforms themselves, but rather that the expanded commercial economy and bureaucracy benefited penisulares and not them. In Argentina, the liberal regime of Rivadavia was

142

tied to the traditional Buenos Aires merchant-bureaucrat elite that had received only relatively minor benefits from the Bourbon reforms when compared to those received by the peninsulares and a very few creole merchants associated with them. The revolution against the Spaniards was theirs, and the Rivadavia program reflected their attempt, even in the face of repeated setbacks caused by the failure to secure Upper Peru, Paraguay, Uruguay, the littoral and interior provinces, to create an economy and society which they could dominate commercially. The program of the liberal Unitarians was based upon a critique of the Spanish colonial system which argued that,

> . . . the economic and social backwardness of Argentina was owing not so much to her lack of material resources as to the economic and fiscal policies of the Spanish regime. Restrictions upon production and distribution, minute regulation of economic activities, oppressive taxes, all of which characterized Spain's economic policies, were contrary to the best interests of the colony but of the mother country as well. The policy of restriction was based upon the notion that the interests of the state (treasury) were opposed to those of the individual.[25]

This was, in fact, almost the same critique which the Spanish Bourbon reformers made of Spain itself in the eighteenth century.[26] It is not surprising then that at least for one group of creoles the solution was similar, centralization of administration, reduction of regional autonomy, the development of agriculture, and the freeing of trade. The Rivadavia plan called for the complete dismantling of colonial restrictions and the reconstruction of the economy on a more "modern" basis under the aegis of a powerful yet paternalistic State.[27] The goal of the Unitarians was thus an intergrated national economy in which foreign trade, foreign investment, and foreign immigration would play a major role.[28]

The opposition to Unitarianism, Federalism, cannot rightly be called "conservative," although in some sense it may be perceived as such. A distinction should also be made between provincial Federalism and porteño (Buenos Aires) Federalism, both of which had liberal and conservative tendencies. Federalism on the whole stood for provincial autonomy in politics and economics against the central State and thus could appeal to rather different interest.[29] In the face of Unitarian supremacy in the executive and legislature, the mass of conflicting interests that made up the opposition could come to no other basis for agreement. Every interest that was threatened by the centralizing scheme of Rivadavia could at least agree on the need to halt it.[30] Perhaps what most turned the provinces against the Rivadavia plan was its call for the elimination of the provincial governments' institutional autonomy which had served as a major prop of the provincial elites. Local political control insured that they would control the local economy and not be forced to compete with foreign or porteño merchants. Yet,

143

they were not against free commerce within the country itself and recognized the need for some kind of political and economic association with Buenos Aires and each other.[31]

Porteño Federalism tended to have greater conservative leanings. The conservative portenos--estancieros and saladeros (owners of meat salting plants)--were perhaps the most privileged economic sector in Buenos Aires province and had, more than any other sector except the politican- intellectuals, reaped the benefits of independence due to the breakdown of inter-provincial commerce and the opening of the economy to foreign trade. They opposed the Unitarians because they believed that the Unitarian policy of trying to force the provinces into a centralized State structure was the chief cause of the instability and rampant warfare so harmful to their businesses.[32] They also resented the Rivadavian Constitution of 1826 which would have nationalized the city of Buenos Aires and denied the province its import-export revenues. This they believed would lead to higher taxation in the province as the only means of financing a seperate provincial government.[33] In any case, the constitution would have negated the privileged position they had gained by virtue of controlling one of the few remaining sources of national wealth, immersing them within a political and economic system in which their influence would be of less consequence.[34] The effective elimination of the Unitarians in Buenos Aires by Juan Manuel de Rosas' Federalist regime did not, however, remove the basis for inter-elite conflicts over the form that the nation would take. It continued in the conflict between porteño Federalists and provincial Federalists. I will return to this conflict in the section on centralism vs federalism.

Liberalism and conservatism in Peru were more clearly defined than in Argentina because the harsh lines of the colonial past were more deeply ingrained there. The liberal tendency, which was predominantly urban based and had sat out the movement for independence--putting their faith in the liberal Spanish Constitution of 1812, finally became the dominant force in 1827 (at least in Lima) after a number of setbacks at the hands of San Martín, whose interests, if not affinities, lay with the more established conservative groups in the capital, and Bolívar, who brought with him his own "foreign" administrators.[35] The liberals, generally weak except in the capital, the depressed areas of the coast in the environs of Lima, and in some provincial towns, favored a considerably more open society than had existed during the colonial regime. They obviously hoped that a system based upon merit rather than inherited status would favor them. They preferred a relatively weak central authority which they could dominate and control through the legislature, the decentralization of political authority--though not federalism--presumably to afford coastal hacendados more direct control over labor distribution and control, and legislative control over the church and military--institutions which were strongholds of colonial, and thus conservative dominance.[36]

The liberals in Peru were particularly successful in constitution writing, having created the Constitutions of 1823,

1828, 1834, 1856 and 1867. However, the application of these instruments was rarely effective. This was a result of two separate but related developments. First, the destruction of the old political structure and its legitimacy created a crisis in administration throughout the country. Promotion and appointment within the bureaucracy was capricious and filled with dangers and disappointments, and the weak liberal establishment in the capital cast suspicion upon the loyalty of administrators far from Lima.[37] Second, the military, that sector of the bureaucracy which because of its function was best able to retain its autonomy from the political center, tended to become dominant. In Peru the relatively professional army derived from the remnants of the Spanish army in America and the independence forces organized by Bolívar became institutionally stronger than the State itself.[38] A military career thus became a surer entrance to political power than any civilian occupation.

Peruvian liberals concentrated their efforts on controlling or eliminating the sources of competition with their State--the military and the church--which were the bulwarks of conservative power. However, liberals were not below putting forth their own military caudillos if a military man could buttress their authority. Unfortunately they chose relatively weak generals like Luis José de Orbegoso and José de La Mar who they could easily control and dominate and so were usually faced with defeat at the hands of more powerful conservative generals like Agustín Gamarra.[39] The liberal Constitution of 1834 reflected their experiences with La Mar, Orbegoso and Gamarra in that it,

> . . . gave to congress the power to designate the size and composition of the armed forces. A supreme council of war was created, its members elected by congress, as a further means of establishing civilian control over the military. . . [it] also stipulated that no additional commissions to officer rank would be given except as vacancies occurred and that promotions were to be based solely upon distinguished service on the field of battle.[40]

Such legislation was always ineffective as the conservative provincial elite continued to provide backing for a host of military caudillos who captured the State, ". . . for the purpose of guaranteeing a perpetuation of the status quo against the "excesses" of the liberalism of the urban intellecturals."[41] Both the crisis engendered by military caudillism and the liberal-conservative conflict over the church in Peru will be discussed below.

CENTRALISM VS FEDERALISM (REGIONALISM)

Conflict over political centralization and decentralization affected countries throughout Spanish America in the first half of the nineteenth century. As we have seen in Chapters 2 and 3, the Bourbon political reforms sought to centralize the old

145

Hapsburg system of administration which had lent the colonies a good deal of local autonomy. Creoles were split on the merit of these reforms depending whether their interests were harmed or furthered by them, but their general opinion was to see the hordes of penisular administrators who attempted to reduce local autonomy as a threat. Within the opposition were two tendencies that became important after political power fell to the creoles. First, there was opposition by those, principally in the viceregal capitals, who were denied positions in the expanding bureaucracy because they were creoles, and second, those in the provinces who suffered the loss of local control. In addition, the administrative decentralization of the Viceroyalty of Peru, which disrupted established patterns of political administration and commerce, made the creation of nations out of the colonies that much more difficult and contentious.

The centralist-federalist (and regionalist) conflicts were at the very heart of the problem of State formation in Spanish America. With the disappearance of the Spanish colonial State and two competing patterns of rule in contention (Bourbon and Hapsburg), the conflict over State formation not only took the form of an internal battle within Spanish American countries, but of an international battle as well. In no other country in Spanish America was this conflict more a central fact of political life than in Argentina. There, according to Joseph Criscenti, when the independence movement got underway there were two quite distinct tendencies regarding what constituted or would constitute the nation. In the interior provinces there was a strong following for a continental solution to the problem of nationhood wherein each province would become an independent unit in its own right, joined to a great federation of all the other provinces on the continent.[42] This solution had obvious roots in the Hapsburg Viceroyalty of Peru. The tendency most predominant in Buenos Aires, however, saw the nation as the geographic extent of the Viceroyalty of Río de la Plata in which the provinces would be subordinate to Buenos Aires.[43] This solution had its roots in the Bourbon viceregal decentralization. A third tendency, however, which proved almost indomitable in the first half of the nineteenth century was the autonomist tendency which had its roots in the conflict between the continental and viceregal visions of the nation.

The continental tendency, which was represented by José de San Martín and Carlos María de Alvear of the Lautaro Lodge, lost a great deal of support in the interior when, as the war against the Spanish forces in America appeared to be headed for defeat, their monarchist leanings became apparent in the search by the Directory for a European aristocrat to preside over America.[44] When the continentalist Constitution of 1819, in which the nation was defined as the "United Provinces of America," was rejected by the provinces, the disintegration of the continentalist idea became complete.[45]

Although autonomism within the continentalist tendency won out over centralizing monarchism, the conflict over what form the nation and the State would take did not end there. The provinces went their own separate ways, forming their own decidedly centralist States and hoping for a continentalist solution that would preserve their political autonomy. This continentalist tendency was most vigorous in Córdoba which, being the most populous and wealthy of the interior provinces, became a natural opponent of Buenos Aires. As each province declared its independence and set up its own State structures pending a general congress which would decide the future of the nation, Córdoba made provisions for its advent by adopting, ". . . on January 30, 1821, a "Reglamento Provisorio" which was to receive the approval of the "authority of the confederation," the "General Congress of the States." Executive power was vested in a "governor of the republic," the legislature in a congress. With the consent of the General Congress of the States the governor could negotiate treaties with one or more provinces."[46] Tucumán and Cuyo followed Córdoba's lead by enacting similar legislation while throughout the interior autonomism led to the further fragmentation of the intendencies into provinces.[47]

Although the autonomist tendency pervaded all of Argentina, the viceregal tendency had a strong base in the city of Buenos Aires. This tendency came to be called Unitarianism. With the fall of the Directory, the Unitarians quickly became the dominant force in the Buenos Aires State. Rather than pushing their plan for the reconstitution of the viceroyalty under the hegemony of Buenos Aires (this had already been rejected by the provinces at the Congress of Tucumán in 1821,[48] and was not popular with the conservative porteño estanciero-saladeros who were beginning to lean towards Federalism),[49] they bided their time hoping that success in creating prosperity and stability in Buenos Aires province would convince the provinces of the value of becoming part of their plan for an Argentine nation.[50] Although the Unitarian program did bring some prosperity to the province, it could not overcome the opposition of the provinces and rural elites of Buenos Aires province who believed that the urban "moneyocracy" which the Unitarians represented did not, and could not, attend to their particular interests.[51]

With the rejection of the Unitarian constitution in 1827, the government of Rivadavia fell and its plans for a centralized national State were destroyed. Manuel Dorrego, a Federalist, was made governor of Buenos Aires province in 1828 and proceeded to put the Federalist program into practice by recognizing the independence of the provinces and concluding treaties with a number of them.[52] Dorrego, however, was too sympathetic towards the interests of the provinces in the opinion of the porteño Federalists and they supported, according to Criscenti, the Unitarian General Juan Lavalle who, at the head of the national army returning from the war with Brazil, overthrew Dorrego. Far from bringing the peace and tranquility that the rural elites desired, Lavalle's execution of Dorrego brought a provincial invasion of Buenos Aires. The estancieros immediately shifted their support to Juan Manuel de Rosas who was acceptable to the provincial Federalists and was able to make a kind of unstable peace with the Unitarian army under General José M. Paz in Córdoba.[53]

The regime of Rosas will be discussed in Chapter 7, but several aspects of his rule are relevant here. Rosas, it seems, as leader of the autonomist tendency in Buenos Aires Federalism, would have been satisfied to have isolated the province and concentrated upon the needs of the class he represented until such time as stability in the region allowed the formation of a federation. However, the successes of the Unitarian Army in the interior forced Rosas to come to the defense of the provincial Federalists, if only to protect his regime in Buenos Aires. Thus began his holy war against the "savage Unitarians."[54] With resistance to his rule rising in both Buenos Aires province and the other provinces by the 1840s, Rosas found that the only sure means of dominating his opponents was a powerful centralized State under his personal control. The provincial leaders were kept within the Rosas fold by the threat of armed force, while his opponents in Buenos Aires province were subjected to terrorist campaigns. Rosas the Federalist became Rosas the centralist.

Rosas ruled the Federalist provinces with an iron grip. Nevertheless, under the leadership of Justo José de Urquiza, they overthrew him in 1852. The overthrow of Rosas, however, did not solve the problem of national organization. It eliminated the logjam created by Rosas, but not the fundamental conflict between Buenos Aires and the provinces. The power and wealth of Buenos aires were built on the basis of policies which strangled the export trade of the riverine provinces and denied the port market to the interior provinces. Urquiza, who was successful in organizing all of the other Argentine provinces in to a Confederation in 1852, was unsuccessful in getting Buenos Aires to join. This was chiefly because the provincial Federalist plan called for the domination of the province of Buenos Aires by the Confederation through the separation of the port from the province.[56] In September 1852, a coalition of urban elites and rural caudillos (former lieutentants of Rosas) overthrew the puppet government of Urquiza in Buenos Aires.[57] However, the new Buenos Aires government attempted to bring the entire Confederation under its sway and was defeated by those same rural caudillos and the forces of the Confederation.[58] Buenos Aires retained its autonomy and fought an economic war against the Confederation until the matter was settled on the field of battle. In September 1861, a porteño army headed by Bartolomé Mitre defeated Urquiza and the Confederation.[59] Mitre, now both governor of Buenos Aires and president of the Confederation, proceeded to enact the plan of Rivadavia and secure the dominance of Buenos Aires over the rest of the Argentine provinces.[60]

The issue of centralism vs federalism (or regionalism) did not so completely dominate the political scene in Peru.[61] But, as in Argentina, there were two aspects to this conflict--one rather mild conflict over the centralization or decentralization of the State, and the other over the geographic extent of, and balance between, the regions that would make up the Peruvian nation. Neither of these conflicts tore Peru apart the way they did Argentina but they contributed to the instability of the era and became grist for the mill of caudillo warfare.

Peruvian liberals evidenced an ideological perference for federalism and the decentralization of the State administration but did not follow up this preference with action. The federalist faction within the liberal congress of 1823 suffered defeat as the liberal majority wrote a decidedly centralized political structure into the Constitution.[62] Although almost all Peruvian constitutions rejected federalism,[63] the federalist tendency existed with more reality in the actual political makeup of the country than any words printed in the constitution. The tradition of rewarding military leaders with the prefectures of the departments, and basing national armies under the control of those prefects upon Indian tribute revenue collected at the department level, gave these military chieftains strong regional bases from which to challenge the central State.[64] At times these military men represented legitimate regional grievances against what was considered the overbearing central administration in Lima; and at times they only represented themselves. Nevertheless, they gave regional animosities the destructive power they might not have had with central control over the military.[65]

Perhaps no reform went further to reduce regional independence than Ramón Castilla's abolition of the Indian tribute. In the sierra, local governments and warlords who relied upon that revenue became dependent upon the revenue passed along to them by the central State in Lima. However, as Frederick Pike comments, ". . . [it] produced a type of centralism that actually still further separated the various part of the country rather than binding them together. The longer this centralism . . . by the capital remained in effect, the more intense became the regional animosities that it generated."[66] Regionalism or federalism continued to be an issue in Peru throughout the nineteenth century, but as José Carlos Mariategui relates, "Actually, the parties were not anxious to abolish centralism. Sincere federalists were not only few in number and scattered among the different parties, but they exercised no real influence on opinion. They did not represent a popular cause."[67] Nevertheless, the imposition of a centralistic order on the departments and their reaction against it added to the political instability of the era and to difficulty in consolidating the State.

The defining of the geographical extent of the nation was a much shorter and violent affair. Two tendencies, though they were not mutually exclusive, were evident and both had economic and political motives. As in Argentina, these tendencies represented attempts by Peru to reconstruct the administrative and economic pattern of the Hapsburg viceroyalty by annexing Ecuador and/or Bolivia. Perhaps the more politically motivated of these movements was the invasion of Colombia (Ecuador was then part of Colombia) by President José de La Mar in 1828, with the encouragement of the "war-mongering" liberal congress.[68] The

149

congress not only sought to annex Ecuador, which had been disputed over by the Viceroyaltys of Peru and New Granada ever since the latter's establishment in 1739,[69] but also to destroy the Bolivarian conservatives in Colombia, hoping for a liberal ascendancy there.[70] La Mar[71] secured Guayaquil, but was defeated by Bolívar's forces at Cuenca.[72] However, he was perhaps defeated more by the plot of Generals Agustín Gamarra and Antonio Gutíerrez de La Fuente to discredit him on the field of battle by having Gamarra retreat and allow defeat.[73] Gamarra then forced the liberal congress to make him president and La Fuente vice president.[74]

The attempt to reconstruct the viceregal patterns of administration and commerce on the southern flank with the annexation of Bolivia by Peru (or Peru by Bolivia) was perhaps the more important and potentially beneficial to both. The seperation of southern Peru from Upper Peru (Bolivia) by the Bourbons in the eighteenth century seriously upset the regional economies of both because they had formed, since at least the Inca period, one political, social, and economic unit. The logic of the Bourbon reformers in separating them was, as we have seen in Chapter 3, strategic--to finance the Viceroyalty of Río de la Plata with the silver mines of Upper Peru. There was then good historical precedent and economic logic to the re-unification of these two areas. The attempt, however, only increased instability in Peru and Bolivia and subjected former to an invasion by Chile.

The idea of a Peru-Bolivian Confederation arose with the desires of Generals Andrés Santa Cruz and Gamarra to re-unite the sierra, although each preferred unification under their own domination. Santa Cruz and Gamarra first agreed to the formation of a Peru-Bolivia Confederation when Gamarra was plotting to overthrow La Mar. The plan was for Gamarra and his army to march into Bolivia and pressure the president of Bolivia, General José de Sucre, to abandon the country. With Sucre gone, Santa Cruz, a native Bolivian, would assume control and declare for a Peru-Bolivia Confederation with himself as its head. Gamarra, having seized power in Peru, would join the Confederation and receive a high position in the new State.[75] Santa Cruz gained control of Bolivia but Gamarra betrayed him and ignored the agreement.[76] However, given Santa Cruz's commitment to a Peru-Bolivia Confederation, Gamarra decided that it would be best if he acted first and prepared to invade Bolivia. Only the mediation of the dispute by Chile in 1831 forstalled war between the two.[77]

The Peru-Bolivia Confederation became a reality in 1836 under the leadership of Santa Cruz after a confusing and violent game of musical presidential chairs in Peru. These macabre events included an attempt by Gamarra to oust the legal president General Luis José de Orbegoso, another deal between Gamarra and Santa Cruz to create a Peru-Bolivia Confederation once Gamarra had seized power in Peru, a revolt by General Felipe Salaverry against Orbegoso, and an alliance between Orbegoso and Santa Cruz against Gamarra and Salaverry which stipulated that Orbegoso agree to a Peru-Bolivia Confederation under the leadership of Santa Cruz.[78] The Santa Cruz-Orbegoso alliance ultimately won the internal struggle and Peru was divided into two republics--South Peru, headed by Santa Cruz and North Peru, headed by Orbegoso. Santa Cruz remained president of Bolivia in addition to becoming the head of the entire Confederation. In the Peruvian highlands, the Confederation had a great deal of support from the elites of both Arequipa and Cuzco who believed that they had at last been freed of the domination of Lima.[79]

In the end though, the Confederation really pleased no particular region,

Lima resented the debilitating division of Peru and domination by a Bolivian. Southern Peru would have preferred union of only itself and Bolivia, a weaker confederation that might have been controlled from Arequipa, the capital of the South. La Paz opposed the selection of Lima as the seat of the general government of the confederation and citizens of both Peru and Bolivia objected to the impairment of their nations' independence.[80]

However, it was the intervention of Chile rather than overwhelming internal discord that sounded the dealth knell of the confederation. Chile, under the sway of Diego Portales, feared its now powerful neighbor to the north, believing that with his success in re-establishing the east-west axis of the old viceroyalty, Santa Cruz would attempt to re-establish the north-south axis and swallow up Chile. In fact, Portales considered the destruction of the Peru-Bolivia Confederation as Chile's "second independence."[81] Chile also had a long standing trade dispute with Peru and Portales believed Santa Cruz was behind an attempt to overthrow his conservative government.[82] In 1839, with the aid of the ever present General Gamarra, Chilean forces defeated Santa Cruz and the Confederation was dissolved--Peru and Bolivia receiving back their respective sovereignties.[83] Gamarra, now president of Peru again, made one last attempt to create a Peru-Bolivia Confederation and died trying. Gamarra was killed on the battlefield at Ingaví, Bolivia, with the defeat of his Peruvian Army.[84]

CHURCH VS STATE

Although the nineteenth century conflict between the church and State had economic and ideological aspects, it was primarily a political conflict that centered upon what role the church as an institution would play in the new nations. The church, as one of the more powerful institutions of colonial society, presented a distinct challenge to the new Spanish American States because of its wealth, legitimacy, and internal institutional strength. During the colonial period, as we have seen in Chapter 2, the church functioned as the right arm of the crown, forming an

151

intergral part of the State through the king's right of patronage over the Catholic church in America. Although the church was a bastion of conservatism and hierarchy within the colonies and thus a prop of the creole elites against the lower classes, it also functioned to control the creoles in the interest of the crown through the Inquisition and its restrictions on the use of the Indian labor force. The church's monopolization of the economy in some areas like Paraguay,[85] and its role as chief rural creditor,[86] often made it the object of creole disfavor.

With independence won, the dual nature of the church's role in society produced contending reactions in favor of the church and against it depending upon the political, economic, and social goals of various creole factions. The early attack on church wealth, for example, received support from almost all elite sectors. In the 1850s and 1860s, when most Spanish American States took over the finances of the church in order to raise much needed funds, they reduced the debts owed to the church by creole landowners to a fraction of their value and liberals as well as conservatives took advantage of the windfall. In Peru, for example, though no figures are available, Arnold Bauer contends that these church obligations, ". . . evaporated in bureaucratic confusion; the documents of others were lost or disposed of in "a most irregular manner."[87] The lands of the regular clergy were confiscated or severely reduced by republican governments with little protest from the conservatives because these estates often competed for land and labor with theirs. They also were able to buy these properties from penurous governments at greatly reduced prices.[88] The Inquisition, hated by all creoles because it was directed at them, was swept away without protest, although the intolerance of un-orthodoxy was not.[89]

Attacks against church wealth only became a source of contention when it was recognized by the conservatives that the social control and political roles of the church, which they sought to maintain, were being erroded by those attacks. However, both liberals and conservatives, when in power, sought to bring the church under the control of the State; the liberals to expel church influence from temporal affairs, the conservatives to use it, much as had the Spanish crown, as an arm of the State. Both liberal and conservative factions of the creole elite then asserted the right of the new States to the patronato of the Spanish kings. Neither sought an independent church and this put the Spanish American States at loggerheads with not only the church hierarchy, but also the Pope.[90]

In the early years of independence conflicts also raged within the clergy itself. High ecclesiastic positions in America were dominated by peninsulares and thus the lower clergy, which was predominantly creole, welcomed, and even participated in, the anti-Spanish independence movements. Liberal clergymen often led the fight for State control over the church, especially in attacks on the regular clergy. However, this liberal interregnum did not last. As these self same clergymen became the rulers the national churches, they also become the most ardent defenders of the autonomy of the church.

In neither Argentina nor Peru did the church-State conflict ever reach the fever pitch or violence that it did in Mexico.[91] But the conflict that did exist was indicative of the difficulty the new States had in asserting their authority and legitimacy. In Argentina, the church and its hierarchy was subjected to attacks by, and the control of, the independence regimes very early. The Bishops of Buenos Aires, Córdoba and Salta were removed from control over their churches by the civil authorities and replaced with priests who were considered "patriotic," while the clergy was forced to propagandize the faithful as to the rightness of the new order.[92] Without the higher clergy in control, the inherent conflict between the regular and secular clergy "led to a fight with fists and knives" which the State often did nothing to halt, the better to control both sides.[93] Church properties, especially those of the regular orders, were confiscated by the State and appointment to high ecclesiatic position was made dependent upon one's adherence to the independence cause. All churchmen were now considered, ". . . as another class within the state, and obliged therefore "to share in the conservation of the whole, on the existence and increase of which the welfare of each part depends."[94] The result of these attacks upon the church was a cowed and ineffective institution whose members, without the guidance of the hierarchy, suffered a "moral" and religious decline.[95]

In 1822, Bernardino Rivadavia, then the principal minister in the Unitarian government, got the congress to abolish the tithe and ecclesiastical fuero, put church finances (including those of the regular orders) under State supervision, restrict the regular orders' recruitment to those over 25 years of age, and set the membership of ecclesiastic houses to a minimum of 16 and a maximum of 30. In addition, some regular orders were suppressed altogether, their property turned over to the State, and the State made responsible for funding the church.[96] The reaction to these reforms was limited yet violent as an ultramontane opposition developed led by Gregorio Tagle who, with the cry of "religion o muerte," attacked the government.[97] This movement was supported by conservative porteño estanciero-saladeros who opposed the secularization program of the Unitarians.[98]

With the rise of the Federalist Rosas in the 1830s, the church believed it had found a friend and supporter. Rosas went to great lengths to reassert the temporal influence of the church, although only under his control and for his purposes. The clergy became ardent supporters of Rosista Federalism, denouncing the "savage Unitarians" from the pulpit and extrolling the "Holy Federal Cause." Some fanatics such as Father Gaeta, ". . . draped his statues in federal colours and badges, and began all his sermons with the exhortation "Parishioners, if there is any filthy unitarian savage among us, crush him."[99] Rosas regarded the Unitarians as "enemies of Jesus Christ" and set to reverse the reforms of Rivadavia, returning church property, re-instating the Dominicans, and even authorizing the return of the Jesuits.[100] The Jesuits returned but were

153

expelled again by Rosas when they refused to become part of the religious arm of his dictatorship.[101] Though the church was nurtured and protected by Rosas, it became a State church, more so than any in Spanish America at the time.

Perhaps the chief basis for church-State conflict in Argentina has been the State's exercise of the right of patronage.[102] The State has never conceded its right to appoint high ecclesiastic officials and rule on communications between the national church and Rome, nor has the Pope conceded to the State the right to exercise these perogatives. This has led to conflict not only between the Argentine State and Rome, but between the State and the national church. The national clergy, hoping to retain its independence vis-à-vis the State by putting itself under the authority of Rome, has been in continuous conflict with the civil authorities who desire to control it. Though this conflict has not been serious, it has remained a cause of considerable friction between the church and State throughout the nineteenth and twentieth centuries.[103]

In Peru, the secular clergy were early participants in the independence governments, but these were the lower clergy, not the hierarchy. Liberal clergymen like Francisco Javier de Luna Pizarro and Mariano José de Arce were important figures in early governments.[104] The lower clergy of Peru were predominently creoles of either pure Spanish or mestizo origins who had been discriminated against by the crown's preference for peninsulares in high ecclesiastic appointments.[105] It is hardly surprising then, that a large contingent of them would be ardent supporters of creole independence. They were also in the forefront of the movement to reform the church and put it under the control of the State, a reflection of their strong position within the congress and the resistance of their Bishops to the independence movement.

The bulk of the clergy, especially the hierarchy, was not in favor of independence and was less in favor of the reforms introduced by the independence governments. Archbishop Bartolomé Maria de Las Heras' opposition to San Martín caused his expulsion from the country, while Bolívar's policies of reducing the number of monasteries and convents, Indian payments to the clergy, and the number of religious holidays, as well as his filling bishoprics without Papal approval, led to intense clerical opposition in the sierra led by the only remaining Bishop in the country, the creole José Sebastían Goyenche of Arequipa. For his opposition, Goyenche was relieved of his authority, though not his office.[106]

In the early national period, liberals and conservatives were apparently in agreement on the principle of State control of the church but with, it seems, two different visions of its role. Liberals wanted to reduce the influence of the church in politics and society. Conservatives favored a church dependent upon the State but functioning as a State directed social control mechanism against the lower classes.[107] The usefulness of the church for the conservatives, and the reason to curb it in the opinion of the liberals, is obvious in an incident described by

S. S. Hill who traveled throughout Peru in the 1850s. Hill found that when the town authorities of Arequipa wanted a pile of dirt removed from an excavation in the town square they called upon the Bishop to help. The Bishop removed a statue of San Juan from a church in a nearby Indian village, set it upon the pile of dirt and told the Indian villagers that it would not be put back in their church until the pile of dirt was cleared away.[108]

The conflict over church-State relations in Peru did not become an important issue until the conservatives took up the cause of the church in earnest in the late 1830s. The liberals felt that the only way to break the temporal power of the church was to weaken its internal cohesion. They therefore began favoring the democratization of the church. Liberals like Manuel Lorenzo de Vidaurre and Francisco de Paula González Vigil called for democratization of the structures of the church, the abolition of ecclesiastic privileges, freedom of thought within the church, freedom from Papal authority and a return to the simplicity and poverty of the early church.[109] In effect, the liberals were calling for the abolition of hierarchy and authoritarianism in the church.[110] Conservatives, unconcerned with past liberal attempts to put the church under State control, saw this new liberal tactic as a threat to themselves and began supporting the church against the State. Having changed their tack on the church-State issue, conservatives began supporting churchmen like Bartolomé Herrera, a confirmed ultramontanist.[111] The conservatives and Herrera came to believe that the only way to save Peru from the constant instability and warfare of the age was for the people to be subject to the authority of the church. For Herrera, only the church could say what the law should be because all authority and sovereignty was derived from God. Herrera's position was thus not only ultramontane, it was intensely theocratic.[112]

Though the debate continued on an ideological level throughout the nineteenth century, the political conflict between liberals and conservatives on this issue was resolved by President Ramón Castilla's compromise Constitution of 1860. In this constitution, the liberals won the suppression of separate ecclesiastical courts and fueros, the prohibiting of State collection of church tithes in favor of a State subsidy to the church, and a system of public education that would end the monopoly of the church in education. The conservatives won safeguards to church wealth and property, relative autonomy for the church's internal organization, the perpetuation of Catholic exclusivism in Peru, and most importantly, a highly centralized authoritarian State.[113] With this assured, the Peruvian conservatives abandoned the ultramontane theocratic position of Herrera, while the liberals, although they did try to reverse this "defeat" in the Constitution of 1867, generally retreated from the battle.[114]

Caudillism, which arose throughout Spanish America in the first half of the nineteenth century, was more a result of political, social, and economic conflicts within the elites than it was the cause of them. A combination of the breakdown of political and social controls and the militarization of Spanish American societies during the Wars of Independence produced this rather informal system of political power and recruitment that was bridled, and then eliminated, only with the consolidation of strong central States in the late nineteenth century.

The phenomenon of caudillism is directly related to both the form and breakdown of the Spanish colonial State. The form of rule within the Spanish bureaucracy which centralized executive, legislative, and judical power in the same office gave legitimacy to the form of one man rule that became the hallmark of caudillism.[115] The breakdown of the Spanish State apparatus in America saw no satisfactory replacement, given the weakness of the independence governments.[116] However, in the countryside and provincial centers, strong authority developed upon those institutions at the local level that were best able to weather the storm of the independence struggle--the military and hacienda based militias.[117]

With the social control mechanisms of the colonial State breaking down and royalists and patriots recruiting of mestizos and pardos into their respective armies, the career of arms became, for a small few of the lower classes, a means to rise to positions, either in the military or in politics, which they would never have attained under the colonial system.[118] The implications of this rise, however, were perhaps exaggerated by its novelty. A very few of the lower classes were able to rise in this manner despite the fears of the creole elites.[119] Not surprisingly, caudillism and the instability it tended to perpetuate found ardent adherents. As Tulio Halperin-Donghi argues, "All that sector of the population which was not to receive its share of the new wealth, the conquest of which was held by many to be the only legitimate goal of the new Spanish American states, could be classified among the potential supporters of civil war."[120]

Evidence supports viewing the caudillo as both the expression of owning class rule and the expression of the rural masses or "folk," as E. Bradford Burns terms them.[121] This is perhaps because caudillos performed contradictory roles. On the one hand, some local caudillos, although they lorded over the local population and were more times than not members of the local elite, protected the local people from outsiders--either other caudillos or representatives of the central government--who "exploited" them.[122] Francois Bourricaud describes a scene from José Maria Arguedas' novel, Yawar Fiesta, in which this protection of the local population by the "good" local patron is illustrated,

When any of the authorities of Cajabamba--mayor or judge--did wrong, the people would come to Don Teodoro in demand of justice. Then he, at the head of the people, would go after the wrongdoer, make him get on a donkey, and ride him out of town with a band of firecrackers. The person expelled like that never returned. Don Teodoro explained: "If we complain to the capital, they will pay no attention to us. In Lima they laugh at the Provinces and dump their scoundrels on us."[80]

Even those caudillos who had their origins as representatives of the central authorities like Juan Facundo Quiroga, the Argentine "tiger of the Pampas," could become the protector of local values and economy.[124] On the other hand, the local caudillo who was a member of the owning class (whether an old member or new one with lands acquired through war) preserved the traditional basis of domination--control over land and administrative positions. If he were not yet a member, he had to take into account the local power structure, even as it opposed and feared him.[125]

In both Argentina and Peru, caudillism was an important aspect of the instability and conflict of the first half of the nineteenth century. In Argentina, the caudillism of the 1820-1860 period had its roots in the breakdown of both the viceregal and independence political structures, the militarization of society with the interminable conflicts of the independence and civil wars, and localist protectionism against the economic and political pretentions of Buenos Aires.

The breakdown of the political administration in Argentina and the ruralization of the bases of political power tended to place the leadership of both the Unitarian and the Federalist causes in the hands of military leaders. For the Unitarians, the generals of the national army began to serve as its leadership, while for the Federalists it was the rural estancieros at the head of their militias.[126] The estanciero became a natural leader of the militia because of his ability to provide, organize, and provision large numbers of men, even when the central government could not. James Scobie describes the Argentine caudillo as,

. . . usually a landowner and decendent of some powerful creole family. In the interior and on the coast, he gathered his gauchos and peons into irregular but effective cavalry forces. With this military power and through his economic and social influence, he became the government, ruling either directly or through puppets. Those with land and capital sought security in his shadow. The rapidly growing lower classes looked to him for protection.[127]

In most provinces local caudillos fought each other for supremacy, the more successful ones like Ricardo López Jordán of Entre Ríos, Juan Facundo Quiroga of La Rioja, Martín Güemes of Salta, Juan Bautista Bustos of Córdoba and, of course, Juan Manuel de Rosas of Buenos Aires, becoming the chiefs and protectors of their provinces.[128]

Rosas was not only the most successful of the caudillos, but the only one who was able to produce a system of national power based upon his domination of all the other provincial caudillos in the Argentine. In his own province of Buenos Aires, Rosas attempted to diminish the powers of the local caudillos by building a strong provincial army not based upon the local estancieros.[129] His system, however centralized it may have been, did not last, nor did it rid Argentina of caudillism, because it did not institutionalize or legitimize the State itself. He was ultimately defeated by the caudillo governor of Entre Ríos, Justo José de Urquiza (who had been one of Rosas' most ardent supporters), who managed to put together a coalition of provincial caudillos for the purpose of removing Rosas from power and organizing a genuine national federal State.[130] The final extirpation of caudillism in Argentina was left to the governments of Bartolomé Mitre and Domingo Sarmiento who, with the expanding power of the national State, put an end to provincial autonomy.[131]

Caudillism in Peru, at least at the national level, tended to be associated with the military proper. Many of the national caudillos of the early nineteenth century like Agustín Gamarra, Andrés Santa Cruz, José de La Mar and Ramón Castilla held commissions in the royalist armies during the Wars of Independence and only switched to the rebels after Peru was invaded by San Martín or Bolívar. These were generally men from modest backgrounds who, with the breakdown of royal power, were catapulted to national leadership in the absence of a strong centralized State in Lima.[132] Their armies, based in the populous and prosperous sierra (at least in relation to the coast), became the basis of regional and personal power with which they vied for the presidency of the nation.[133]

The caudillo's relationship with the owning classes was inherently problematic. Several caudillos, for example José de La Mar, Felipe Santiago Salaverry and Manuel Ignacio Vivanco, had strong connections with, or were themselves members of, the upper classes. But most of the others related to the elite on the basis of mutual suspicion. If the State was too weak to put a brake on social disintegration, the owning classes were willing to acquiesce and support the strongmen of the military.[134] It was not exclusively the conservative forces that put their faith in caudillism, the liberals of Lima and the coast also offered up their share of caudillos like General Orbegoso. If they could not impose liberalism through the constitution, they would use the mailed fist.[135]

The regime of Ramón Castilla, military caudillo from Arequipa, did a good deal to finally end caudillism in Peru, although not in his own lifetime. Castilla strengthened and centralized the Peruvian State with windfall revenues secured by the government's monopoly of the guano trade. Under Castilla, the State itself became the greatest power base in Peru and its largesse began to produce a group--bureaucrats, merchants, businessmen and coastal plantation owners--who, in succeeding years, would form a class basis for an effective Peruvian State.[136] However, guano revenues were an unstable basis for the establishment of State power and it would take the maturation of this class in the late nineteenth century to rid Peru of caudillism.

States in Spanish America in the first half of the nineteenth century were inherently weak given the breakdown of the legitimacy and political structures of the colonial era. The chief post colonial problem in almost all Spanish American countries was the re-establishment of a legitimate State structure. As we have seen, this was hampered by both the legacy of the colonial system and its destruction. Political conflicts wracked the new nations making a new political order almost impossible to construct. Yet, it was only through the reconstruction of political order that such conflicts would cease to tear the nations apart. In the middle and latter half of the nineteenth century there began to emerge, in most Spanish American countries, States which began to consolidate a class basis for political order by managing the conflicts we have just examined. It was in the process of managing these conflicts and creating a basis for State power that States had a profound effect upon the Spanish American economies. It was in large measure because of the policies of these States that their economies became export economies.

NOTES

[1] William H. Breezley, "Caudillism: An Interpretive Note," Journal of Inter-American Studies XI (July 1969), 347.

[2] James Lang, Conquest and Commerce: Spain and England in the Americas (New York: Academic Press, 1975), 235.

[3] See O. Carlos Stoetzer, The Scholastic Roots of the Spanish American Revolution (New York: Fordham University Press, 1979).

[4] See the discussion on this point in Glen Dealy, "The Spanish American Political Tradition," in The Borzoi Reader in Latin American History, Volume II, ed. Helen Delper (New York: Knopf, 1972), 13-14.

[5] Ibid.

[6] Charles Anderson, Politics and Economic Change in Latin America (New York: Van Nostrand, 1967), 17.

[7] Ibid., 17-18.

[8] Jorge I. Domínguez, Insurrection or Loyalty: The Breakdown of the Spanish American Empire (Cambridge, Massachusetts: Harvard

University Press, 1980), 253.

[9]Breezley, 348.

[10]Charles Hale, "The Reconstruction of Nineteenth Century Politics in Spanish America: A Case for the History of Ideas," Latin American Research Review VIII, Number 2 (Summer 1973), 61.

[11]Frederick B. Pike, "Heresy, Real and Alleged in Peru: An Aspect of the Liberal-Conservative Struggle, 1830-1875," Hispanic American Historical Review XLVII (February 1967), 50-51.

[12]John Lynch, The Spanish American Revolutions: 1808-1826 (New York: W. W. Norton, 1973), 343.

[13]Frank Safford, "Bases of Political Alignment in Early Republican Spanish America," in New Approaches to Latin American History, eds., Richard Graham and Peter H. Smith (Austin: University of Texas Press, 1977), 90-91.

[14]Ibid., 80-88.

[15]Robert N. Schwartz, Peru (Los Angeles: Inter American Publishing Company, 1970), 106-107.

[16]Safford, 80-86.

[17]Ibid., 88.

[18]Ibid., 103.

[19]See Alan Wolfe, The Limits of Legitimacy (New York: Free Press, 1977), 7, 18-19.

[20]Hale, 58.

[21]Dealy, 13-14.

[22]Safford, 83.

[23]Some large towns, like Cuzco and Arequipa in Peru, and Córdoba in Argentina, also had relatively large bureaucratic establishments.

[24]Hamnett makes this claim for Mexican liberalism and conservatism in Brian Hamnett, Politics and Trade in Southern Mexico, 1750-1821 (Cambridge: Cambridge at the University Press, 1971), 154-155. This claim is also made by Hale, 62.

[25]Miron Burgin, The Economic Aspects of Argentine Federalism 1820-1852 (New York: Russell and Russell, 1946, 1971), 87.

[26]Jaime Vicens Vives, An Economic History of Spain, trans. Frances M. López-Morillas (Princeton: Princeton University Press, 1969), 473-476.

[27]Burgin, 88.

[28]Ibid., 89.

[29]Ibid., 107.

[30]Ibid.

[31]Ibid.

[32]Joseph T. Criscenti, "Argentine Constitutional History, 1810-1852: A Re-examination," Hispanic American Historical Review XLI, Number 3 (August 1961), 400-401.

[33]Burgin, 105.

[34]Ibid., 105-106.

[35]Frederick B. Pike, The Modern History of Peru (New York: Praeger, 1967), 35-44, 47-55; and David Werlich, Peru: A Short History (Carbondale: Southern Illinois University Press, 1978), 50-76.

[36]Pike, Modern History, 53-54.

[37]Tulio Halperin-Donghi, The Aftermath of Revolution in Latin America (New York: Harper, 1973), 40-41.

[38]See the discussion in Ibid., 20-21.

[39]Pike, Modern History, 69-90.

[40]Ibid., 76.

[41]Stephen M. Gorman, "The State, Elite and Export in Nineteenth Century Peru: Toward an Alternative Reinterpretation of Political Change," Journal of Inter-American Studies XXI, Number 3 (1979).

[42]Criscenti, 370-371.

[43]Ibid., 371.

[44]Ibid., 380-384.

[45]They opposed the constitution not so much because the provinces were to be put under the authority of the Supreme Director, but because they objected to the institution of a monarchy which they believed would be the next step, see Ibid., 383-384.

[46]Ibid., 387.

[47]Ibid., 387-389.

[48]Burgin, 85-86.

[49]Criscenti, 390-394.

[50]Burgin, 86-87.

[51]Ibid., 103-109; and Tulio Halperin-Donghi, Politics,

Economics and Society in Argentina in the Revolutionary Period (Cambridge: Cambridge University Press, 1975), 343.

[52]Criscenti, 400.

[53]Ibid., 400-401. Also see John Lynch, Argentine Dictator, Juan Manuel de Rosas 1829-1852 (London: Oxford University Press, 1981), 44-45.

[54]Lynch, Argentine Dictator, 158-159.

[55]James Scobie, "The Significance of the September Revolution," Hispanic American Historical Review XLI, Number 2 (May 1961), 236-237.

[56]Ibid., 241-245.

[57]Ibid., 248.

[58]Ibid., 249-258.

[59]A. J. Walford, "The Economic Aspects of the Argentine War of Succession, 1852-1861," Inter-American Economic Affairs I, Number 2 (September 1947), 70-76. Also see F. A. Kirkpatrick, A History of the Argentine Republic (Cambridge: Cambridge at the University Press, 1931), 168-169.

[60]Kirkpatrick, 169.

[61]Werlich, 68.

[62]Pike, Modern History, 54.

[63]The Constitutions of 1856 and 1867 had provisions for the decentralization of government by adding elected department juntas to State appointed prefects, see Ibid., 106-108.

[64]Halperin-Donghi, Aftermath, 19. Also see, Henry F. Dobyns and Paul L. Doughty, Peru: A Cultural History (New York: Oxford University Press, 1976), 144.

[65]Dobyns and Doughty, 158-159.

[66]Pike, Modern History, 113.

[67]José Carlos Mariategui, Seven Interpretive Essays on Peruvian Reality, trans. Marjory Urquidi (Austin: University of Texas Press, 1971), 155.

[68]Pike, Modern History, 71.

[69]The Peruvians were worried about the loss of the Pacific port of Guayaquil which they thought might become a competitor to Callao.

[70]Pike, Modern History, 71.

[71]La Mar was from Guayaquil and, understandably, thought

that it should be a part of Peru.

[72]Werlich, 69; and Pike, Modern History, 71.

[73]William S. W. Ruschenberger, Three Years in the Pacific (Philadelphia: Carey, Lea and Blanchard, 1834), 432; and Pike, Modern History, 72.

[74]Ruschenberger, 432; and Pike, Modern History, 72-73.

[75]Pike, Modern History, 71-72.

[76]Ibid., 73. Robert Burr gives another account of this conspiricy in which Gamarra drove Santa Cruz out of Peru at gunpoint and thus created the animosity between the two generals, see Robert N. Burr, By Reason or Force: Chile and the Balancing of Power in South America, 1830-1905 (Berkeley and Los Angeles: University of California Press, 1965), 25.

[77]Pike, Modern History, 73; and Burr, 26-27.

[78]A full description of these events can be found in Pike, Modern History, 79-81; Werlich, 70-71; Burr, 33-36; and Lane Kendall, "Andrés Santa Cruz and the Peru-Bolivia Confederation," Hispanic American Historical Review XVI, (February 1936), 29-39.

[79]Werlich, 71.

[80]Ibid.

[81]Burr, 38-40.

[82]Both of these issues are discussed in Ibid., 36-39.

[83]Werlich, 72.

[84]Ibid.

[85]John Hoyt Williams, The Rise and Fall of the Paraguayan Republic, 1800-1870 (Austin: University of Texas Press, 1979), 8-13.

[86]Arnold J. Bauer, "The Church and Spanish American Agrarian Structure 1765-1865," The Americas XXVII (July 1971), 78-98.

[87]Ibid., 90.

[88]Ibid., 83-85.

[89]Halperin-Donghi, Aftermath, 97-98.

[90]J. Lloyd Mecham, Church and State in Latin America (Chapel Hill, North Carolina: University of North Carolina Press, 1934), 61-67 & passim.

[91]Mexican State-church relations have been particularly violent in both the nineteenth and twentieth centuries, see

Emilio Portes Gil, The Conflict Between the Civil Power and the Clergy (Mexico, D. F.: 1935); Robert E. Quirk, The Mexican Revolution and the Catholic Church, 1910-1929 (Bloomington: University of Indiana Press, 1973); and D. Baily, Viva Cristo Rey: The Cristero Rebellion and the Church-State Conflict in Mexico (Austin: University of Texas Press, 1974).

[92]Halperin-Donghi, Argentina, 180-181.

[93]Ibid., 182.

[94]Ibid., 183; and Mecham, 225.

[95]Halperin-Donghi, Argentina, 185; and Mecham, 226.

[96]Mecham, 226; and Peter Masten Dunne, "Church and State in Argentina," Review of Politics VII, Number 4 (October 1945), 398.

[97]Mecham, 227.

[98]Lynch, Argentine Dictator, 32.

[99]Ibid., 184.

[100]Ibid., 184-185.

[101]Ibid., 185.

[102]Dunne, 401.

[103]Mecham, 233-250.

[104]Pike, Modern History, 54.

[105]A. Tibesar, "The Peruvian Church at the Time of Independence in Light of Vatican II," The Americas XXVI (April 1970), 352.

[106]Mecham, 163-164.

[107]Pike, Hispanic American Historical Review, 51-52.

[108]S. S. Hill, Travels in Peru and Mexico, 2 Vols., (London: Longman, Green, Longman and Roberts, 1860), I:98-99.

[109]Pike, Hispanic American Historical Review, 52-59.

[110]Frederick B. Pike, "Church and State in Peru and Chile Since 1840," American History Review LXXIII (October 1967), 31-32; and Pike, Hispanic American Historical Review, 55.

[111]For a review of the thought of Herrera see Daniel Gleason, "Anti-Democratic Thought in Early Republican Peru: Bartolomé Herrera and the Liberal-Conservative Ideological Struggle," The Americas XXXVIII, Number 2 (October 1981), 205-217. Also see Pike, Hispanic American Historical Review, 55.

[112]Gleason, 205-217.

[113]Pike, Hispanic American Historical Review, 67.

[114]Ibid., 67-69; and Pike, American History Review, 35-37.

[115]Breezley, 346.

[116]Ibid., 347.

[117]Eric Wolf and Edward Hansen, "Caudillo Politics: A Structural Analysis," Comparative Studies in Society and History IX (1976), 169; and Halperin-Donghi, Aftermath, 14-24.

[118]Halperin-Donghi, Aftermath, 22.

[119]Ibid., 22-37. Stephen Gorman finds that the social rise of the mestizo in Peru at this time may be exaggerated. He believes that at least half of the caudillos who became president were white creoles, Gorman, 398 note 4.

[120]Halperin-Donghi, Aftermath, 23.

[121]These contradictory views are examined in Jacques Lambert, Latin America: Social Structures and Political Institutions, trans., Helen Katel (Berkeley: University of California Press, 1967), 153-166; Francois Chevalier, "The Roots of Personalismo," in Dictatorship in Spanish America, ed. Hugh M. Hamill (New York: Knopf, 1965), 35-51; and E. Bradford Burns, The Poverty of Progress: Latin America in the Nineteenth Century (Berkeley: University of California Press, 1981), 90-94.

[122]Burns, 92-93; and Stanley Stein and Barbara Stein, The Colonial Heritage of Latin America (New York: Oxford University Press, 1970), 162.

[123]Francois Bourricaud, Power and Society in Contemporary Peru, trans. Paul Stevenson (New York: Oxford University Press, 1970), 162.

[124]Lynch, Revolutions, 345.

[125]Halperin-Donghi, Aftermath, 19.

[126]This is a major theme of Halperin-Donghi, Argentina.

[127]James Scobie, Argentina, 2nd ed. (New York: Oxford University Press, 1971), 91.

[128]Ricardo Levene, A History of Argentina, trans. William Spence Robertson (Chapel Hill, North Carolina: University of North Carolina Press, 1957), 396-403.

[129]Lynch, Argentine Dictator, 112, 189-196.

[130]Ibid., 315-327; and Levene, 434-442.

[131]Levene, 464-479; and Irene Nicholson, The Liberators: A Study of the Independence Movements in Spanish America (New York:

Praeger, 1969), 278.

[132]Halperin-Donghi, _Aftermath_, 19.

[133]Ibid., 19-20; and Gorman, 398-399.

[134]Halperin-Donghi, _Aftermath_, 19-20.

[135]Pike, _Modern History_, 79-82.

[136]Gorman, 401-406.

7
The State and the Origin of the Export Economy: Peru and Argentina

The second half of the nineteenth century saw the beginnings of the consolidation of the State in most Spanish American countries and with that, the rise of full-blown export economies. Rather than the one creating the other, there arose a dialectical relatonship between the two, with the State clearly the determining instance. As we have seen, States in the early nineteenth century were relatively weak and clearly unable to manage the intense conflicts between fractions of the owning classes. In fact, the State itself was most often the object of those conflicts. Yet, the position of the State within a socio-economic formation--the space it occupies as the "public power"--forces those who occupy its apparatuses to manage class conflict and create a class hegemony within the dominant class, not only in the interest of the dominant class, but in the interest of the State itself.[1]

The economic effect of the State is derived from this purely political role. Absolutist States, for example, had the effect of encouraging the development of capitalism in Western Europe, not because they consciously sought to develop capitalism, but because in encouraging bourgeois development the States were strengthened and thus better able to perform their political role--managing class conflict.[2]

In the second half of the nineteenth century, Spanish American States seeking to create political order in their countries steered their economies, often unconsciously, into the international economy as agro/mineral export economies. There is no doubt that this would have been impossible without the existence of the international economy and the increasing demand for agro/mineral products created by capitalist industrialization in Europe. Nevertheless, Spanish American economies did not lock step to the tune of European demand without the mediation of their States. Rather than the demand of the international economy, it was the internal constellation of political forces, and the actions of the State in each Spanish American country, that would decide how and to what degree they would be intergrated into the international economy.[3]

In 1913, Francisco García Calderón, in his Latin America: Its Rise and Progress, observed that Spanish Americans had left foreigners to develop their national wealth. He attributed this to the inordinate "bloating" of the State which necessitated large customs revenues to pay for huge military and bureaucratic establishments.[4] In this analysis he was not so far from the truth. The failure to create, early on, a unified ruling class in most Spanish American nations led to the growth of State structures which far exceeded what might have been necessary. The resources which these States needed in order to impose order on conflict ridden societies turned them towards the only sources of finance available to them--foreign trade. Unable to draw resources out of their own internal economies which were hardly within their control, Spanish American States, from the very beginning, relied almost exclusively on the customs house. In this we find the first step in the creation of dependent economies.

THE STATE AND THE CREATION OF THE PERUVIAN EXPORT ECONOMY

Nineteenth century Peru is probably the clearest example of a State induced export economy. Not only was its first important link with the international economy, guano, produced by the State itself, but succeeding links can be traced to the effects of that first tie. In the aftermath of the independence wars the peruvian economy was, as we have seen, almost prostrate. The coastal plantations, in decline since the colonial period, were in ruins; the mines never returned to their former productivity or wealth; and trade, dependent upon the other two, seriously declined. Early independence governments were bankrupt, surviving on forced and foreign loans.[5] The State was forced to rely upon colonial taxes and the customs house for revenues which were substantially less than those of the colonial period.

Although the liberals who took charge of the government were dedicated to dismantling the colonial system--especially in the sierra, by force of circumstance they had to continue to rely upon the Indian tribute, now called the contribución de indígenas, for State revenues. The tribute was abolished in 1808, re-established in 1815, abolished again by San Martín in 1821 but re-instituted in 1826 when it became clear that no other source of income could be found.[6] The "contribución" was the only source of revenue upon which the State could count, as revenues from customs were subject to the ebb and flow of commerce. Until revenues from the guano trade became important, the "contribución" provided almost half of the total revenes collected by the State.[7]

Tariffs in Peru, however, were not set for the sole purpose of raising revenues. They were chiefly protective and this indicates the influence that the local craftsmen and artisans of Lima had on the liberal congress (which ideologically favored free trade), and the limited ability of the Peruvian market to absorb imports.[8] The tariff of 1826 provided for an 80% duty on all goods similar to those produced in Peru and 30% on all other goods. In 1828, the tariff was revised to completely prohibit the import of goods "more or less similar" to those produced in Peru.[9] Included on the prohibited list were olives, olive oil, brandy, alcohol, rice, sugarcane, sulfur, cacao, coffee, shoes, leather, chocolate, vermicelli, flour, soap, liquors, corn, lard, butter, dried vegetables, horse harnesses and saddles, furniture, dried fruit, gunpowder, ready-made clothing, saltpeter, salt, straw hats, tobacco, coarse wool and cotton cloth, tallow and wax candles.[10] This tariff was abolished during the Confedereation period but re-established with the return of independence.[11] Protection did have some beneficial effects by contributing to a revival of the textile industry, but Peru had never been an important producer of agricultural or manufactured goods and those sectors continued to languish.[12] Its economy revolved around the mines in the highlands and they continued to weaken despite government aid in financing the miners' mercury debt and the infusion of British capital and machinery.[13]

The lack of resources available to the State contributed as much to political instability in Peru as did political conflict itself. In fact, the two were inextricably linked. If the State was to perform its function of managing the intra-class conflicts of the elite, it had to have the resources necessary to impose order effectively. Only this would win it legitimacy in the eyes of the elite sectors. The State's weakness in the face of caudillos whose economic and political bases were beyond its control, led to a succession of caudillo led revolts whose aim was the capture of the State itself. The spoils of success could enhance the power and wealth of a caudillo and his followers, but such success only bred further caudillo led revolts. The State never proved strong enough, regardless of what caudillo headed it, to impose order.[14] The central State was strengthened and political conflict attenuated only when Ramón Castilla rose to the Peruvian presidency and discovered that guano, a fertilizer of which Peru held a virtual monopoly, could be marketed in Europe very profitably.

Castilla was a typical military caudillo of the first half of the nineteenth century. Born in Tarapacá in 1799, his parents were of the "lower middle class," his father a merchant-miner working the refuse silver ores of the mines of El Carmen. He spent a short period of study in Chile, but when the Wars of Independence broke out, he quickly joined the royalist army in Peru. He was captured by the rebels of Buenos Aires, but escaped to rejoin the royalist forces in Lima. After Peruvian independence was declared by San Martín in 1821, Castilla joined the rebellion and served at the battles of Junín and Ayacucho. He was rewarded by being appointed prefect of his native Tarapacá and then Tacna. In a dizzying display of false loyalty Castilla played the game of Peruvian caudillism, first opposing Gamarra and fighting for Orbegoso, then breaking with Orbegoso, reconciling with Gamarra and fighting against Orbegoso and Santa Cruz. For his "loyalty" to Gamarra, Castilla was rewarded with the ministry of the treasury.[15] Castilla developed his political base in Arequipa where he married and cemented important connections with the elite.[16] Of him Mariátegui has said, "Castilla was the military caudillo at his best."[17]

Yet, skilled and connected as he was, Castilla would not have been able to succeed in strengthening the State had he not been fortunate enough to come to power just when guano revenues dramatically increased. Guano (from the Indian word for the Guanay bird) is bird excrement which, deposited for centuries on coastal islands off of Peru, proved to be an excellent fertilizer and became much in demand in European agriculture. Roberto Cortés Conde explains that,

> The cold currents off Peru make its climate belie its tropical location. They also account for the dryness of the coastal zone which constituted an agricultural disadvantage in the central zone, accounted for the accumulation of enormous deposits of animal excrement in the islands off the coast of Peru. The coldness of the water (the Humboldt Current) attracted fish, hence, birds. The atmospheric dryness permitted the preservation and calcination of their deposits, which had a high concentration of nitrogen.[18]

On this collection of rocks called the Chincha Islands, guano deposits reached one hundred feet in depth and only needed to be hacked off with picks and shovels, loaded onto waiting cargo ships and sent to Europe. There was no need for processing and thus capital inputs were neglibible--a few tools and a labor force.[19]

The State, under the direction of Castilla as treasury minister, laid claim to the islands in 1840 and ran the guano trade as a monopoly of the Peruvian State.[20] In the following years guano revenues were to become the basis for an expanded State bureaucracy and army, the re-capitalization of coastal agriculture, and the building of railroads which began creating a unified national political structure. Guano, more than any other factor, led to the rise of a strong Peruvian State which could finally impose relative political stability. In 1865 Pedro Dávalos y Lissón wrote,

> With abundance, anarchy flees . . . . Until then [before guano] the government survived on customs and Indian tribute, and was at the mercy of funds sent by the Provinces . . . . With guano, now the government did not have to fear uprisings, vitality flowed to where the money was; and Lima became, for the first time, the social head of the nation.[22]

For the State, guano changed everything. As revenues grew, the State acquired resources against which regional caudillo revolts were to prove ineffective. These revenues did not require the State to be beholden to any domestic force and allowed it to become "relatively autonomous" from the clashing upper class sectors in society.[22]

But guano did not become important in Peruvian State finances until Castilla became president in 1845. The first guano contract was given, in 1840, to Francisco de Quiroz, a legislator and president of the Peruvian Chamber of Commerce, who proposed to pay the government 10,000 pesos per year, for six years, and advance it 40,000 pesos immediately for the exclusive right to export guano.[23] However, when the government learned that guano, which Quiroz said would net £12 per ton in London, fetched 18, it cancelled his contract and asked for new bids.[24] Few bids came in and the contract again went to Quiroz who, with his London backers, agreed to pay the State 64% of his net receipts and loan it 287,000 pesos against its anticipated share. Three months later, the government cancelled this arrangement and again contracted with the Quiroz group for a five year monopoly in which the treasury would receive advances of nearly half a million pesos, the first 30 dollars per ton obtained from the sale of guano plus 75% of any remaining profits.[25] The benefits of guano, however, did not materialize until the late 1840s. The British found the only other source of guano in the world available for the taking on Ichabone Island in the South Atlantic off of Africa. Guano exports from Peru could hardly match those of Ichabone. In 1846, Peru exported only 25,100 tons compared with Ichabone's 254,527 tons. But by 1847, the deposits at Ichabone were exhausted.[26]

Castilla came to the presidency in 1845, after a horrendous period of civil war between 1841 and 1845.[27] Castilla, popular with a cross section of the political spectrum, steered a course geared towards avoiding conflict with either the liberals or conservatives.[28] As guano income to the State rose, he was able to increase the size of the buraucracy, strengthen the armed forces and create a solid class basis for the State based on guano revenue disbursements.[29] Throughout Castilla's two presidencies, the intervening period of the Echenique government, and into the 1870s, guano revenues rose through a series of lucrative contracts between the State and domestic and foreign consignees.[30] By 1852, guano revenues made up over one third of the national budget, and by 1861 they rose to almost 80%.[31] Peruvian budgets rose dramatically, totaling 8,669,000 pesos in 1852, 21,246,000 pesos in 1861 and 42,236,000 pesos in 1869.[32] Between 1851 and 1861, Castilla was able to double government spending on the bureaucracy and more than triple the military budget.[33] The bureaucracy was stabilized, regularly paid and expanded so that by 1861 it counted over 33,000 employees--about 1.6% of the total population.[34]

The key to the success of the State created by Castilla was not its ability to impose order. It did that rather poorly during the "guano age." Its success lay in the creation of what Shane Hunt calls a "rentier economy."[35] Peru became, as it had been during the colonial era with silver, a society that revolved around one commodity which was controlled by the State. With this control, the State could use the carrot and stick method of rule--those who supported it received guano contracts, sinecures, grants and favors, those who did not received the army. This method, of course, did not that appreciably reduce political instability as Castilla's own revolts against the governments of José Rufino Echenique and Mariano Ignacio Prado clearly show,[36] but the nature of the revolts against the government changed. No longer were they revolts against the capital, they were now initiated to share in the largesse of the State.[37]

With the huge revenues derived from guano, some 454 million pesos over the 40 year period, the State created a class, principally on the coast, which was integrally tied to the State through guano. Not only did the Peruvian elite benefit indirectly through jobs in the bureaucracy and army, but in 1849, Castilla was convinced to allow Peruvians direct participation in the guano trade. Peruvians received lucrative consignment contracts from the government and, although it was not until the 1860s that they could take full control of the trade, large fortunes were made.[38] These fortunes became the basis for the development of a native banking and credit system which did much to re-capitalize the large sugar and cotton plantations on the coast.[39]

Castilla used guano revenues to begin retiring Peru's outstanding foreign and domestic debt. The foreign debt was a result of the borrowings of penurous governments during the Wars of Independence and the costs of Chilean and Colombian assistance during the wars. The British debts of 1822 and 1825 were converted into bonds guaranteed by half the government's share of revenues from guano consignments shipped to Britain.[40] However, more important for Peruvian development was the consolidation of the domestic debt. After the State had begun to repay its foreign debt, protests were heard from Peruvians who demanded that the government's policy be balanced and recognize the obligations of past governments to Peruvians as well.[42] Castilla agreed to recognize the legitimate debt incurred by the armies and governments of Peru throughout the entire post-independence period. The laws of 1847, 1848, and 1850 allowed Peruvians to present their claims--often the scribbled notes of military caudillos--to a special tribunal which would make a determination on the legitimacy of the claim.[43] These debts would be converted into bonds paying a yearly interest rate of 6%. Claims amounting to 4.3 million pesos were recognized in the first few years and Castilla believed that the final accounting would reach between 6 and 7 million pesos.[44] In 1851, however, Echenique became president and claims skyrocketed to over 19,154,000 pesos by 1852. "Realizing the questionable nature of much of this newly created debt, the government feared the possibility that a future administration would repudiate it. To avoid this, in 1853 it entered into a secret contract with European financial houses whereby some 9 million pesos of the total was converted from internal to external debt."[45] When this "secret" loan became known, Castilla led a revolution against Echenique. Yet, although a tribunal of investigation found that over 12 million pesos of these claims were spurious, the debt was not repudiated.[46] Echenique's attitude towards his prodigality was prophetic, "'What does it matter,' he asked,

172

'that a few have enriched themselves whose wealth has also remained in the country and contributed to the development of these benefits'."[47]

Guano revenues were additionally made available to the coastal elite through the abolition of slavery in 1854. In order to win the support of liberal abolitionist José Gálvez, and to enlist the slaves in his revolt against Echenique, Castilla declared the abolition of slavery.[48] However, this was not an attack on the slave-holding coastal elite.[49] Slave owners were compensated for the loss of their slaves with bonds worth 300 pesos per slave, including many already escaped slaves. According to Laura Randall, "By 1855, 15,871 certificates of liberation were issued, and payments of 4,761,500 pesos made: 1,432,000 in cash and 3,329,500 in bonds. By 1860, 25,505 slaves were freed at a cost of 7,651,000 pesos."[50] Although Frederick Pike writes that, "The sudden abolition . . . produced serious difficulties within the private sector of the economy,"[51] William Bollinger argues that there was, ". . . a smooth transition out of slavery through the massive importation of indentured servants financed by generous government compensation for each freed slave."[52] In either case, the State policy of compensated manumission freed a great deal of capital, heretofore tied up in chattels, for further investment on coastal plantations.

At the same time he abolished slavery, Castilla abolished the contribución de indígenas. Though this had been a major source of revenue for the State, guano revenues gave Castilla the freedom to abolish it.[53] Its abolition had far reaching political and economic effects. Politically, it weakened the sierra elite because this internal tax was the basis of provincial finances. Without it, as Pike argues, "These governments now found themselves dependent upon the largesse of the central bureaucracy in Lima. Most frequently money was doled out from Lima not to aid the development of the provinces, but to entrench in power supporters of the political machine that was at the moment in control of the capital."[54] The "contribución" had also been an important coercive device in the hands of the sierra hacendados. It was used by them to force the Indians to work on their lands (as Indians needed cash to pay the tax) and its abolition led to an economic depression in the highlands.[55] However, the re-imposition of the tax by Mariano Ignacio Prado in 1866 (in order to make up for guano revenues when the Spanish Navy seized the Chincha Islands in 1864),[56] led to an Indian revolt in the highlands which was put down by the government and hacendados. This outbreak led to the re-imposition of hacienda predominance in the highlands through the breakup of Indian comunidades and land confiscations.[57]

Much of the revenue from guano was dissipated in wasteful expenditures, but Shane Hunt has found that the greater part of it found its way into the Peruvian economy.[58] The consolidation of the domestic debt, slave compensation, and guano contracts became the basis for the rise of an export elite in the late nineteenth century. Coastal agriculture became its first

173

base, as Peter Klarén relates,

> Important for the resurgence of coastal agriculture during this period. . . was the guano boom of the 1840s and 1850s, which for the first time since independence produced large amounts of capital for reinvestment in the agrarian sector. Profits from this "new industry" rapidly soared, enriching in the process the old creole families and parvenue landholders of the independence period--many of whom now turned to the problem of reorganizing and revitalizing coastal agriculture.[59]

Flush with guano money, coastal agriculture began a slow but steady rise. Cotton, though helped along by the price rise and shortage caused by the U.S. civil war, found new prosperity, while sugar prices zoomed. Yet, neither could have reacted to these new markets had guano not provided the capitalization for production, as Hunt relates,

> Landowners had acquired the means to purchase coolie contracts, partly through payments received for manumissions of slaves, partly through finance available from newly created banks and concentrations of private wealth created by guano prosperity. This finance did more than merely purchase a labor force: It permitted coastal haciendas a spending spree on borrowed funds. New machinery, new buildings and new consumption standards came along with new workers and new plantings.[60]

As State largesse was converted into large personal fortunes, banks, and coastal prosperity, and as the expenses of an expanded bureaucracy and military grew, total revenues began to fall below budget needs. The war with Spain led to an accumulated deficit of 17 million pesos by 1869/70.[61] In order to deal with the deficit, the State, under José Balta and his treasury minister Nicholás de Píerola, cancelled all the contracts of Peruvian consignees in 1868 and contracted the lucrative commerce to the French firm of Dreyfus and Company in 1869.[62]

The Dreyfus Contract was heavily criticized, particularly by the jilted Peruvian guano consignees, but it did solve, at least temporarily, the crisis of State finances and provided the government with the funds for an ambitious railroad building scheme.[63] Dreyfus was given a monopoly on the sale of 2 million tons of guano in Europe for which the Peruvian State received a 2.4 million sole advance against sales, and a promised 700,000 soles per month for twenty months. In addition, Dreyfus assumed the 16 million sole obligation of the government to the Peruvian consignees and agreed to service Peru's foreign debt to the tune of 5 million soles per year, while the State was to pay 5% interest of all advances made to it by Dreyfus.[64] Dreyfus also became responsible for floating large loans for the government's railroad building program.[65]

With the Dreyfus Contract, State finances were put in order

174

and Peru's international credit rose, allowing Dreyfus to float loans of £12 million in 1870, and £15 million in 1872 for the purpose of railroad construction.[66] Balta and Piérola contracted with Henry Meiggs to build a dizzying array of railways whose economic benefits were, even then, suspect.[67] The railways cost Peru 91.9 million pesos, a bit less than one quarter of all the guano revenue received by the State between 1847 and 1878. By 1872, foreign debts consumed almost all of the 700,000 sole per month advance made by Dreyfus.[68] The engineering feats of Meiggs were, though, truly amazing, he,

> . . . connected the southern port of Mollendo with Arequipa and then extended the line to Puno, on Lake Titicaca. About 325 miles in length and reaching heights of over 14,600 feet, the Southern Railway was the longest and highest railroad in South America at the time . . . As a complement to the Southern, Meiggs transported two steamboats over the Andes in pieces and reassembled them on Lake Titicaca. He also began work on a railroad from Cuzco to Puno. An even more spectacular engineering achievement was the Central Railway, an extension of the Lima-Callao line to La Oroya, in the central highlands. Climbing more than 15,000 feet in only 78 miles . . . the central had 65 tunnels, totaling 30,000 feet in length, 61 bridges including an iron span of 580 feet.
>   Meiggs also built a 93-mile railroad from the harbor at Pacasmayo inland toward the sierra city of Cajamarca, another one of 50 miles from the coastal town of Chimbote up the Santa River valley and a 60 mile line connecting Moquega with the port of Ilo.[69]

Although the shorter coastal lines did contribute to the economy, the lines to the sierra were, at least in the short run, a total disaster. The British minister, Spencer St. John, reported that the railroad from Callao to the sierra, "passes through sterile country without population, resources or trade," and silver shipments required only one car per month. The Arequipa - Mollendo line ran one passenger train per day and the line between Arequipa and Puno only two per week.[70] The lines could not even compete with llamas and mules which were still more economic, if slower, means of transport.[71]

Railroad construction, however, was not only geared towards economic development and this must explain the patently un-economic lines. As Pike suggests, "Balta in particular came to believe that by criss-crossing Peru with railroads, the full economic potentialities of so richly endowed a country could be readily realized, while at the same time anarchy and revolutionary activities would be stamped out."[72] Charles McQueen also argues that Balta was looking for a way to unify the country and end internal strife, while at the same time secure an alternative source of State revenues.[73] Randall agrees, arguing that, ". . . the government was building a "railroad to nowhere," for political, rather than economic reasons."[74] The "political" railways understandably did nothing to create

175

economic development in Peru. The rails, bridges, and rolling stock were all imported, as was the bulk of the labor force.[75] In later years they would contribute substantially to the Peruvian export economy, but in the 1870s they led inexorably to the near bankruptcy of the State. By the close of the 1870s, Peru had the largest rail system in South America; it also had the largest foreign debt.

State expenditures on the railways and the near bankruptcy of the State became a scandal in Peru. They were also to lead to the beginnings of the consolidation of the coastal plutocracy in the form of the Civilista Party. The Civilista Party was founded in 1871 under the leadership of Manuel Pardo and was the first coherent expression of the new coastal elite created by the guano policies of the State.[76] The party avoided the old liberal-conservative disputes and organized both tendencies into a broad based coalition.[77] After a brief attempt by elements of the military to remove him, Pardo took over the presidency in 1872. Pardo and the Civilistas believed, in line with the interests of the coastal plutocracy, that the pie-in-the-sky programs of the Balta regime would only lead to ruin. What was needed, they argued, was for the government to put the State's finances in order and promote "modernization" which, ". . . within the plutocratic lexicon meant an expansion of export . . . ."[78]

Under Pardo, however, State finances were in serious shape. Guano income hardly covered the foreign debt service and the budget faced an 8.5 million sole deficit.[79] Pardo also continued the Balta railroad program because some of the lines were useful to the coastal elite and to protect the enormous investment the State had already made.[80] He therefore set out on a program to strengthen State finances by reducing the size of the bureaucracy and military, imposing new taxes, negotiating a new guano contract with Dreyfus, and nationalizing Peru's nitrate wealth.

Although the military budget was reduced, the bureaucracy thinned, and customs and internal taxes increased, the centerpiece of the Civilista plan was to make nitrate a State monopoly like guano. Nitrate revenue, they felt, would provide the State with the means to pay its foreign debt and, at the same time, expand the infrastructure for the export economy which the coastal plutocracy desired.

Nitrate, found in the Atacama desert, had been known as a fertilizer in Peru since the days of the Incas and was mined throughout the colonial period under a monopoly from the crown to the Jesuits. Small quantities were sent to Britain in the 1820s, 1095 quintals (hundredweights) exported in the 1830s, 3,679,951 during the 1840s, 8,895,993 in the 1850s, and during the 1860s, 10,587,390.[81] Peruvians were involved in its manufacture, but only as small producers. The bulk of the nitrate business was in the hands of foreigners--Chileans and Britons. Nitrate production in Peru, until the late 1870s, was an example of a classic enclave economy in which labor, capital, and inputs were brought in from the outside, while profits were sent

176

overseas.[82]   Nitrate production, however, was not like guano
production.   It required costly machines to process and remove
the various impurities of the ore and the establishment of a vast
infrastructure of railways, towns, and ports.[83]   Large firms
like the Tarapacá Nitrate Company thus became the chief producers
of nitrate.

Nitrate paid only a 4 centavo per quintal export tax to the
Peruvian State, so the first act by Pardo was to propose an
increase in the tax to 25 centavos per quintal.   The congress,
however, proposed and approved a plan to turn nitrate into a
State monopoly a-la guano.[84]   The justification for this was
clear--Peruvians, in and out of congress, believed that the
growth of nitrate exports was responsible for the fall in guano
sales in Europe.   Between 1869 and 1873 guano sales fell from
575,000 tons to less than 350,000 tons.   If the State could
control the export of both fertilizers, the price and sales of
guano could be increased and Peru's foreign debt, which was tied
to guano, paid.[85]   The estanco proposal, as it was called,
would not have taken the nitrate fields away from their owners.
Rather, it would have instituted a Peruvian State monopoly of its
purchase.   The State would have bought nitrate at 2.4 soles per
quintal and shared with the owners any profit when nitrate sold
for over 3.1 soles per quintal.[86]   In addition, production
quotas were to be assigned to each nitrate field working and
those unworked would become the property of the State.[87]

The estanco never got off the ground.   First, there was clear
opposition to the plan from the nitrate companies who feared that
government quotas would hurt their businesses.   They increased
production dramatically in anticipation of quotas and sent the
price of nitrate plummeting to 1.87 soles per quintal.   At that
price the State would have had to pay the nitrate producers more
than it received on the European market.[88]   Second, the
Peruvian State neither had the estimated 8 million soles, nor the
legions of trained administrators needed to run the
monopoly.[89]   In March 1873, the plan was shelved in favor of an
export tax of 15 centavos per quintal.[90]

A rise in export taxes on nitrates, however, did not solve
the problem of State finances.   In fact, they worsened as the now
lower priced nitrate continued to replace guano in Europe.[91]
In 1875, a new solution was proposed by the congress and accepted
by the president whereby the State would expropriate the nitrate
fields with funds received by floating a £7 million loan in
Europe.   The loan would be serviced by revenues from the sale of
nitrate.[92]

The plan immediately ran into difficulties when the State
could not raise the funds in Europe and was forced to purchase
the nitrate fields with government certificates due in two years
and paying 8% interest.   It was agreed that the owners of the
fields would work them for the State under quotas set by the
State.[93]   By 1877, the government had issued 18,550,000 soles
in certificates.[94]   In order to ship and market the nitrate in
Europe, the State came to agreement with the London firm of
Antony Gibbs and Sons which had interests in nitrate and had been

a State guano consignee in the past. In 1876, Gibbs was given the exclusive monopoly of the sale of State nitrate and agreed to advance to the Peruvian banks managing the business for the State £40,000 at 6% interest, return to them a 2% commission on all sales, and pay 1.7 soles per quintal to the nitrate producers.[95]

The State nitrate monopoly was a complete disaster and led to the greatest crisis in Peruvian history since the Wars of Independence. The State never completed the expropriation of the nitrate fields and the independence of the largest producers undermined the value of Gibbs' monopoly; in 1878, it withdrew from the trade.[96] Peru's attempt to secure a monopoly in the nitrate trade went far to bring about a Chilean declaration of war.[97] The War of the Pacific (1879-1883)[98] was an utter catastrophe for the Peruvian State and economy. Much of what had been built up during the "guano age" was either destroyed or lost to national control. The Chileans occupied Lima and the rich coastal provinces, demanding forced "contributions" to support the occupation. They carried off the books in the National Library, stripped the National Archives, sent the Lima Zoo animals to Santiago, and dismantled and shipped to Chile much of the Southern Railway.[99] Peru lost the nitrate province of Tarapacá outright, while Chile was to administer the provinces of Tacna and Arica until a plebiscite was held ten years hence to decide their fate.[100] It also lost the guano islands and thus the means to pay off its foreign debts. Its productive capacity was in total ruins and the value of its exports dropped to 2,400,000 soles. The currency became virtually worthless.[101]

In debt to foreigners, its economy in a shambles, the State gave away what was left. The debts arising from the loans of 1869, 1870, and 1872, were retired by giving the national railways (for 66 years) to the Peruvian Corporation of London, a company organized by the holders of defaulted Peruvian bonds. In addition, the Corporation received free navigation of, and the right to the steamboat concession on Lake Titicaca, 3 million tons of guano, and £80,000 per year for 33 years.[102] In return, the Corporation agreed to extend and repair several railways and arrange for new government loans of up to £5 million.[103] This agreement, known as the Grace Contract, ushered Peru into an age of foreign exploitation and dependency. The country was thrown open to foreign capitalists who bought up ruined coastal plantations, sierra mines, invested heavily in them and built in Peru a modern export sector.[104] The coastal plutocracy regained control of the State in 1895, but by then it was no more than a comprador class.

Peru began its independent history as a very minor participant in the international economy. By the end of the nineteenth century it had become a typical export economy. Instrumental in that transformation was the Peruvian State. The State, as we have seen, did not act consciously as an engine of economic development. It acted politically, in its own interest and that of the Peruvian elite. The guano revenue of the State went to enhancing its ability to solve the problem of political order in Peru and, in the process, it created a hegemonic ruling class which, when it did capture the State, destroyed it and the Peruvian economy. The basis of the Peruvian export economy was thus laid by the State in the "guano age."

THE STATE AND THE CREATION OF THE ARGENTINE EXPORT ECONOMY

The foundation of the Argentine export economy was laid much earlier than that of Peru, but the role of the State was fundamental there too. For Argentina, it was precisely the trap pointed to by García Calderón--a reliance upon customs revenues--that led succeeding Argentine governments to favor the growth of import-export trade. This occurred almost immediately with the Wars of Independence as independence governments, cut off from the traditional viceregal source of income--the silver mines of Upper Peru, opened the port of Buenos Aires to international trade as a means of financing the government and the war.[105] Early Argentine governments had to rely upon forced loans (particularly from peninsular merchants), the printing of paper money, and the export of cattle products which would provide import-export revenue.[106]

The importance of customs revenues cannot be overemphasized. They made up 82.5% of total State revenues in 1822, 78.3% in 1824, and almost 82% in 1829.[108] Other taxes provided very little revenue to the government. The contribución directa, introduced in 1821, provided only 1% of total revenues in 1822, and by 1829, did not exceed 3%.[109] The stamp tax provided between 3 and 4%, and port dues another 1%. The balance was made up by equally insignificant taxes.[110] It is no wonder that the State supported and encouraged import-export commerce.

The expense of the war of liberation, followed closely by that of the civil war, forced the authorities in Buenos Aires to rely heavily upon customs revenues. The costs of the war with Spain and the civil war were high and military requirements made up the bulk of the budget.[111] Yet, there was no intention on the part of those in control of the State to create a dependence upon foreign commerce. Rather, the creole bureaucrat-merchant elite of Buenos Aires sought to re-establish the former viceregal patterns of trade and administration for their exclusive benefit. When this failed because of provincial rebellion, the Buenos Aires elite was forced to fall back on the only resource at their disposal--the pastoral products of the Buenos Aires countryside.

The Unitarians, who took power in Buenos Aires in the wake of the defeat of Directory by the provinces in 1820, did not allow that defeat to deter them from their plans for Argentina. Although convinced "free traders," the Unitarians, under Martín Rodríguez and Bernardino Rivadavia, did not see the future of Argentina in cattle product exports. Their vision of a future Argentina was much more grandiose and ultimately led to their downfall. Rivadavia planned to use the State to create in Argentina an "integrated national economy."[112] The Unitarians

179

believed that Argentina contained all the necessary resources for the construction of a "well balanced economy," but it lacked the capital, labor, and technical skills to bring them to fruition. These, they believed, could be attracted through foreign trade, foreign investment, and foreign immigration.[113]

The most important aspect of the Rivadavia plan was the settling of the land, with the aim of creating a prosperous small farmer--not rancher--economy. Unable to sell public lands which were put up as collateral against a British loan, Rivadavia developed a system of emphyteusis in which the land was rented for a period of twenty years at the rate of 8% of the value of the land used for pasturage, and 4% for land used for agriculture. The State reserved the right to revise rents after a period of ten years.[114]

There is some controversy over the intentions of Rivadavia's emphyteusis plan. On the one hand, it has been interpreted as a means of halting the accumulation of large tracts of land by estancieros and providing an impetus to agriculture, and on the other, simply as a means of halting the accumulation of land that would be used solely for the purposes of speculation.[115] Miron Burgin argues that if it was meant to limit the accumulation of land by the large estancieros, it was singularly unsuccessful in that it did not limit the amount that one could rent.[116] Although Burgin's claim seems to be borne out by the fact that by 1827, 112 corporations and individuals had received 65,500,000 acres under emphyteusis,[117] it seems clear that this was not Rivadavia's intention as, in 1827, he complained that,

> The lack of limitation with which, until now, public land has been ceded in enfiteusis, in all the extent which has been solicited, has given rise to an abuse whose consequences already are beginning to be felt. Immense areas are denounced claimed without intention or possibility of settling them, but with the security of selling in the distant future at a good price the right which has been acquired at little public cost. Thus it is that the entire extension of public lands included within the new frontier line, even though the majority of them are unpopulated, are already almost entirely distributed. The accumulation of such large areas in so few hands is necessarily going to retard their settlement and cultivation. Nor is it just, on the other hand, that a few appropriate to themselves exclusively a benefit which the law made available in order to favor the industry of all.[118] (author's emphasis)

As an adjunct to this plan, Rivadavia sought to encourage European immigration which he believed would change the character of the countryside. In his opinion, the country people of Buenos Aires province were "immoral" and unwilling to work.[119] Thus, as Scobie argues, "Rather than adapt to the existing conditions, he hoped to submerge the gaucho with industrious European peasants, to cover the grasslands with crops, and to create a democracy of smallholders."[120] For this purpose a Colonization

Commission was established and colonization companies were encouraged.[121]

The Unitarians also sought foreign investment to build the Argentina of their vision. It was at this time that Argentina first contracted large foreign debts. In 1822, in order to raise funds to finance harbor improvements, frontier settlements, and a municipal waterworks, the State authorized the floating of a loan for 5 million gold pesos in London. The contract for this loan was concluded with Baring Brothers of London in 1824. After all costs had been deducted, the State received only 3 million gold pesos.[122] The loan, though, was never used for its intended purposes. The war with Brazil intervened and the funds were dissipated in military expenditures.

In an attempt to find alternative sources of government revenue, Rivadavia sought foreign investment to re-activate the mining industry which had provided viceregal governments with almost half of their revenues. Since the mines of Potosí had been lost, Rivadavia's hopes were placed on the development of the Fatima mine in La Rioja province. To this end he encouraged the formation of a company in London, the Compañía de Minas de Las Provincias Unidas del Río de La Plata. The company did some preliminary surveying, but the project was halted by the government of La Rioja which was opposed to the proto-national State at Buenos Aires giving concessions to foreigners in mines that were not within its jurisdiction.[123]

The expansion of trade, investment, and industry further required an expansion of credit. The Unitarians established a National Bank under the strict control of the State, which they hoped would form the basis for the economic unification of the country through the creation of a national market. The bank was definitely not designed to meet the needs of the cattle industry. As Burgin argues, "The fact that in defining the functions of the bank no recognition was accorded to the needs and interests of agriculture and cattle breeding was not due to oversight."[124] Its primary purpose was to lend funds to the government and finance commerce. Loans due in 90 days, as were the credits of the National Bank, could not provide a source of cheap credit to the cattle industry whose cycle of production was more lengthly.[125]

Theoretical free traders, the Unitarians nevertheless recognized the dependence of the State on customs revenues, as well as the interests of the small manufacturing and agricultural sectors of the province of Buenos Aires. Their tariff polity was a balance between the revenue needs of the State and the protection of domestic production. The tariff of 1822 provided for a basic rate of 15% ad valorem on all foreign imports. While lowering the rate to 5% for some commodities, particularly those needed for the State's economic development plan, such as mercury, agricultural tools, mining machinery, construction materials, saltpeter, and bricks, it raised others in an effort to protect national industries. An impost of 20% was laid upon foreign sugar, coffee, cocoa, yerba mate, tea, rice, and foodstuffs; 25% on furniture, clocks, carriages, shoes, vinegar, cider, mirrors, saddles, clothing, wines, beer, and tobacco; and 30% on brandy, liquors, and cana. Increased protection was afforded to the hat industry as foreign imports were required to pay a tax of 3 pesos per hat. Wheat and flour imports were subject to a sliding scale tax by which wheat paid 4 pesos per fanega (1.5 bushels) when the domestic price was 6 pesos per fanega and decreased to 1 peso per fanega when the domestic price reached 9 pesos per fanega--flour imports were similarly taxed to balance the interests of the producer and consumer.[126] Throughout the 1820s, tariffs on overseas imports generally rose, affording greater protection to domestic industries.

Rivadavia's plan was never fully put into effect. Strong opposition rose in several powerful sectors of Argentina. The provinces rejected it not only because the tariff was not protective enough, but becasue Rivadavia sought an economic policy directed by a strong central State. In the aftermath of Cepeda, each province developed its own State with its own interest, and these were not the same as that of the national State Rivadavia was attempting to construct. Provincial governments, in financial straits due to the breakdown of internal trade and production caused by the independence struggles, would accept Rivadavia's plan only if the central State shared the revenues of the port of Buenos Aires with them. This was unacceptable to the Buenos Aires State.[127]

The estancieros of Buenos Aires province opposed the Rivadavia plan because the Unitarians were intent on destroying their province's dominant position in the polity and economy of Argentina by separating the port of Buenos Aires from the province. This they believed would lead to an increase in taxes to support a provincial government, as well as reduce their influence in national policy.[128] They also resented the policy of "national" economic development, feeling, with some justification, that the State would ignore the needs of the cattle industry. For the estancieros, the major difficulties in the development of the economy in Buenos Aires province were the expansion of the frontier and Indian attacks. Although the Unitarian State recognized the problems, it did nothing to solve them.[129]

The Rivadavia plan did not even find favor among the farmers, artisans or lower bureaucrats of Buenos Aires. The farmers felt that the tariff of 1822 did not provide adequate protection, while the artisans continued to complain about competition from foreign imports. The protective characteristics of the 1822 tariff had been eroded by inflation caused by large emissions of the National Bank and so these protests had validity, but on the opposite side, high duties on foodstuffs brought complaints from the city's consumers.[130]

The failure of the Rivadavia plan was not that it was unrealistic and did not take into account the realities of Argentina's potential in the 1820s, as Burgin claims,[131] it was rather that no important sector of the economy or polity was willing to make the kind of sacrifices it called for, nor was the State powerful enough to enforce them. The problem of economic

development in Argentina was intergrally linked to the problem of
political unification. As we have seen in Chapters 4, 5 and 6,
the political and economic crisis of Argentina in the
independence period initiated a decided shift of political power
to rural elites. Political and military power were decentralized
and fell into the hands of those who used them for their own
narrow interests. The incipient State was weak, and by the time
the Unitarians were able to lay the constitutional foundation
(Constitution of 1826) for a State that could impose its
development plan on the country, the real basis of power had
shifted to its opponents. As H. S. Ferns argues,

> The policy of Rivadavia was in its design logical and
> realistic . . . . But in the 1820s it was not successful. It
> required for its implementation political stability, peace
> and the determined support of at least one predominant
> element in the community . . . the appeal of Rivadavia's
> plans could excite the enthusiasm and win the support of only
> those with sufficiently long view of the community interest,
> but there was nothing about them either as ideas or
> activities which immediately and strongly engaged the
> interest and support of the men on horseback in the province
> of Buenos Aires, Entre Rios or Corrientes.[132]

There is, perhaps, no better example of how the interests of
the State steer economic development than the regime of Juan
Manuel de Rosas. Rosas, a porteño Federalist, became governor of
Buenos Aires province in 1829 in the wake of the Unitarian
defeat. He was one of the largest and wealthiest
estanciero-saladeros of the province and there is no doubt that
he favored his class. Yet, in some cases his regime, as with its
tafiff policy and nationalist stance against foreign intervention
in the Río de La Plata, was in direct opposition to the interests
of the estanciero-saladeros. This contradiction can best be
explained by the fact that Rosas, as head of the Buenos Aires
State, was not only responsible to the class that put him into
power but also to the State itself.
The estanciero-saladero Federalists of Buenos Aires quickly
came into conflict with the provincial Federalists after the
defeat of the Unitarians. The provincial Federalists and a
fraction of the porteño Federalists were committed to national
unification, though under a federal, not centralized, national
State. This group sought to bring Buenos Aires under the control
of the provinces, but that was exactly what the majority of
porteño Federalists opposed.[133] These estanciero-saladeros
understood the economic advantages which Buenos Aires had over
the other provinces and sought to maintain them through a policy
of political separation from the other provinces.[134] This
contradiction--that in order to dominate the provinces the Buenos
Aires State had to be politically separated from the
provinces--plagued Argentina for over twenty years. Rosas was
able to create in Argentina what Rivadavia failed to--a strong
centralized State--by virtue of porteño economic domination of

the country and the political isolation of its State. Because the provinces were dominated economically and militarily, the emphasis shifted from the kind of centralized administration which Rivadavia had suggested to armed force and economic exclusion. The power of Rosas' State against the provinces depended upon the economic position of Buenos Aires, and that position depended upon the cattle industry. Yet, when the interests of the cattle industry and the State came into conflict, the interests of the State prevailed.

Rosas may have taken over the Buenos Aires State in the interest of the cattle industry, but the exigencies of that State very quickly impressed themselves upon his regime. The land policy of Rosas is most often pointed to in support of the argument that he favored the interests of the cattle industry over those of the rest of the province.[135] However, what choice did Rosas have given the dependence of the State upon the revenues generated by pastoral exports? His land policy had three purposes, (1) to extend cattle production in the province and thus provide increased revenues to the State, (2) to provide income for the State through the sale of land, and (3) to provide political support for the State and reduce the cost of his large army by paying soldiers off in land. Although the major thrust of his land distribution policy was the extension of cattle raising in order to raise customs revenues, it also had other fiscal and, more importantly, political functions. Fiscally, the Rosas land policy was designed to provide the State with extraordinary income. The income from emphyteusis could hardly assist the budget. In 1833, rents amounted to only 198,000 pesos and, although they were doubled when the leases came up in that year, they dropped to 196,000 pesos in 1839. Obviously many tenants were not paying their rents or many did not pay them in full. Rather than continue this policy, Rosas began to sell public lands outright. In 1836, the State was authorized to sell 1,500 square leagues of public lands.[137]

The land sales, however, were not very successful either. By 1839, they had only yielded about one million pesos, and in 1840, only about 100,000 pesos. Much of the land went unsold in a buyers market.[138] Rosas was then forced to give land away, hoping that it would find its way into production and thus into the balance of imports and exports upon which State finances depended.[139] Land was additionally used to pay the army and administration. Rosas himself received land in this manner as the leader of the Desert Campaign which pushed the Indian frontier south and put millions of acres of land into the hands of the State. In 1834, Rosas was awarded for his services with the Island of Choele-Choel on the Río Negro--which he promptly exchanged for 60 square leagues of pasture land. Officers and common soldiers were also awarded land as payment.[140]

Payment of the army in land became a State policy with Rosas as governor and, when a rebellion against the State arose in 1839, rewards of land, cattle, and sheep were made to the army that put down the rebellion. Six square leagues were awarded to generals, five for colonels, one half for non-commissioned officers, and one quarter for privates.[141] Altogether, 8,500 boletos de premios entierras were awarded by the State and eventually became a kind of money with which the wealthy speculated. Although thousands were issued to soldiers and minor bureaucrats, they almost always ended up in the hands of the large estancieros.[142] More than anything else, land was a political tool for Rosas. With it he could gain adherents to the State and, by taking it away (confiscations), he could harm its enemies.[143] As John Lynch observes, ". . . land was the richest source of patronage available, a weapon for Rosas, a welfare system for his supporters."[144]

Without focusing on Rosas as the head of the Buenos Aires State, his tax and tariff policies seem terribly contradictory. Here we have the representative of the estanciero-saladero class raising internal taxes and imposing protective tariffs, both of which were opposed by that class. Rosas' first aim, of course, was to maximize the revenues taken in through the customs house, but he also sought to reduce State reliance on these through increases in internal taxes. The contribución directa, a poor source of income throughout the independence period, was doubled in 1838. In 1839, he hoped that it would produce 3 million pesos, 27% of the State budget. However, the tax brought in only 891,000 pesos in 1839, about one million in 1840, and then dropped to 868,000 in 1841. In that year Rosas demanded that the legislature revise the system of assessment, but it would not act and the tax remained a minor part of State revenues throughout his regime.[145] The contribución directa failed mainly because assessments were made to the tax collectors by the property owners themselves and thus there were, by declaration, quite a few "poor" residents in Buenos Aires province. Though Rosas railed against such a poor system of tax assessment arguing that the law,

> . . . made no provision for an equitable and objective evaluation of taxable wealth. This omission was not only injurious to the treasury but it was also unjust to the taxpayer, for "nothing was more cruel and inhuman than to compel an individual to give an account of his private wealth." Had this law . . . been more in accord with the conception of justice, had it been based upon the principles of liberalism and equality, the tax would have been more productive of revenue, and might also encourage economy and frugality, the true source of public and private wealth.[146]

the contribución failed to live up to his expectations.[147]

The tariff issue clearly illustrates the contradiction of Rosas' position as the representative of the estancieros and his positon as the head of the Buenos Aires State which was also a proto-national State. Since Rosas denied the other provinces direct trade with Europe, and their commerce was required to pass through the port of Buenos Aires, he had to incorporate their interests into the policies of the State if he was to conciliate them to the predominance of Buenos Aires. This may not have been in the interest of the estancieros of Buenos Aires, but it was certainly in the interest of Rosas' State.

If the issue of centralism vs federalism was the chief conflict between Federalists and Unitarians, the issue of tariff protection was the chief conflict between porteño federalism and provincial federalism.[148] The provincial Federalists argued strenuously for the protection of their agricultural and manufacturing industries that were being damaged by the relatively light duties charged on foreign imports by Buenos Aires. The porteño Federalists argued that protective tariffs would ruin the economy of Buenos Aires, raise the prices of goods to consumers, and protect industries there, and in the provinces, that were uneconomic and should by all economic logic be allowed to fail.[149] That Rosas supported the views of the porteno Federalists makes his later volte-face on this issue all the more interesting.

The Tariff Act of 1835 (for 1836) constituted a decided shift by Rosas to protectionism. The basic import duty was set at 17% ad valorem on all commodities not specifically provided for in the law. Goods which did not compete with those of Buenos Aires and the provinces, or were required for their industries, paid relatively low duties. Hides, horsehair, crude wool, crude tallow, horns, bones, jerked beef, ostrich feathers, and precious metals were allowed in free. A tax of 5% was imposed on plaster, coal, bricks, tin plates, steel, bronze, mercury, raw wool, paintings, printed matter, watches, jewelry, and agricultural implements; 10% on silk, tar, rice, sack cloth, and arms; and 24% on sugar, coffee, cocoa, tea, yerba mate, cotton, wool, and food stuffs.[150] The tariff then became protective with a 35% duty on shoes, clothing, furniture, wine, brandy, liquors, tobacco, oil, leather goods, cheese, guitars (!), ink, and mirrors; 50% on beer, saddles, spaghetti, and other flour products, while hats were to pay a stiff 13 pesos per hat.[151] For the first time since 1821, a large number of goods were prohibited altogether, these included brass and tin plate wares, ornamental iron, iron and steel goods, all kinds of kitchen utensils, textiles, wood products, maize, peas, beans and other vegetables, butter, and mustard. Wheat was prohibited unless its price in Buenos Aires exceeded 50 pesos per fanega, and it could then be imported only by special permit.[152] Overland trade between Buenos Aires and the provinces was free except for certain products of Paraguay (still considered a province), Corrientes and Missiones.[153] About his new policy Rosas argued that, ". . . foreign competition was the principal obstacle to industrial and agricultural recovery and that the tafiff 'should result in progressive growth of foreign and domestic commerce as well as higher revenues'."[154]

There certainly were interests in Buenos Aires province, particularly in the city and agricultural sector in its suburbs, to which this policy could be laid. But they were politically weak in comparison to the estancieros and consumers of the city who would have to pay higher prices in the absence of cheap imported foreign articles. Thus, rather than it being the result of political pressure from within Buenos Aires Province, Rosas instituted this policy because he believed that it was in the best political interest of the Buenos Aires State. "In the eyes of the provinces Rosas became the most Argentine of all porteño governors, the only governor in fact who placed the economic interests of the nation above those of foreign merchants. The Buenos Aires government revealed itself as a national government and Rosas became the recognized leader of the nation."[155]

It is not unlikely that Rosas favored the creation of an Argentine confederation under the leadership of Buenos Aires and that the tariff was a first step in reconciling the provinces to the Buenos Aires State. Such a step was impossible earlier because from 1829 to 1831 the commerce of the city of Buenos Aires was in a "wretched state" due to the lack of trade with the provinces and civil war, and the drought of 1829-1832 had turned the pampas "into an arid desert" where cattle died like flies. In addition, the National Bank failed and thus the State had no means of raising revenues except through customs.[156] The Buenos Aires State was in no condition fiscally or politically to make concessions to the other provinces. By 1835, however, these problems had receded and it is possible that Rosas was making a bid for unification. Juan Facundo Quiroga, the La Rioja caudillo, is reported to have said that Rosas was in accord with him on the need to form an Argentine Confederation and that as soon as the provinces were at peace again he would, with Quiroga, take steps to convoke a congress of the provinces for that purpose.[157] Rosas himself, writing to Quiroga said that, "No one can be more fully convinced than you and I of the necessity of organizing a general government and that this procedure is the only means of insuring existence and respectability to our republic . . ."[158]

However the protective tariff was very quickly revoked when Buenos Aires became embroiled in conflicts with France and Britain which led to blockades of the port. As a result of the Federal Pact of 1831, a defensive-offensive alliance between Buenos Aires and the riverine provinces, the Buenos Aires State received the role of representing those provinces in international relations.[159] When, in the late 1830s, Rosas refused certain demands of the French for special commercial privileges and immunities for its nationals, a French naval squadron blockaded the port of Buenos Aires. In 1838, the French found support for their blockade in Uruguay (whose independence Rosas did not recognize) and the riverine provinces which opposed the Rosas' policy of denying them direct access to overseas trade. Although the dispute with the French was settled by 1840, Buenos Aires opposition to Uruguayan independence continued, and in 1845, brought about a blockade of the port by both the French and the British.[160]

The blockades themselves are beyond the scope of this work,[161] however, it is clear that any hope of Argentine unity on the basis of Rosas' tariff was all but lost by this assertion of nationalism by the Buenos Aires State. The blockades forced the abandonment of the protective tariff policy as import-export revenues dropped and Buenos Aires sought to make running the blockade attractive through lower duties.[162] The French blockade and intervention lit the fires of disunity. Buenos Aires was attacked by a "Coalition of the North" in 1839 led by the hated Unitarians and, in the same year, by an army raised by disgruntled estancieros of southern Buenos Aires province who blamed Rosas for the blockade and cutoff of exports.[164] Rosas was able to defeat both the internal and external challenges to his regime, but he became convinced that the only way to deal with his opponents in Buenos Aires and the provinces was through force.[165] The dictatorship imposed by Rosas ruled out formal national unity. If any unity existed in Argentina during the 1840s, it was that imposed by Rosas' praetorian State. Rosas' failure was a result of the impossibility of reconciling the role of the State as the expression of Buenos Aires province with its role as the expression of the Argentine nation. For Burgin,

. . . as long as Rosas' government remained essentially a provincial government it served a useful purpose and was economically justified. But when by force of circumstance, the porteño government assumed the functions of a national government it not only forsook the interests of Buenos Aires but it also fanned the flames of bitter resentment in the Interior and the Litoral.[166]

The importance of the Rosas period for the development of the Argentine export economy in the late nineteenth century cannot be underestimated, although at this time Argentina was only marginally integrated into the international economy compared to what it would become by the turn of the century.[167] Patterns of economic and political development laid by the politico-economic conflict over the formation of the State were to relegate the Argentine economy to the status of an export economy. The intransigence of the political structure in Buenos Aires finally bore fruit in the 1860s and 1870s with the failure of the provinces to create a State in which Buenos Aires was subservient to the provinces.[169] Argentine unification arose on the basis of Buenos Aires and its pattern of development--stockraising. Railroads opened up the pampas to world trade, but the previous pattern of landholding reduced the impact of immigration and the growth of agriculture. Argentina bacame a major producer of grains, but the benefits of this development did not emerge because the Argentine farmer became a tenant or laborer on the lands of large estancias rather than an independent smallholder.[170] The cities and towns, which in the U.S. arose as a result of the opening of the frontier to food crop agriculture, and provided the markets necessary for the rise of modern industrialization, were absent in Argentina.[171] Industry received very little impetus from the poor Argentine tenant farmer because he never became a permanent fixture in the countryside. Estancieros would rent a section of their land to the tenant for a period of from three to six years and at the end of the contract require the tenant to grow alfalfa for his cattle. The evicted tenant therefore had no incentive to improve the land or build permanent structures. Every three to six years he was forced to pick up stakes and find a new home.[173] Immigrants generally concentrated in Buenos Aires, servicing the export sector. Capitalist development in Argentina was thus stunted by the economic patterns created as a result of the political conflicts of the first half of the nineteenth century. Argentina entered the twentieth century as an export economy.

It is a paradox that in both Peru and Argentina the political conflicts between sectors of the dominant classes which made the consolidation of the State so difficult were also what made the consolidation of strong States so imperative. It was because the States themselves were the objects of such conflicts that they could not perform their mediating role and produce a stable class basis for rule. The Spanish colonial administration had been able to perform the function of mediating class conflict by virtue of its "relative autonomy" from the Spanish American classes but, in the early republican era, the basis of rule in Spanish America had been dramatically transformed. Whereas the authority and legitimacy, as well as the "relative autonomy," of the colonial administration had been based upon its representation of the Spanish monarchy, the new republican State administrations were based upon the notion of "popular sovereignty" (although narrowly defined to include only members of the dominant classes) which automatically made the public authority--the State--the target and prize of intra-class conflict. State and dominant class consolidation were thus hampered by the lack of "relative autonomy" and maneuverability of the new States.

The authority of early Peruvian and Argentine States was rarely effective outside of the capitals and/or major ports. Although, as we have seen, efforts were made to consolidate State authority on the basis of programs of national development and integration, these were made impossible by political conflicts between sectors of the dominant classes and the political and economic weakness of the new States. Both the Peruvian and Argentine States, therefore, came to rely more and more upon the factor which they could easily tap into--foreign trade. A stopgap measure designed to shore up State finances in the face of the enormous costs of the independence struggles, customs revenues became the major source of State finance in Peru (up until guano revenues replaced customs revenues in the 1850s) and Argentina, as well as in most other Spanish American countries. Such reliance led States to encourage the growth of agro/mineral export enterprises as a means of enlarging State revenues and thus the ability of States to impose political order. The results of this strategy led, as we have seen, to a strengthening of the export elite in Argentina and the creation of one in Peru, as well as the hardening of a pattern of agro/mineral export growth in both. In the late nineteenth century these patterns formed the basis for the dramatic expansion of agro/mineral export development fueled by active State support.

189

NOTES

[1] Theda Skocpol, States and Social Revolutions (Cambridge: Cambridge University Press, 1979), 30; and Nicos Poulantzas, Political Power and Social Classes (London: New Left Books, 1973), 245-252. Also see Chapter 1 above.

[2] Perry Anderson, Lineages of the Absolutist State (London: New Left Books, 1975), 15-42. Also see Chapter 1 above.

[3] Charles Hale has commented on how the importance of the State in the nineteenth century may have been improperly ignored by many observers, see Charles Hale, "The Reconstruction of Nineteenth Century Politics in Spanish America: A Case for the History of Ideas," Latin American Research Review VIII, Number 2 (Summmber 1973), 61.

[4] Francisco García Calderón, Latin America: Its Rise and Progress (London: T. F. Unwin, 1913), 381-383.

[5] For the Peruvian loans see J. Fred Rippy, British Investments in Latin America, 1822-1949 (Minneapolis: University of Minnesota Press, 1959), 17-22; and Laura Randall, A Comparative Economic History of Latin America 1500-1914. Vol. 4 Peru (Published for the Institute of Latin American Studies, Columbia University, by University Microfilms International. Ann Arbor, Michigan: 1977), 71-73.

[6] Randall, 74; Thomas M. Davies, Indian Integration in Peru: A Half Century of Experience, 1900-1948 (Lincoln: University of Nebraska Press, 1970, 1974), 23; and Roberto Cortés Conde, The First Stages of Modernization in Spanish America (New York: Harper, 1974), 37.

[7] Charles Alfred McQueen, Peruvian Public Finances United States Department of Commerce, Bureau of Foreign and Domestic Commerce. Trade Promotion Series #30. (Washington, D.C.: U.S. Govt. Printing Office, 1926), 37.

[8] William Mathew, "The Imperialism of Free Trade: Peru 1820-1870," Economic History Review XXI (December 1968), 567.

[9] Randall, 74.

[10] Ibid.

[11] Ibid., 75; and Mathew, 566-567.

[12] Randall, 75

[13] Ibid.; and Shane Hunt, Growth and Guano in Nineteenth Century Peru, Research Program in Economic Development. Woodrow Wilson School. Discussion Paper #34 (Princeton: Woodrow Wilson School of Public and International Affairs at Princeton

University, February, 1973), 43-51.

[14]Stephen Gorman, "The State, Elite and Export in Nineteenth Century Peru: Toward an Alternative Reinterpretation of Political Change," Journal of Inter-American Studies XXI, Number 3 (1979), 397-399; and Roanld Berg and Frederick Stirton Weaver, "Toward a Reinterpretation of Political Change in Peru During the First Century of Independence," Journal of Inter-American Studies XX, Number 1 (February 1978), 71.

[15]Frederick B. Pike, The Modern History of Peru (New York: Praeger, 1967), 71; and Clement R. Markham, Travels in Peru and India (London: John Murray, 1862), 296-297.

[16]Gorman, 398.

[17]José Carlos Mariátegui, Seven Interpretive Essays on Peruvian Reality, trans. Marjory Urquidi (Austin: University of Texas Press, 1971), 50.

[18]Cortés Conde, 13.

[19]Hunt, 59.

[20]David Werlich, Peru: A Short History (Carbondale: Southern Illinois University Press, 1978), 80-81; Cortés Conde, 13-14; Berg and Weaver, 72-73; and Hunt 59.

[21]Quoted in Randall, 79.

[22]Berg and Weaver, 72.

[23]Werlich, 80; and Cortés Conde, 13.

[24]Werlich, 80-81; and Cortés Conde, 13.

[25]Werlich, 80-81.

[26]Cortés Conde, 17.

[27]Pike, 87-89.

[28]Ibid., 93.

[29]Berg and Weaver, 73-76; Gorman, 400-401; and William Bollinger, "The Bourgeois Revolution in Peru: A Conception of Peruvian History," Latin American Perspectives Issue 14, Number 3 (Summer 1977), 31.

[30]Hunt, 65-66; and Cortés Conde, 13-27.

[31]Hunt, 70 Table #8. Also see McQueen, 37.

[32]Hunt, 70 Table #8.

[33]Ibid., 73 Table #9.

[34]Bollinger, 31 note 6; and Pike, 94.

[35]Hunt argues strenuously against the thesis of Jonathan Levin who claims that guano was a classic "enclave economy." Hunt argues that guano was hardly an enclave when the government received in excess of 70% of the value produced by the commodity and distributed a large portion of it to native Peruvians, see Hunt, 60, 110-112; and Jonathan Levin, The Export Economies (Cambridge, Massachusetts: Harvard University Press, 1960), Chapter 2.

[36]Pike, 101-103, 117-119.

[37]Gorman, 403.

[38]Ibid., 400; Werlich, 82; and Hunt, 65.

[39]Gorman, 402; and Jean Piel, "The Place of the Peasantry in the National Life of Peru in the Nineteenth Century," Past and Present XLVI (February 1970), 124.

[40]Randall, 81; and Mathew, 574.

[41]Randall, 81; Mathew, 574; and Hunt, 75.

[42]Werlich, 83.

[43]Ibid.; and Cortés Conde, 23.

[44]Cortés Conde, 23.

[45]Hunt, 76.

[46]Ibid.; and Pike, 100-103.

[47]Quoted in Randall, 84.

[48]Bollinger, 30.

[49]Berg and Weaver claim that, "Castilla unequivically demonstrated the power of the executive vis-à-vis the most powerful domestic classes by the abolition of slavery and the abolition of the Indian head tax," see Berg and Weaver, 74. Bollinger and Piel disagree, see Bollinger, 30; and Piel, 124-125.

[50]Randall, 87; and Werlich, 84.

[51]Pike, 112.

[52]Bollinger, 30-31.

[53]Hunt, 71.

[54]Pike, 113.

[55]Davies, 29; and Werlich, 101-102.

[56]The incident which led the Spanish to seize the Chincha Islands occurred in 1863 when a dispute between some Basque settlers who had been contracted to work on a coastal plantation

and its owner led to an armed clash. Many Basque settlers were killed and Spain demanded an apology and indemnities from the Peruvian government. Peru refused and a Spanish naval squadron seized the guano islands. The end result was a crisis of State in which Ramón Castilla once again attempted to seize power but died in the trying in 1867. For a full discussion of the incident see Pike, 115-119.

[57]Davies, 30-31.

[58]Hunt, 69-113.

[59]Peter F. Klarén, Modernization, Dislocation and Aprismo: Origins of the Peruvian Aprista Party 1870-1932 (Austin: University of Texas Press, 1973), 4.

[60]Hunt, 55.

[61]Randall, 104; McQueen, 6; Werlich, 92; and Pike, 123.

[62]Werlich, 92; and Pike, 124.

[63]Werlich, 93; and Pike, 123.

[64]Werlich, 93; and Randall, 104-105.

[65]McQueen, 7; Randall, 106; and Pike, 125.

[66]McQueen, 7; and Randall, 106.

[67]Pike, 126.

[68]Hunt, 78 Table #10; and Werlich, 93.

[69]Werlich, 94.

[70]Robert G. Greenhill and Rory M. Miller, "The Peruvian Government and the Nitrate Trade 1873-1879," Journal of Latin American Studies V (May 1973), 109.

[71]Ibid.; and Werlich, 95.

[72]Pike, 125.

[73]McQueen, 7.

[74]Randall, 103.

[75]According to Randall, 20,000 to 30,000 Chileans, as well as Chinese, worked on the Peruvian railways, see Randall, 107.

[76]Gorman, 406; Bollinger, 31-32; and Berg and Weaver, 76.

[77]Werlich, 95.

[78]Gorman, 406.

[79]Randall, 122.

[80]Werlich, 97.

[81]Randall, 123.

[82]Greenhill and Miller, 113-114.

[83]Ibid., 114.

[84]Ibid., 113.

[85]Ibid., 112-113.

[86]Ibid., 113; and McQueen, 40.

[87]Greenhill and Miller, 113.

[88]Ibid., 114-115.

[89]Ibid., 114; and McQueen, 40.

[90]Greenhill and Miller, 115.

[91]Ibid., 116.

[92]Ibid., 117; and McQueen, 40.

[93]Greenhill and Miller, 117; and McQueen, 40.

[94]McQueen, 40.

[95]Greenhill and Miller, 117-118.

[96]For a complete discussion of these events see Ibid., 122-128.

[97]Gorman, 407.

[98]For an account of the War sympathetic to Peru see Clement R. Markham, The War Between Peru and Chile 1879-1882 (London: Sampson, Low, Matson, Searle and Rivington, 1882). For an account sympathetic to Chile see Gonzalo Bulnes, Chile and Peru: The Causes of the War of 1879 (Santiago: Imprinta Universitaria, 1920). Also see William S. Cober, "The War of the Ten Centavos: The Geographic, Economic and Political Causes of the War of the Pacific," Southern Quarterly VII (January 1969), 113-129; Robert N. Burr, By Reason or Force: Chile and the Balancing of Power in South America, 1830-1905 (Berkeley and Los Angeles: University of California Press, 1965), 135-166; William F. Sater, "Chile During the First Months of the War of the Pacific," Journal of Latin American Studies (May 1973), 133-158; and Werlich, 106-119.

[99]Werlich, 117.

[100]Ibid., 118; and Pike, 149.

[101]Randall, 125.

[102]Ibid., 127.

103Pike, 153.

104Gorman, 407-408; and Werlich, 120-127. For a favorable view of the Grace Contract see Lawrence A. Clayton, "A Shared Prosperity: W. R. Grace and Co. and Modern Peru," West Georgia College Studies in the Social Sciences XVII (1978), 1-12.

105Laura Randall, A Comparative Economic History of Latin America 1500-1914. Vol. 2 Argentina (Published for the Institute of Latin American Studies, Columbia University, by University Microfilms International. Ann Arbor, Michigan: 1977), 32.

106Ibid., 32-34.

107Ibid., 34; and Clifton Kroeber, The Growth of the Shipping Industry in the Río de la Plata 1794-1860 (Madison: University of Wisconsin Press, 1957), 56.

108Miron Burgin, The Economic Aspects of Argentine Federalism 1820-1852 (New York: Russell and Russell, 1946, 1971), 47.

109Ibid., 48.

110Ibid., 49 Table #7.

111Alexander Caldcleugh, Travels in South America During the Years 1819-20-21, 2 Vols. (London: J. Murray, 1825), I:198.

112Burgin, 88.

113Ibid., 89.

114Ibid., 96-98.

115These positions are set forth in Ibid., 98-99.

116Ibid., 97-98.

117Randall, Argentina, 39.

118Quoted in Ibid.; and Burgin, 99.

119Randall, Argentina, 40-41.

120James Scobie, Argentina, 2nd ed. (New York: Oxford University Press, 1971), 79.

121Burgin, 91-92.

122Ibid., 54-55; and Randall, Argentina, 45-46.

123Burgin, 91.

124Ibid., 95.

125Ibid., 59.

126All of these taxes are listed in Ibid., 70-71.

[127] Ibid., 82.

[128] John Lynch, Argentine Dictator, Juan Manuel de Rosas 1829-1852 (London: Oxford University Press, 1981), 32; and Ibid., 104.

[129] Lynch, 30-31; and Burgin, 105.

[130] Burgin, 102-103.

[131] Ibid., 79-111.

[132] H. S. Ferns, The Argentine Republic, 1516-1971 (London and New York: Barnes and Noble, 1973), 27-28.

[133] Burgin, 147-148.

[134] Ibid., 148.

[135] Ibid., 252-254; and Lynch, 51-59.

[136] Lynch, 57; and Burgin, 199.

[137] Burgin, 199.

[138] Lynch, 58-59.

[139] Ibid., 59; and Burgin, 255.

[140] Lynch, 59, 72-73.

[141] Ibid., 60; and Burgin, 255.

[142] Lynch, 62-63.

[143] Ibid., 59-67.

[144] Ibid., 62.

[145] Burgin, 190-194.

[146] Paraphrased in Ibid., 191.

[147] Ibid., 196; and Lynch, 61.

[148] Lynch, 137-140; and Burgin, 151-154.

[149] Lynch, 138-140; and Burgin, 234-237.

[150] Burgin, 237-238.

[151] Ibid.

[152] Ibid., 238.

[153] Ibid., 239.

[154] Ibid.

[155] Ibid., 240.

[156]Joseph T. Criscenti, "Argentine Constitutional History, 1810-1852: A Re-examination," Hispanic American Historical Review XLI, Number 3 (August 1961), 406.

[157]Ricardo Levene, A History of Argentina, trans. William Spence Robertson (Chapel Hill, North Carolina: University of North Carolina Press, 1957), 401.

[158]Ibid., 402.

[159]Ibid., 394.

[160]For discussions of the French and Anglo-French blockades see Ibid., 423-429; Lynch, 267-294; and F. A. Kirkpatrick, A History of the Argentine Republic (Cambridge: Cambridge at the University Press, 1931), 150-157.

[161]Randall, Argentina, 63-64

[162]Lynch, 149-150; and Burgin, 243-245.

[163]Lynch, 206-207; and Levene, 419-420.

[164]Lynch, 206-207.

[165]Ibid., 209-246.

[166]Burgin, 286.

[167]Aldo Ferrer, The Argentine Economy, trans. Marjory Urquidi (Berkeley: University of California Press, 1967), 91-92.

[168]Ibid., 63.

[169]See F. J. McLynn, "The Corrientes Crisis of 1868," North Dakota Quarterly XLVII, Number 3 (Summer 1979), 45-58; James Scobie, "The Significance of the September Revelution," Hispanic American Historical Review XLI, Number 2 (May 1961), 236-258; and A. J. Walford, "The Economic Aspects of the Argentine War of Succession, 1852-1861," Inter-American Economic Affairs I, Number 2 (September 1947), 70-96.

[170]On this development see James Scobie, Revolution on the Pampas: A Social History of Argentine Wheat 1860-1910 (Austin: University of Texas Press, 1946). Also see Hector Pérez Brigiola, "The Economic Cycle in Latin American Agriculture: Export Economies (1880-1930)," Latin American Research Review XV, Number 2 (1980), 14-17; Carl Solberg, "Farm Workers and the Myth of Export Led Development in Argentina," The Americas XXXI, Number 2 (1974), 121-138; and Richard M. Morse, "Trends and Patterns of Latin American Urbanization 1750-1920," Comparative Studies in Society and History XVI Number 4 (1974), 431-432.

[171]Morse, 431.

[172]Scobie, Argentine Wheat, 58-60.

[173]Ibid., 6.

8
Conclusion:
Spanish America and
the International Economy

In both Peru and Argentina, State policies aimed at strengthening the State and creating political and social order laid the foundation for the development of the export economies of the late nineteenth century. Though the aims of the Peruvian and Argentine States were political, the effects of their policies tended to steer their countries into economic roles in the international economy that are today associated with dependency.

Political instability, of course, did not disappear. In the late nineteenth century, Peru saw some of the fiercest political conflict in its history. This conflict was brought about by Peru's defeat in the War of the Pacific as each faction blamed the other for the ruination of the country.[1] Yet, the rapidity with which a powerful State was reconstructed indicates that the terms of the conflict were decidedly different than in the early nineteenth century. In 1895, after a short period of military rule under Andrés Caceres (the only recognized hero on the War of the Pacific), the two contending factions of the coastal plutocracy--Democrats (Píerolistas) and Civilistas--joined together to oust him in a bloody civil war.[2] Under the presidency of Democrat Nicolás de Píerola (1895-1899), the hegemonic class created by the policies of the State in the "guano age" took charge and rebuilt the economy on the basis of their own interests--export production.[3]

With Píerola, Peru marched rapidly into the international economy as an export producer. The State was employed by his administration, and succeeding ones, to steadily advance the growth of exports. Peru converted to the gold standard in order to attract foreign investment and stabilize the currency so that Peruvian financiers would shift their interests from currency speculation to productive investment.[4] Since currency stabilization required an expansion of exports to finance a gold backed money, the State encouraged the growth of mining and coastal agriculture. Between 1895 and 1897, the total value of Peruvian exports rose by 40%.[5]

With the currency stabilized and the fiscal position of the State strengthened, the decade after Píerola's term saw even more spectacular growth of the export economy. The quantity of exports expanded by 41% between 1900 and 1904, and by 1907 by 164%.[6] New export industries were rapidly integrated into the economy. Rubber exports grew from 16 toneladas (tons) in 1900 to 3,193 toneladas in 1912,[7] while oil production in the rich La Brea Pariñas fields tripled between 1904 and 1908 under the leadership of the foreign owned Pacific Petroleum Company which had purchased the rights to the fields from the State in 1889.[8] The mining industry, freed from taxation by the State for 25 years starting in 1890, and allowed to import machinery free of duty, expanded rapidly, with copper exports doubling between 1901 and 1902.[9] In 1902, the U.S. Cerro de Pasco Corporation was formed and in the next twenty-five years became one of the largest agro/mineral producers in the world.[10]

The leading role of the State in this "economic miracle" is indisputable. Currency stabilization, laws providing for the development of corporations that facilitated large scale agro/mineral exploitation, the creation of the National Agricultural Society, National Mining Society, and National Industrial Society, improvements in port facilities, roads, and communication--all geared towards export promotion--were the legacy of the plutocratic Peruvian State.[11] This State was so successful that it could accommodate the coastal plutocracy, foreign capital, and even the sierra elite.[12]

If Peru's strides in intergrating its economy into the international market were prodigious, Argentina's were astounding. With Barolomé Mitre's defeat of Urquiza's Confederation at the battle of Pavón in 1861, Buenos Aires and the economic pattern produced by its State prevailed over the whole of Argentina. However, the definitive unification of Argentina under the hegemony of the Buenos Aires State and its class supports--merchants and landowners--did not come about until the State set out on a policy to destroy the autonomy of the provinces by removing all barriers to their incorporation into the nation, as defined by Buenos Aires. The tools used were the Constitution of 1853 and railroad construction.

The Constitution of 1853 was designed by the provinces of the Confederation to once and for all eliminate the influence of Buenos Aires in Argentina. In the hands of the provinces, the constitution would have been able to limit the autonomy which gave Buenos Aires such overwhelming mastery.[13] But in the hands of the Buenos Aires State, it meant the subordination of the provinces, and ultimately the subordination of Buenos Aires province itself.[14] Under Mitre and Domingo Faustino Sarmiento the Argentine State was centralized and the provinces brought to submission (although Buenos Aires province was not reduced until 1880, when the city was separated from the province). Between 1862 and 1880, some 22 instances of Federal State intervention in the provinces were recorded.[15] During the late 1860s, Mitre and Sarmiento used the cover of the Paraguayan War to reduce the power of provincial strongman Urquiza and his supporters,[16] while the isolation of the interior provinces and rural Buenos Aires (which had always provided bases for opposition to the

State), was destroyed by a wave of State railway building.

Railroad construction had political as well as economic purposes. In 1852, Juan Bautista Alberdi wrote, "Without the railroad political unity cannot be had in a country where distance makes central political power impossible . . . Political unity can only begin through territorial unity, and only the railroad can make places separated by five hundred leagues a unified country."[17] The dual role of railway construction was clearly recognized by those in charge of the Argentine State. Mitre, in his speech at the groundbreaking ceremonies for the Central Argentine Railroad in 1863 said, "Everyone must rejoice on the opening of this road, for it will tend to give riches where there is poverty and to institute order where there is anarchy."[18]

Perhaps no State policy was more responsible for Argentina's dramatic export growth in the late nineteenth century than the financing of the railroads. The railways were not built by British capitalists seeking to expand Argentina's export production. They were built by the State through its guarantees to reluctant British investors. If the railroads did not pay for themselves, the Argentine government would assure them a profit. British investors were thus assured a 7% return on capital invested whether the railroads were profitable or not.[19]

The progress of the railroads and Argentine export growth went hand in hand. The railroads made possible what James Scobie calls the "revolution on the pampas" by bringing immigration into the pampas to convert vast areas over to grain cultivation and by carrying crops to the ports for export.[20] In 1872-1873, only 325,000 acres were devoted to wheat. By 1887-1888, it had increased to 2,000,000 acres. Wheat exports jumped from 9 toneladas in 1871 to 327,894 in 1890, while corn exports rose from 15,032 tons in 1880 to 707,282 in 1890.[21] By 1904, agriculture had displaced stock raising as Argentina's major exporter.[22] The sugar industry in Tucumán also received enormous stimulation with the coming of the railroad, production doubling between 1880 and 1886.[23]

Better transport and the development of refrigeration led to a shift in emphasis in the cattle industry as the export of salted meat was replaced by the export of frozen and chilled meat. Salted meat, which made up 48% of all meat exports in 1887, dropped to only 4% by 1904, while frozen meat rose to 51%.[24] Between 1870 and 1900, the total value of Argentine exports rose from 30 million gold pesos to over 150 million gold pesos.[25]

It is obvious that without external demand Argentina would not have experienced such dramatic growth in so short a time. But even so, it would not have been able to respond to that demand had not the State taken an active role in the promotion of export activities.[26] In 1894, investments in infrastructure for the export economy accounted for 63.1% of the entire public debt, while such investments made up 36.6% of the national budget. By making government guarantees available to foreign investment for the construction of railroads, port facilities,

201

and other export related infrastructure, the State was able to attract foreign capital amounting to 3.5 million pesos by 1913.[27] In fact, as Roberto Cortés Conde argues, "One could say that government action in directing this process of growth by specifically promoting, encouraging, and guaranteeing basic investment in infrastructure played a much more important role than is generally assumed . . ."[28] In order to finally do away with provincial autonomy, in order to "civilize" the Argentine, in order to promote the dominance of the political center, Argentine statesmen steered the economy into rapid export growth in the second half of the nineteenth century.

Exclusive agro/mineral export development in Peru and Argentina, as well as in most other Spanish American countries of this era, ultimately resulted in what writers such as Andre Gunder Frank, Theotonio Dos Santos, and Fernando Henrique Cardoso and Enzo Faletto have described as underdevelopment and dependency. Nevertheless, although these writers may claim that Spanish American underdevelopment and dependency was a result of capitalist exploitation expressed as a system of international trade within which the Spanish American economies were relegated to the role of raw materials producers, the historical evidence does not bear out their thesis. As I have argued throughout this work, the Spanish American countries did not develop agro/mineral export economies as a result of the influences of the international economy.

By shifting the focus of analysis away from the international system of trade to the historical development of the social relations of production, inter-class conflict, intra-class conflict, and the consolidation of the State within Spanish American countries, it has become dear that the agro/mineral export economies were chiefly the result of the complex interaction of these forces. The international economy, rather than being the determinant factor, influenced the development of the Spanish American economies in the nineteenth century by offering the possibility of export development as an alternative to inward focused economic development. Of course, there is no reason to believe, as the dependentistas do, that inward focused economic development would have created progressive capitalist economies--that such a possibility existed would have to be proven, not assumed.[29] Nevertheless, as I have argued, a choice was made to develop outwardly--to develop export economies--through a process in which essentially domestic crisis, class conflicts, and State development played the dominant roles.

More important than the international economy in determining the direction of the Spanish American economies in the nineteenth century was the specific manner in which each new Spanish American State attempted to resolve the political turmoil that erupted with the demise of the colonial administrative apparatus. The secret of that administration's success in regulating inter-class and intra-class conflicts during the colonial period had been its "relative autonomy" from the classes in conflict. However, the weakness of the new Spanish American

States made the regulating of those conflicts and the fashioning of unified ruling classes impossible. In fact, the State was the primary focus of intra-class conflict between sectors of the dominant classes because each required different, and often incompatible, political-administrative-legal requisites for the reproduction of their exploitative relationship with the laboring classes. Thus, they engaged in predominantly political, not economic, battles with one another over the administrative and legal form of the new States.

What the new Spanish American States lacked was the "relative autonomy" which had served the colonial bureaucratic administration so well. Without the resources to impose their political sway in the new countries, they could neither regulate inter-class and intra-class conflicts nor prevent attacks on their own structures. Their lack of authority and legitimacy further prevented their appropriating the resources needed to strengthen themselves from wholely or predominantly domestic sources. Thus, as we have seen, these resources were acquired primarily through external economic links--revenues from the custom houses (and thus the encouraging of production for export), foreign loans to finance State expenditures, trade/production monopolies (such as guano in Peru), and foreign investment, principally in railroad construction which, while serving to encourage export expansion, also gave the States the means with which to eliminate local political autonomy and opposition. Spanish American States were thus the mediation through which the Spanish American economies were articulated with the international economy. It is clear then that the general pattern of economic articulation with the international economy--agro/mineral export--was not originally an economic policy of the States, nor was it economically imposed by international capitalism. It was, rather, primarily the result of an effort by the Spanish American States to solve their political crises.

By the late nineteenth century, Spanish America leapt to meet the expanding international economy with open arms. "Modernization"--the link with the outside, Europeanization--became the panacea for all the conflicts of the nineteenth century. It was--for a time. States were strengthened, political conflicts were confined within the institutional structures of the States, and hegemonic ruling classes tied to export growth emerged. But the veneer of capitalism could not create the effects of the real thing. The export economies' dynamic center lay elsewhere--in the industrial capitalist nations--and it would not be long before Spanish Americans realized that they had exchanged the possibilities of development for growth and dependence.

Although the argument in this study has centered on the origin of dependency in nineteenth century Spanish America, it clearly has implications for the debate on the contemporary relationship between the developed and less developed countries. As in their thesis on the causes of nineteenth century dependency in Spanish America, dependency theorists lean heavily on the effects of international economic forces to explain the causes of contemporary dependency. The popularity this view has spawned even grander theories, such as the "world systems theory" of Immanuel Wallerstein. Wallerstein holds that the development of individual economies can only be analyzed and understood within the context of the capitalist world system which, he argues, had its origin in Europe in the sixteenth century. Development and underdevelopment are thus two aspects of the development of this system. Although classes are acknowledged within this theoretical perspective (though only in their international character as a "world proletariat" and "world bourgeoisie"), the world capitalist system is a system of countries, some of which constitute the "core" (the developed countries), others the "semi-periphery" (the semi-developed countries), and still others the "periphery" (the under or less developed countries). While a country's position in the system is determined by its internal economic structure, that structure is determined by the system.[30]

The displacement of attention from the political and economic processess within countries to the economic relations between countries has led Marxists and non-Marxists alike to similar approaches to the problem of underdevelopment. Samir Amin, for example, sees world revolution arising from the contradictions between rich and poor nations--in effect, proletarian countries versus bourgeois countries.[31] In a somewhat similar vein both left and right wing governments of the less developed countries have focused their energies at the United Nations on the creation of a "new international economic order" in which the developed countries will be forced to redistribute their wealth to the less developed on the assumption that an unequal economic relationship between the two has been the cause of the latter's underdevelopment. Thus, in the less developed countries, the exploiters of the working classes represent themselves as the exploited of the capitalist world system in the hope that the class struggles in their countries will be derailed through appeals to nationalism. This trend has also found favor in the developed countries as depression, unemployment, and reduced living standards are blamed on the international economy. Workers there, no doubt, feel better knowing that the cause of their economic woes lay beyond their effective influence. With their attention focused on the international level, workers become less troublesome opponents for the national bourgeoisies.

Dependency and world systems theory have, consequently, obfuscated what this study has sought to illuminate--that countries become underdeveloped and dependent primarily as a result of political and economic forces internal to those countries. If they are to break free of this condition, it will depend upon changes within those countries that can only come about through those same internal forces. The class struggle, the State, and the political process in the less developed countries, as I have argued, should be the focus of any analysis of the causes of underdevelopment and dependency because these social formations are, and have been, the arenas within which the maintenance or transformation of economic patterns are decided. While dependency and world systems theory have been valuable in directing attention to the "effects" of international economic relations, their emphasis on these as main explanatory variables lead only to misguided analysis, ideological confusion and reactionary practice.

NOTES

[1]Frederick B. Pike, The Modern History of Peru (New York: Praeger, 1967), 142-150.

[2]Ibid., 156-157.

[3]Magali Sarfatti Larson and Arlene Eisen Bergman, Social Stratification in Peru, Politics of Modernization Series #5 (Berkeley: Institute of International Studies, University of California, 1969), 260.

[4]Laura Randall, A Comparative Economic History of Latin America 1500-1914. Vol. 4 Peru (Published for the Institute of Latin American Studies, Columbia University, by University Microfilms International. Ann Arbor, Michigan:1977), 32.

[5]Ibid., estimated from Table #13-14 p. 206.

[6]Ibid., 136-137.

[7]Ibid., 137.

[8]Ibid., 143-144; and Pike, 121-223.

[9]Randall, 139.

[10]Pike, 194.

[11]Randall, 142, 144; and Henry F. Dobyns and Paul L. Doughty, Peru: A Cultural History (New York: Oxford University Press, 1976), 220-221.

[12]William Bollinger, "The Bourgeois Revolution in Peru: A Conception of Peruvian History," Latin American Perspectives IV, Issue 14, Number 3 (Summer 1977), 32.

[13]James Scobie, "The Significance of the September Revolution," Hispanic American Historical Review XLI, Number 2 (May 1961), 237.

[14]J. Fred Rippy, "Argentina," in Argentina, Brazil and Chile Since Independence, ed. A. Curtis Wilgus (Washington, D.C.: George Washington University Press, 1935), 109-110.

[15]Ibid., 110.

[16]F. J. McLynn, "The Corrientes Crisis of 1868," North Dakota Quarterly XLVII, Number 3 (Summer 1979), 45-48; and F. J. McLynn, "The Causes of the War of the Triple Alliance: An Interpretation," Inter-American Economic Affairs XXXIII, Number 2 (Autumn 1979), 21-43.

[17]Quoted in Raymond H. Pulley, "Railroads and Argentine National Development, 1852-1914," The Americas XXIII (July 1966), 63.

[18]Quoted in Winthrop R. Wright, British-Owned Railways in Argentina: Their Effect on Economic Nationalism, 1854-1948 (Austin: University of Texas Press, 1974), 32.

[19]Pulley, 65.

[20]James Scobie, Revolution on the Pampas: A Social History of Argentine Wheat 1860-1910 (Austin: University of Texas Press, 1946).

[21]Laura Randall, A Comparative Economic History of Latin America 1500-1914. Vol. 2 Argentina (Published for the Institute of Latin American Studies, Columbia University, by University Microfilms International. Ann Arbor, Michigan:1977), 102; and H. S. Ferns, The Argentine Republic, 1516-1971 (London and New York: Barnes and Noble, 1973), 90.

[22]Randall, Argentina, 218 Table #7-19.

[23]Ibid., 102-103.

[24]James Scobie, Argentina, 2nd ed. (New York: Oxford University Press, 1971), 120.

[25]Ibid., 119.

[26]Roberto Cortés Conde, The First Stages of Modernization in Spanish America (New York: Harper, 1974), 126-151.

[27]Ibid., 137.

[28]Ibid., 128-129, 138-144.

[29]This point is made by Bill Warren, Imperialism: Pioneer of Capitalism (London: New Left Books, 1980), 166-168.

[30]Immanuel Wallerstein, The Modern World System (New York: Academic Press, 1974); and Immanuel Wallerstein, "The Rise and Future Demise of the World Capitalist System," Comparative Studies in Society and History XVI, Number 4 (September 1974), 387-415.

[31]Samir Amin, Accumulation on a World Scale, 2 Vols. (New York: Monthly Review Press, 1974), I:24.

Bibliography

Alier, Juan Martínez. "Relations of Production in Andean Haciendas: Peru." In Land and Labour In Latin America, 141-164. Edited by Kenneth Duncan and Ian Rutledge. Cambridge: Cambridge University Press, 1977.

Amin, Samir. Accumulation on a World Scale. 2 Vols. New York: Monthly Review Press, 1974.

Anderson, Charles. Politics and Economic Change in Latin America. New York: Van Nostrand, 1967.

Anderson, Perry. Lineages of the Absolutist State. London: New Left Books, 1975.

Anna, Timothy. "Economic Causes of San Martín's Failure in Lima." Hispanic American Historical Review LIV, Number 4 (November 1974): 657-681.

Anna, Timothy. The Fall of the Royal Government in Peru. Lincoln, Nebraska: University of Nebraska Press, 1979.

Anna, Timothy. "The Peruvian Declaration of Independence: Freedom By Coercion." Journal of Latin American Studies VII, Part 2 (November 1975): 221-248.

Apter, David. "A Comparative Method for the Study of Politics." American Journal of Sociology LXIV, Number 3 (November 1958): 221-237.

Archer, Christon. "Pardos, Indians and the Army of New Spain: Interrelationships and Conflicts 1780-1810." Journal of Latin American Studies VI, Part 2 (November 1974): 231-255.

Bachrach, Peter. The Theory of Democratic Elitism. New York: Little, Brown, 1967.

Bachrach, Peter; and Baratz, Morton. "Two Faces of Power." American Political Science Review LVI (December 1972): 947-952.

Baily, D. Viva Cristo Rey: The Cristero Rebellion and the Church-State Conflict in Mexico. Austin: University of

Texas Press, 1974.

Bamat, Thomas. "Relative State Autonomy and Capitalism in Brazil and Peru." Insurgent Sociologist VII, Number 2 (1977): 74-84.

Barbier, Jacques A. "Elite and Cadres in Bourbon Chile." Hispanic American Historical Review LII (August 1972): 416-435.

Bauer, Arnold J. Chilean Rural Society from the Spanish Conquest to 1930. Cambridge: Cambridge University Press, 1975.

Bauer, Arnold J. "Rural Workers in Spanish America: Problems of Peonage and Oppression." Hispanic American Historical Review LIX, Number 1 (February 1979): 34-63.

Bentley, Arthur. The Process of Government. Chicago: University of Chicago Press, 1908.

Berg, Ronald; and Weaver, Frederick Stirton. "Toward a Reinterpretation of Political Change in Peru During the First Century of Independence." Journal of Inter-American Studies XX, Number 1 (February 1978): 69-84.

Bernstein, Harry. Modern and Contemporary Latin America. New York: Russell and Russell, 1956.

Bettelheim, Charles. "Appendix I." Arghiri Emmanuel. Unequal Exchange., 271-322. New York: Monthly Review Press, 1972.

Bollinger, William. "The Bourgeois Revolution in Peru: A Conception of Peruvian History." Latin American Perspectives IV, Issue 14, Number 3 (Summer 1977): 18-56.

Bonilla, Frank; and Girling., T. eds. Structures of Dependency. Princeton: Princeton University Press, 1973.

Booth, David. "Andre Gunder Frank: An Introduction and Appreciation." In Beyond the Sociology of Dependence, 50-85. Edited by Ivan Oxaal, Tony Barnett and David Booth. London: Routledge and Kegan Paul, 1975.

Bottomore, T. B. Elites and Society. Harmondsworth, England: Penguin, 1964.

Bourricaud, Francois. Power and Society in Contemporary Peru. Translated by Paul Stevenson. New York: Praeger, 1970.

Brading, D. A. Miners and Merchants in Bourbon Mexico, 1763-1810. Cambridge: Cambridge at the University Press, 1971.

Breezley, William. "Caudillism: An Interpretive Note." Journal of Inter-American Studies XI (July 1969): 345-352.

Brenner, Robert. "The Origins of Capitalist Development: A Critique of Neo-Smithian Marxism." New Left Review Number 104 (July-August 1977): 25-93.

Brown, Jonathan C. "The Dynamics and Autonomy of a Traditional Marketing System: Buenos Aires, 1810-1860." Hispanic American Historical Review LVI, Number 4 (November 1976): 605-629.

Brown, Jonathan C. A Socio-Economic History of Argentina 1776-1860. New York: Cambridge University Press, 1979.

Bruchey, Stuart. The Roots of American Economic Growth. New York: Harper, 1965.

Bulnes, Gonzalo. Chile and Peru: The Causes of the War of 1879. Santiago, Chile: Imprinta Universitaria, 1920.

Burgin, Miron. The Economic Aspects of Argentine Federalism 1820-1852. New York: Russell and Russell, (1946), 1971.

Burkholder, Mark A. "From Creole to Peninsular: The Transformation of the Audencia of Lima." Hispanic American Historical Review LII (August 1972): 395-415.

Burns, E. Bradford. The Poverty of Progress: Latin America in the Nineteenth Century. Berkeley: University of California Press, 1981.

Burr, Robert N. By Reason or Force: Chile and the Balancing of Power in South America, 1830-1905. Berkeley and Los Angeles: University of California Press, 1965.

Caldcleugh, Alexander. Travels in South America During the Years 1819-20-21. 2 Vols. London: J. Murray, 1825.

Campbell, Leon G. "The Army of Peru and the Tupac Amaru Revolt 1780-1783." Hispanic American Historical Review LVI (February 1976): 31-57.

Campbell, Leon G. "Black Power in Colonial Peru: The 1779 Tax Rebellion in Lambayque." Phylon XXXIII (Summer 1972): 140-152.

Campbell, Leon G. "The Changing Racial and Administrative Structure of the Peruvian Military Under the Later Bourbons." The Americas XXXII (July 1975): 117-133.

Campbell, Leon G. "A Colonial Establishment: Creole Domination of the Audencia of Lima During the Late Eighteenth Century." Hispanic American Historical Review LII (February 1972): 1-25.

Campbell, Leon G. The Military and Society in Colonial Peru. Philadelphia: American Philosophical Society, 1978.

Campbell, Leon G. "Recent Research on Andean Peasant Revolts 1750-1820." Latin American Research Review XIV, Number 1 (1979): 3-49.

Campbell, Leon G. "Social Structure of the Tupac Amaru Army in Cuzco, 1780-1781." Hispanic American Historical Review LXI, Number 4 (November 1981): 675-693.

Cardoso, Fernando Henrique. "The City and Politics." In

209

Urbanization In Latin America, 157-190. Edited by Jorge E. Hardoy. New York: Doubleday, 1975.

Cardoso, Fernando Henrique. "The Consumption of Dependency Theory in the United States." Latin American Research Review XII, Number 3 (1977): 7-24.

Cardoso, Fernando Henrique. "Imperialism and Dependency in Latin America." In Structures of Dependency, 7-16. Edited by Frank Bonilla and T. Girling. Princeton: Princeton University Press, 1973.

Cardoso, Fernando Henrique; and Faletto, Enzo. Dependency and Development in Latin America. Berkeley: University of California Press, 1979.

Carr, Raymond., ed. Latin American Affairs. (St. Antony's Papers Number 22). London: Oxford University Press, 1966.

Carr, Raymond. Spain, 1801-1839. London: Oxford University Press, 1966.

Chaplin, David. The Peruvian Labor Force. Princeton: Princeton University Press, 1967.

Chevalier, Francois. "The Roots of Personalismo." In Dictatorship in Spanish America, 35-51. Edited by Hugh M. Hamill, Jr. New York: Knopf, 1965.

Chilcote, Ronald; and Edelstein, Joel. Latin America: The Struggle With Dependency and Beyond. New York: Wiley, 1974.

Clayton, Lawrence A. "A Shared Prosperity: W. R. Grace and Company and Modern Peru." West Georgia College Studies in the Social Sciences XVII (1978): 1-12.

Cober, William S. "The War of the Ten Centavos: The Geographic Economic and Political Causes of the War of the Pacific." Southern Quarterly VII (January 1969): 113-129.

Cockcroft, James D.; Frank, Andre Gunder; and Johnson, Dale L., eds. Dependence and Underdevelopment. New York: Doubleday, 1972.

Cohen, Ronald; and Service, Elman R. Origins of the State: The Anthropology of Political Evolution. Philadelphia: ISHI, 1978.

Collier, Simon. Ideas and Politics of Chilean Independence: 1808-1833. Cambridge: Cambridge University Press, 1967.

Cook, Shelburne F., and Borah, Woodrow. Essays in Population History: Mexico and the Caribbean. 2 Vols. Berkeley and Los Angeles: University of California Press, 1971-1974.

Cornblit, Oscar. "Society and Mass Rebellion in Eighteenth Century Peru and Bolivia." In Latin American Affairs, 9-44. Edited by Raymond Carr. (St. Antony's Papers Number 22), London: Oxford University Press, 1970.

Cortés Conde, Roberto. The First Stages of Modernization in

Spanish America. New York: Harper, 1974.

Cox, Oliver Cromwell. Caste, Class and Race. New York: Monthly Review Press, 1959.

Criscenti, Joseph T. "Argentine Constitutional History, 1810-1852: A Re-examination." Hispanic American Historical Review XLI, Number 3 (August 1961): 367-412.

Dahl, Robert. A Preface to Democratic Theory. Chicago: University of Chicago Press, 1956.

Davies, Thomas M. Indian Intergration in Peru: A Half Century of Experience, 1900-1948. Lincoln, Nebraska: University of Nebraska Press, 1970, 1974.

Davies, Thomas M. "Indian Integration in Peru, 1820-1948; An Overview." The Americas XXX (October 1973): 184-208.

Davis, Ralph. The Rise of the Atlantic Economies. Ithica: Cornell University Press, 1973.

Dealy, Glen. "The Spanish American Political Tradition." In The Borzoi Reader in Latin American History, Vol. II, 4-14. Edited by Helen Delper. New York: Knopf, 1972.

Delper, Helen., ed. The Borzoi Reader in Latin American History. Vol. II. New York: Knopf, 1972.

Descola, Jean. Daily Life in Colonial Peru. London: George Allen and Unwin, 1968.

Dietz, James. "Capitalist Development: The Development of Capitalism in Latin America." Latin American Perspectives VI, Issue 20, Number 1 (Winter 1979): 88-92.

Dobb, Maurice. Studies in the Development of Capitalism. New York: International Publishers, 1947.

Dobyns, Henry F., and Doughty, Paul L. Peru: A Cultural History. New York: Oxford University Press, 1976.

Domhoff, G. William. Who Rules America? Englewood Cliffs, New Jersey: Prentice Hall, 1967.

Domínguez, Jorge I. Insurrection or Loyalty: The Breakdown of the Spanish American Empire. Cambridge, Massachusetts: Harvard University Press, 1980.

Dore, Elizabeth, and Weeks, John. "Class Alliances and Class Struggle in Peru." Latin American Perspectives IV, Issue 14, Number 3 (Summmber 1977): 4-17.

Dos Santos, Theotonio. "The Crisis of Development and the Problem of Dependence in Latin America." In Underdevelopment and Development. Edited by Henry Bernstein. Harmondsworth, England: Penguin, 1973.

Dos Santos, Theotonio. "The Structure of Dependency." American Economic Review LX, Number 2 (1970): 231-236.

Draper, Hal. Karl Marx's Theory of Revolution: State and Bureaucracy. New York: Monthly Review Press, 1977.

Duffield, Alexander James. Peru in the Guano Age. London: R. Bentley and Son, 1877.

Duncan, Kenneth; and Rutledge, Ian., eds. Land and Labour in Latin America. Cambridge: Cambridge University Press, 1977.

Duncan Baretta, Silvio R., and Markoff, John. "Civilization and Barbarism: Cattle Frontiers in Latin America." Comparative Studies in Society and History XX, Number 4 (October 1978): 587-620.

Dunne, Peter Masten. "Church and State in Argentina." Review of Politics VII, Number 4 (October 1945): 395-417.

DuPlessis, Robert S. "From Demesne to World System: A Critical Review of the Literature on the transition From Feudalism to Capitalism." Radical History Review III, Number 4 (Winter 1977): 3-41.

Eisen, Arlene. "The Indians in Colonial Spanish America." In Spanish Bureaucratic-Patrimonialism in America, 98-120. By Magali Sarfatti. Berkeley: University of California Institute of International Studies, 1966.

Emmanuel, Arghiri. Unequal Exchange. New York: Monthly Review Press, 1972.

Engels, Frederick. The Origins of the Family, Private Property and the State. New York: International Publishers, 1972.

Eyzaguirre, Jaime. "Promise and Prejudice in Spanish America." In The Origins of the Latin American Revolutions, 1808-1826, 256-260. Edited by R. A. Humphreys and John Lynch. New York: Knopf, 1965.

Fagen, Richard. "Studying Latin American Politics: Some Implications of a Dependencia Approach." Latin American Research Review XII, Number 2 (1977): 3-26.

Farriss, Nancy. Crown and Clergy in Colonial Mexico, 1759-1821: The Crisis of Ecclesiastical Privilege. London: Athlone Press, 1968.

Favre, Henri. "The Dynamics of Indian Peasant Society and Migration to Coastal Plantations in Southern Peru." In Land and Labour in Latin American, 253-267. Edited by Kenneth Duncan and Ian Rutledge. Cambridge: Cambridge University Press, 1977.

Felstiner, Mary. "Kinship Politics in the Chilean Independence Movement." Hispanic American Historical Review LVI, Number 1 (February 1976): 50-80.

Ferns, H. S. The Argentine Republic, 1516-1971. London and New York: Barnes and Noble, 1973.

Ferrer, Aldo. The Argentine Economy. Translated by Marjory M.

Urquidi. Berkeley: University of California Press, 1967.

Ferrer, José. "The Armed Forces in Argentine Politics to 1830." Unpublished Ph.D. Dissertation, University of New Mexico, 1966.

Fisher, John R. Government and Society in Colonial Peru. The Intendant System 1784-1814. London: Athlone Press, 1970.

Fisher, John R. "Imperial 'Free Trade' and the Hispanic Economy, 1778-1796." Journal of Latin American Studies XIII, Part I (May 1981): 21-56.

Fisher, John R. "The Intendant System and the Cabildos of Peru 1784-1810." Hispanic American Historical Review XLIX (August 1969): 430-453.

Fisher, John R. "Royalism, Regionalism and Rebellion in Colonial Peru, 1808-1815." Hispanic American Historical Review LIX, Number 2 (May 1979): 232-257.

Fisher, John R. "Silver Mining and Silver Mines in the Viceroyalty of Peru 1776-1824: A Prolegomenon." In Social and Economic Change in Modern Peru, (Center of Latin American Studies Monograph Number 6). Edited by Rory Miller, Clifford Smith and John Fisher. Liverpool: University of Liverpool Press, 1976.

Fisher, Lillian E. The Intendant System in Spanish America. Berkeley: University of California Press, 1929.

Fisher, Lillian E. The Last Inca Revolt, 1780-1783. Norman, Oklahoma: University of Oklahoma Press, 1966.

Fisher, Lillian E. Viceregal Administration in the Spanish American Colonies. Berkeley: University of California Press, 1926.

Frank, Andre Gunder. Dependent Accumulation and Underdevelopment. New York: Monthly Review Press, 1979.

Frank, Andre Gunder. Capitalism and Underdevelopment in Latin America. New York: Monthly Review Press, 1967, 1969.

Frank, Andre Gunder. "The Development of Underdevelopment." In Dependence and Underdevelopment, 3-17. Edited by James Cockcroft, Andre Gunder Frank and Dale Johnson. New York: Doubleday, 1972.

Frank, Andre Gunder. "Economic Dependence, Class Structure and Underdevelopment Policy." In Dependence and Underdevelopment, 19-45. Edited by James Cockcroft, Andre Gunder Frank and Dale Johnson. New York: Doubleday, 1972.

Frank, Andre Gunder. Lumpenbourgeoisie : Lumpendevelopment. New York: Monthly Review Press, 1972.

Frank, Andre Gunder. World Accumulation, 1492-1789. New York: Monthly Review Press, 1978.

Fried, Morton. The Evolution of Political Society. New York: Random House, 1967.

Friedrich, Carl. The Age of Baroque, 1610-1660. New York: Harper, 1952.

Fuentes, Manuel A. Lima or Sketches of the Capital of Peru. London: Trubner and Company, 1866.

Furtado, Celso. The Economic Development of Latin America. London: Oxford University Press, 1970.

Galdames, Luis. A History of Chile. Translated by Isaac Joshua Cox. Chapel Hill, North Carolina: Universtiy of North Carolina Press, 1941.

Galeano, Eduardo. Open Veins of Latin America. New York: Monthly Review Press, 1973.

García Calderón, Francisco. Latin America: Its Rise and Progress. London: T. F. Unwin, 1913.

Genovese, Eugene. The Political Economy of Slavery. New York: Random House, 1965.

Germini, Gino. "The Stages of Modernization in Latin America." In Latin America: The Dynamics of Social Change, 1-43. Edited by Stefan A. Halper and John R. Sterling. New York: St. Martin's Press, 1972.

Gibson, Charles. Spain in America. New York: Harper, 1966.

Gilmore, Robert L. "The Imperial Crisis, Rebellion, and the Viceroy: Nueva Granada in 1809." Hispanic American Historical Review XL, Number 1 (February 1960): 1-24.

Glade, William P. The Latin American Economies. New York: Van Nostrand, 1969.

Glassman, Ronald. Political History of Latin America. New York: Funk and Wagnalls, 1969.

Gleason, Daniel. "Anti-Democratic Thought in Early Republican Peru: Bartolomé Herrera and the Liberal-Conservative Ideological Struggle." The Americas XXXVIII, Number 2 (October 1981): 205-217.

Godelier, Maurice. "Infrastructures, Societies and History." New Left Review Number 112 (November-December 1978): 84-96.

Góngora, Mario. Studies in the Colonial History of Spanish America. Cambridge: Cambridge University Press, 1975.

Góngora, Mario. "Urban Social Stratification in Colonial Chile." Hispanic American Historical Review LV, Number 3 (August 1975): 422-448.

Gorman, Stephen M. "The State, Elite, and Export in Nineteenth Century Peru: Toward an Alternative Reinterpretation of Political Change." Journal of Inter-American Studies XXI, Number 3 (1979): 395-418.

Graham, Richard; and Smith, Peter H., eds. New Approaches to Latin American History. Austin: University of Texas Press, 1977.

Greenhill, Robert G., and Miller, Rory H. "The Peruvian Government and the Nitrate Trade 1873-1879." Journal of Latin American Studies V (May 1973), 107-131.

Griffin, Charles C. "Economic and Social Aspects of the Era of Spanish American Independence." Hispanic American Historical Review XXIX, Number 2 (May 1949): 170-187.

Griffin, Charles C. "The Enlightenment and Latin American Independence." In Latin America and the Enlightenment, 119-143. Edited by Arthur P. Whitaker. Ithica: Cornell University Press, 1961.

Guy, Donna J. "The Rural Working Class in Nineteenth Century Argentina: Forced Plantation Labor in Tucumán." Latin American Research Review XII, Number 1 (1978): 135-145.

Guy, Donna J. "Women, Peonage and Industrialization: Argentina, 1810-1914." Latin American Research Review XVI, Number 3 (1981): 65-89.

Haigh, Roger. The Formation of the Chilean Oligarchy: 1810-1821. Salt Lake City: Historical S. & D. Research Foundation, 1972.

Haigh, Roger. "Martin Güemes: A Study of the Power Structure of Salta, 1810-1821." Ph.D. dissertation, University of Florida, 1963.

Hale, Charles. "The Reconstruction of Nineteenth Century Politics in Spanish America: A Case for the History of Ideas." Latin American Research Review VIII, Number 2 (Summber 1973): 53-73.

Hall, Stuart. "The 'Political' and the 'Economic' in Marx's Theory of Classes." In Class and Class Structure, 15-60. Edited by Alan Hunt. London: Lawrence and Wishart, 1977.

Halper, Stefan A., and Sterling, John R., eds. Latin America: The Dynamics of Social Change. New York: St. Martin's Press, 1972.

Halperin-Donghi, Tulio. The Aftermath of Revolution in Latin America. New York: Harper, 1973.

Halperin-Donghi, Tulio. Politics, Economics and Society in Argentina in the Revolutionary Period. Cambridge: Cambridge University Press, 1975.

Hamill, Hugh., ed. Dictatorship in Spanish America. New York: Knopf, 1965.

Hamnett, Brian. "The Counter Revolution of Morillo and the Insurgent Clerics of New Granada 1815-1820." The Americas XXXII, Number 4 (April 1976): 597-617.

Hamnett, Brian. Politics and Trade in Southern Mexico, 1750-1821. Cambridge: Cambridge at the University Press, 1971.

Hanke, Lewis., ed. Readings in Latin American History. 2 Vols. New York: Thomas Crowell, 1966.

Hardoy, Jorge E., ed. Urbanization in Latin America. New York: Doubleday, 1975.

Haring, Charles. The Spanish Empire in America. New York: Harcourt, Brace, 1947.

Herr, Richard. The Eighteenth Century Revolution in Spain. Princeton: Princeton University Press, 1958.

Hill, S. S. Travels in Peru and Mexico. 2 Vols. London: Longman, Green, Longman and Roberts, 1860.

Hilton, Rodney., ed. The Transition from Feudalism to Capitalism. London: New Left Books, 1976.

Hindess, Barry; and Hirst, Paul Q. Pre-Capitalist Modes of Production. London: Routledge and Kegan Paul, 1975.

Huck, Eugene R. "Economic Experimentation in a Newly Independent Nation: Colombia Under Francisco de Paula Santander 1821-1840." The Americas XXIX, Number 1 (July 1972): 17-29.

Humphreys, R. A., and Lynch, John., eds. The Origins of the Latin American Revolutions, 1808-1826. New York: Knopf, 1975.

Hunt, Alan., ed. Class and Class Structure. London: Lawrence and Wishart, 1977.

Hunt, Shane. Growth and Guano in Nineteenth Century Peru. (Research Program in Economic Development. Woodrow Wilson School. Discussion Paper #34). Princeton: Woodrow Wilson School of Public and International Affairs at Princeton University, February 1973.

Imaz, José Luis de. Los Que Mandan. Translated by Carlos Astiz. Albany: State University of New York Press, (1964), 1970.

Jane, Cecil. Liberty and Despotism in Spanish America. Oxford at the Clarendon Press, 1929.

Johnson, John. Political Change in Latin America: The Rise of the Middle Sectors. Stanford: Stanford University Press, 1958.

Johnson, John. Simon Bolívar and Spanish American Independence 1783-1830. Princeton: Van Nostrand, 1968.

Kahl, Joseph Alan. Modernization, Exploitation and Dependency in Latin America. New Brunswick, New Jersey: Transaction Books, 1976.

Kay, Geoffrey. Development and Underdevelopment: A Marxist Analysis. New York: St. Martin's Press, 1975.

Keith, Robert G. "Encomienda, Hacienda and Corregimiento in Spanish America: A Structural Analysis." Hispanic American Historical Review LI, Number 3 (August 1971): 431-446.

Keith, Robert G., ed. Haciendas and Plantations in Latin America. New York: Holmes and Mier, 1977.

Kendall, Lane C. "Andres Santa Cruz and the Peru-Bolivia Confederation." Hispanic American Historical Review XVI (February 1936): 29-48.

Kiernan, V. G. "Foreign Interests in the War of the Pacific." Hispanic American Historical Review XXXV (February 1955): 14-36.

Kinsbruner, Jay. "The Political Influence of British Merchants Resident in Chile During the O'Higgins Administration 1817-1823." The American XXVII (July 1970): 26-39.

Kinsbruner, Jay. "The Political Status of Chilean Merchants at the End of the Colonial Period: The Concepción Example 1790-1810." The Americas XXIX (July 1972): 30-56.

Kirkpatrick, F. A. A History of the Argentine Republic. Cambridge: Cambridge at the University Press, 1931.

Klarén, Peter F. Modernization, Dislocation and Aprismo: Origins of the Peruvian Aprista Party 1870-1932. Austin: University of Texas Press, 1973.

Klein, Herbert S. "Structure and Profitability of Royal Finance in the Viceroyalty of Río de La Plata in 1790." Hispanic American Historical Review LIII (August 1973): 440-469.

Kossok, Manfred. "Common Aspects and Distinctive Features in Colonial Latin America." Science and Society XXXVII (Spring 1973): 7-30.

Kroeber, Clifton B. The Growth of the Shipping Industry in the Rio de La Plata Region 1794-1860. Madison, Wisconsin: University of Wisconsin Press, 1957.

Kubler, George. The Indian Caste of Peru 1795-1940: A Population Study Based Upon Tax Records and Census Reports. Smithsonian Institute. Institute of Social Anthropology Pub. #14. Washington, D.C.: Government Printing Office, 1952.

Kula, Witold. An Economic Theory of the Feudal System. London: New Left Books, 1976.

Laclau, Ernesto. Politics and Ideology in Marxist Theory. London: New Left Books, 1977.

Lambert, Jacques. Latin America: Social Structures and

Political Institutions. Translated by Helen Katel. Berkeley: University of California Press, 1967.

Lang, James. Conquest and Commerce: Spain and England in the Americas. New York: Academic Press, 1975.

Larson, Magali Sarafatti; and Bergman, Arlene Eisen. Social Stratification in Peru. Politics of Modernization Series #5. Berkeley: Institute of International Studies, University of California, 1969.

Lea, Henry Charles. "The Inquisition in Colonial Peru." In The Conflict Between Church and State in Latin America, 38-52. Edited by Frederick B. Pike. New York: Knopf, 1964.

Leiserson, Alcira. Notes on the Process of Industrialization in Argentina, Chile and Peru. Berkeley: Institute of International Studies, University of California, 1966.

Lenin, V. I. Imperialism: The Highest Stage of Capitalism. New York: International Publishers, 1939.

Levene, Ricardo. A History of Argentina. Translated by William Spence Robertson. Chapel Hill, North Carolina: University of North Carolina Press, 1957.

Levin, Jonathan. The Export Economies. Cambridge, Massachusetts: Harvard University Press, 1960.

Leys, Colin. "Underdevelopment and Dependency: Critical Notes." Journal of Contemporary Asia VII, Number 1 (1977): 92-107.

Lockhart, James. "Encomienda and Hacienda: The Evolution of the Great Estate in the Spanish Indies." Hispanic American Historical Review XLIX (August 1969): 411-429.

Lofstrom, William. "Attempted Economic Reforms and Innovations in Bolivia Under José de Sucre 1825-1828." Hispanic American Historical Review L, Number 2 (May 1970): 279-299.

Lofstrom, William. "From Colony to Republic: A Case Study in Bureaucratic Change." Journal of Latin American Studies V, Part II (1973): 177-197.

Long, Norman; and Roberts, Byran R., eds. Peasant Cooperation and Capitalist Expansion in Central Peru. Austin: University of Texas Press, 1978.

Lublinskaya, A. D. "The Contemporary Bourgeois Conception of Absolute Monarchy." Economy and Society I, Number 1 (1972): 65-91.

Lublinskaya, A. D. French Absolutism: The Crucial Phase 1620-1629. Cambridge: Cambridge University Press, 1968.

Lynch, John. Argentine Dictator, Juan Manuel de Rosas 1829-1852. London: Oxford University Press, 1981.

Lynch, John. Spain Under the Hapsburgs. 2 Vols. New York:

Oxford University Press, 1969.

Lynch, John. The Spanish American Revolutions: 1808-1826. New York: W. W. Norton, 1973.

Lynch, John. Spanish Colonial Administration, 1762-1810: The Intendant System in the Viceroyalty of the Río de La Plata. London: Athlone Press, 1958.

McAlister, Lyle. "Social Structure and Social Change in New Spain." In Readings in Latin American History, Vol. I, 154-170. Edited by Lewis Hanke. New York: Crowell, 1966.

MacDermot, B. C. "Historical Introduction." In The British in Paraguay, 1850-1870, i-xxv. By J. Pla. Surrey, England: Richmond Publishing Company, 1976.

MacKay, Angus. Spain in the Middle Ages. New York: St. Martin's Press, 1977.

McLellan, David., ed. Karl Marx: Selected Writings. London: Oxford University Press, 1977.

McLynn, F. J. "The Causes of the War of the Triple Alliance: An Interpretation." Inter-American Economic Affairs XXXIII, Number 2 (Autumn 1979): 21-43.

McLynn, F. J. "The Corrientes Crisis of 1868." North Dakota Quarterly XLVII, Number 3 (Summber 1979): 45-58.

McQueen, Charles Alfred. Peruvian Public Finance. U.S. Dept. of Commerce, Bureau of Foreign and Domestic Commerce. Trade Promotion Series #30. Washington, D.C.: U.S. Govt. Printing Office, 1926.

Macridis, Roy C., and Brown, Bernard E., eds. Comparative Politics: Notes and Readings. 5th Ed. Homewood, Illinois: Dorsey Press, 1977.

de Madariaga, Salvador. "The Church and the Inquisition in the Spanish American Colonies." In The Conflict Between Church and State in Latin America, 53-64. Edited by Frederick B. Pike. New York: Knopf, 1964.

Mandle, Jay R. "The Plantation Economy: An Essay in Definition." Science and Society XXXVI, Number 1 (Spring 1972): 49-62.

Mariategui, José Carlos. Seven Interpretive Essays on Peruvian Reality. Translated by Marjory Urquidi. Austin: University of Texas Press, 1971.

Markham, Clement R. Travels in Peru and India. London: John Murray, 1862.

Markham, Clement R. The War Between Peru and Chile 1879-1882. London: Sampson, Low, Matson, Searle and Rivington, 1882.

Marx, Karl. Capital. 3 Vols. New York: International Publishers, 1967.

219

Marx, Karl. A Contribution to the Critique of Political Economy. Moscow: Progress Publishers, 1970.

Marx, Karl. The Economic and Philosophical Manuscripts of 1844. New York: International Publishers, 1964.

Marx, Karl. Grundrisse. Translated by Martin Nicolaus. Harmondsworth, England: Penguin, 1973.

Marx, Karl. The Poverty of Philosophy, Karl Marx: Selected Writings, ed. David McLellan. London: Oxford University Press, 1977.

Marx, Karl. Revolution in Spain. New York: International Publishers, 1939.

Marx, Karl; and Engels, Frederick. Selected Works. 3 Vols. Moscow: Progress Publishers, 1969.

Mathew, W. M. "The Imperialism of Free Trade: Peru 1820-1870." Economic History Review XXI (December 1968): 562-579.

Matos Mar, José. "Sharecropping on the Peruvian Coast." In Haciendas and Plantations in Latin American History, 163-167. Edited by Robert G. Keith. New York: Holmes and Meier, 1977.

Means, Philip. The Fall of the Inca Empire. New York: Scribners, 1932.

Mecham, J. Lloyd. Church and State in Latin America. Chapel Hill, North Carolina: University of North Carolina Press, 1934.

Mellafe, Rolando. The Latifundio and the City in Latin American History. The Latin American in Residence Lectures #II in the Series. Toronto: University of Toronto Press, 1970-71.

Mellafe, Rolando. Negro Slavery in Latin America. Berkeley: University of California Press, 1975.

Merrington, John. "Town and Country in the Transition to Capitalism." In The Transition from Feudalism to Capitalism, 170-195. Edited by Rodney Hilton. London: New Left Books, 1976.

Miliband, Ralph. The State in Capitalist Society. New York: Basic Books, 1969.

Miller, John. The Memoirs of General Miller in the Service of the Republic of Peru. London: Longman, Rees, Orne, Brown and Green, 1828-1829.

Miller, Rory; Smith, Clifford; and Fisher, John., eds. Social and Economic Change in Modern Peru. Center of Latin American Studies Monograph Number 6. Liverpool: University of Liverpool Press, 1976.

Mollenkopf, John. "Theories of the State and Power Structure

Research." Insurgent Sociologist V, Number 3 (Spring 1975): 245-264.

Moore, John Preston. The Cabildo in Peru Under the Bourbons: A Study in the Decline and Resurgence of Local Government in the Audencia of Lima 1700-1824. Durham, North Carolina Duke University Press, 1966.

Moreno, Frank J. Legitimacy and Stability in Latin America: A Study of Chilean Political Culture. New York: New York University Press, 1969.

Mörner, Magnus., ed. Race and Class in Latin America. New York: Columbia University Press, 1970.

Mörner, Magnus. Race Mixture in the History of Latin America. Boston: Little, Brown, 1967.

Morse, Richard M. "A Framework for Latin American Urban History." In Urbanization in Latin America, 57-107. Edited by Jorge E. Hardoy. New York: Doubleday, 1975.

Morse, Richard M. "The Development of Urban Systems in the Americas in the Nineteenth Century." Journal of Inter-American Studies XVII, Number 1, (1975): 4-24.

Morse, Richard M. "The Heritage of Latin America." In The Founding of New Societies, 123-177. Edited by Louis Hartz. New York: Harcourt, 1964.

Morse, Richard M. "Trends and Patterns of Latin American Urbanization 1750-1920." Comparative Studies in Society and History XVI, Number 4 (1974): 416-447.

Moses, Bernard. "Flush Times in Potosí." In Papers on the Southern Spanish Colonies in America. Berkeley: University of California Press, 1911.

Moulder, Frances V. Japan, China and the Modern World Economy. London: Cambridge University Press, 1977.

Murray, Martin. "Recent Views on the Transition From Feudalism to Capitalism." Socialist Revolution (Spring 1976): 64-91.

Necochea, Hernán Ramírez. "The Economic Origins of Independence." In The Origins of the Latin American Revolutions, 1808-1826, 169-183. Edited by R. A. Humphreys and John Lynch. New York: Knopf, 1975.

Nicholson, Irene. The Liberators: A Study of the Independence Movements in Spanish America. New York: Praeger, 1969.

O'Brien, Phillip. "A Critique of Latin American Theories of Dependency." In Beyond the Sociology of Development, 7-27. Edited by Ivar Oxaal, Tony Barnett, and David Booth. London: Routledge and Kegan Paul, 1975.

Orlove, Benjamin S. Alpacas, Sheep and Men: The Wool Export Economy and Regional Society in Southern Peru. New York: Academic Press, 1977.

221

Oszlak, Oscar. "The Historical Formation of the State in Latin America." Latin American Research Review XVI, Number 2 (1981): 3-32.

Oxaal, Ivar; Barnett, Tony and Booth, David., eds. Beyond the Sociology of Development. London: Routledge and Kegan Paul, 1975.

Parkin, Frank. Marxism and Class Theory: A Bourgeois Critique. New York: Columbia University Press, 1979.

Pérez Brigioli, Hector. "The Economic Cycle in Latin American Agriculture: Export Economies (1880-1930)." Latin American Research Review XV, Number 2 (1980): 3-33.

Phelan, John Leddy. "Authority and Flexibility in the Spanish Imperial Bureaucracy." Administrative Science Quarterly V (1960): 47-65.

Phelan, John Leddy. The People and the King: The Comunero Revolution in Colombia, 1781. Madison, Wisconsin: University of Wisconsin Press, 1978.

Piel, Jean. "The Place of the Peasantry in the National Life of Peru in the Nineteenth Century." Past and Present XLVI (February 1970): 109-133.

Pike, Frederick B. "Aspects of Class Relations in Chile 1850-1960." Hispanic American Historical Review XLII, Number 1 (February 1963) 14-33.

Pike, Frederick B. "Church and State in Peru and Chile Since 1840." American History Review LXXIII (October 1967): 30-50.

Pike, Frederick B. "Heresy, Real and Alleged, in Peru: An Aspect of the Liberal-Conservative Struggle, 1830-1875." Hispanic American Historical Review XLVII (February 1967): 50-74.

Pike, Frederick B. The Modern History of Peru. New York: Praeger, 1967.

Pike, Frederick B., and Stritch, Thomas., eds. The New Corporatism. South Bend, Indiana: University of Notre Dame Press, 1974.

Pla, Josefina. The British in Paraguay, 1850-1870. Surrey, England: Richmond Publishing Company, 1976.

Platt, D. C. M. "Dependency in Nineteenth Century Latin America: An Historian Objects." Latin American Research Review XV, Number 1 (1980): 113-130, 147-149.

Platt, D. C. M. Latin America and British Trade, 1806-1914. New York: Barnes and Noble (Harper), 1973.

Poggi, Gianfranco. The Development of the Modern State. Stanford: Stanford University Press, 1978.

Portes Gil, Emilio. The Conflict Between the Civil Power and the Clergy. Mexico, D. F., 1935.

Poulantzas, Nicos. Classes in Contemporary Capitalism. London: New Left Books, 1975.

Poulantzas, Nicos. Political Power and Social Classes. London: New Left Books, 1973.

Poulantzas, Nicos. State, Power, Socialism. London: New Left Books, 1978.

Pulley, Raymond H. "Railroads and Argentine National Development, 1852-1914." The Americas XXIII (July 1966): 63-75.

Quirk, Robert E. The Mexican Revolution and the Catholic Church, 1910-1929. Bloomington, Indiana: University of Indiana Press, 1973.

Randall, Laura. A Comparative Economic History of Latin America 1500-1914. Vol. 2 Argentina. Published for the Institute of Latin American Studies, Columbia University, by University Microfilms International. Ann Arbor, Michigan: 1977.

Randall, Laura. A Comparative Economic History of Latin American 1500-1914. Vol. 4 Peru. Published for the Institute of Latin American Studies, Columbia University, by University Microfilms International. Ann Arbor, Michigan:1977.

Ray, David. "The Dependency Model of Latin American Underdevelopment: Three Fallacies." Journal of Inter-American Studies XV, Number 1 (February 1973): 4-20.

Reynolds, Keld J. "The Lautaro Lodges of Revolutionary Spanish America." The Americas XXIV (July 1967): 18-32.

Rippy, J. Fred. British Investments in Latin America, 1822-1949. Minneapolis: University of Minnesota Press, 1959.

Rostow, Walt Whitman. The Stages of Economic Growth. London: Cambridge University Press, 1960.

Rout, Leslie B. The African Experience in Spanish America: 1502 to the Present. Cambridge: Cambridge University Press, 1976.

Roxborough, Ian. Theories of Underdevelopment. Atlantic Highlands, New Jersey: Humanities Press, 1979.

Ruschenberger, William S. W. Three Years in the Pacific. Philadelphia: Carey, Lea and Blanchard, 1934.

Safford, Frank. "Bases of Political Alignment in Early Republican Spanish America." In New Approaches to Latin American History, 71-111. Edited by Richard Graham and Peter H. Smith. Austin: University of Texas Press, 1977.

Safford, Frank. "Foreign and National Enterprise in Nineteenth Century Colombia." Business History Review XXXIX (Winter 1965): 503-526.

Safford, Frank. "Social Aspects of Politics in Nineteenth Century Spanish America: New Grenada 1825-1850." Journal of Social History V, Number 3 (1972): 344-370.

Sanchez-Albornoz, Nicholas, The Population of Latin America: A History. Berkeley: University of California Press, 1974.

Sarafatti, Magali. Spanish Bureaucratic-Patrimonialism in America. Berkeley: Institute of International Studies. University of California Press, 1966.

Sater, William F. "Chile During the First Months of the War of the Pacific." Journal of Latin American Studies (May 1973): 133-158.

Schwartz, Robert N. Peru. Los Angeles: Inter-American Publishing Company, 1970.

Scobie, James R. Argentina. 2nd ed. New York: Oxford University Press, 1971.

Scobie, James R. Revolution on the Pampas: A Social History of Argentine Wheat 1860-1910. Austin: University of Texas Press, 1946.

Scobie, James R. "The Significance of the September Revolution." Hispanic American Historical Review XLI, Number 2 (May 1961): 236-258.

Scott, James C. Comparative Political Corruption. Englewood Cliffs, New Jersey: Prentice-Hall, 1972.

Service, Elman R. "Indian-European Relations in Colonial Latin America." American Anthropologist LVII (June 1955): 411-425.

Service, Elman R. Origins of the State and Civilization. New York: Norton, 1975.

Skocpol, Theda. States and Social Revolutions. Cambridge: Cambridge University Press, 1979.

Slatta, Richard W. "Rural Criminality and Social Conflict in Nineteenth Century Buenos Aires Province." Hispanic American Historical Review LX, Number 3 (August 1980): 450-472.

Smith, Archibald. Peru As It Is. 2 vols. London: Richard Bentley, 1839.

Smith, Peter H. "Political History in the 1980s: A View From Latin America." Journal of Interdisciplinary History XII, Number 1 (Summber 1981): 3-27.

Socolow, Susan. "Economic Activities of the Porteño Merchants." Hispanic American Historical Review LV,

Number 1 (February 1975): 1-24.

Socolow, Susan. The Merchants of Buenos Aires, 1778-1810. Cambridge: Cambridge University Press, 1978.

Solberg, Carl. "Farm Workers and the Myth of Export Led Development in Argentina." The Americas XXXI, Number 2 (1974): 121-138.

Soustelle, Jacques. Daily Life of the Aztecs. Stanford: Stanford University Press, 1961.

Spalding, Karen. "Class Structure in the Southern Peruvian Highlands 1750-1920." Radical History Review III (Fall-Winter 1975): 5-27.

Spalding, Karen. "Hacienda-Village Relations in Andean Society to 1830." Latin American Perspectives II, Issue 4, Number 1 (Spring 1975): 107-21.

Stavenhagen, Rudolfo. Social Classes in Agrarian Societies. New York: Doubleday, 1975.

Stein, Stanley. "Bureaucracy and Business in the Spanish Empire, 1759-1804: Failure of a Bourbon Reform in Mexico and Peru." Hispanic American Historical Review LXI, Number 1 (February 1981): 2-28.

Stein, Stanley; and Stein, Barbara. The Colonial Heritage of Latin America. New York: Oxford University Press, 1970.

Stepan, Alfred. The State and Society: Peru in Comparative Perspective. Princeton: Princeton University Press, 1978.

Stephens, Richard H. Wealth and Power in Peru. Metuchen, New Jersey: Scarecrow Press, 1971.

Stewart, Watt. Chinese Bondage in Peru. Durham, North Carolina: Duke University Press, 1951.

Stoetzer, O. Carlos. The Scholastic Roots of the Spanish American Revolution. New York: Fordham University Press, 1979.

Super, John C. "Querétaro Obrajes: Industry and Society in Provincial Mexico 1600-1810." Hispanic American Historical Review LVI, Number 2 (May 1976): 197-216.

Svec, William Rudolph. "A Study of the Socio-economic Development of the Modern Argentine Estancia 1852-1914." Unpublished Ph.D. Dissertation, University of Texas at Austin, 1966.

Taylor, John G. From Modernisation to Modes of Production. London: Macmillan Press, 1979.

Taylor, William B. "Landed Society in New Spain: A View From the South." Hispanic American Historical Review LIV, Number 3 (August 1974): 387-413.

Therborn, Göron. Science, Class and Society. London: New Left

Books, 1976.

Tibesar, A. "The Peruvian Church at the Time of Independence in the Light of Vatican II." The Americas XXVI (April 1970): 349-375.

Truman, David. The Governmental Process. New York: Knopf, 1951.

Tschudi, J. J. Von. Travels in Peru 1838-1842. Translated by Thomasina Ross. London: D. Bogue, 1847.

Urrutia, Miguel. The Development of the Colombian Labor Movement. New Haven: Yale University Press, 1969.

Valenzuela, J. Samuel; and Valenzuela, Arturo. "Modernization and Dependency." Comparative Politics X, Number 4 (July 1978): 535-557.

Vázquez, Marco C. "Immigration and Mestizaje in Nineteenth Century Peru." In Race and Class In Latin America, 73-95. Edited by Magnus Morner. New York: Columbia University Press, 1970.

Véliz, Claudio. The Centralist Tradition of Latin America. Princeton: Princeton University Press, 1980.

Verlinden, Charles. The Beginnings of Modern Colonization. Ithica: Cornell University Press, 1970.

Vicens Vives, Jaime. An Economic History of Spain. Translated by Frances M. López-Morillas. Princeton: Princeton University Press, 1969.

Villalobos, Sergio R. "The Creole Desire for Office." In The Origins of the Latin American Revolutions, 1808-1826, 250-255. Edited by R. A. Humphreys and John Lynch. New York: Knopf, 1965.

Villalobos, Sergio R. "Opposition to Imperial Taxation." In The Origins of the Latin American Revolutions, 1808-1826, 124-137. Edited by R. A. Humphreys and John Lynch. New York: Knopf, 1965.

Walford, A. J. "The Economic Aspects of the Argentine War of Succession, 1852-1861." Inter-American Economic Affairs I, Number 2 (September 1947): 70-96.

Wallerstein, Immanuel. The Modern World System. New York: Academic Press, 1974.

Wallerstein, Immanuel. "The Rise and Future Demise of the World Capitalist System: Concepts for a Comparative Analysis." Comparative Studies in Society and History XVI, Number 4 (September 1974): 387-415.

Warren, Bill. Imperialism: Pioneer of Capitalism. London: New Left Books, 1980.

Watchtel, Nathan. The Vision of the Vanquished. New York:

Barnes and Noble Books, 1977.

Weaver, Frederick Stirton. "American Underdevelopment: An Interpretive Essay on Historical Changes." Latin American Perspectives III, Issue 11, Number 4 (Fall 1976): 17-53.

Weaver, Frederick Stirton. "Political Disintegration and Reconstruction in Nineteenth Century Spanish America: The Class Basis of Political Change." Politics and Society V, Number 2 (1975): 161-183.

Weeks, John. "Backwardness, Foreign Capital and Accumulation in the Manufacturing Sector of Peru. 1954-1975." Latin American Perspectives IV, Issue 14, Number 3 (Summer 1977): 124-145.

Weeks, John; and Dore, Elizabeth. "International Exchange and the Causes of Backwardness." Latin American Perspectives VI, Issue 21, Number 2 (Spring 1979): 62-87.

Werlich, David. Peru: A Short History. Carbondale, Illinois: Southern Illinois University Press, 1978.

Whitaker, Arthur Preston. The Huancavelica Mercury Mines. Cambridge, Massachusetts: Harvard University Press, 1941.

Whitaker, Arthur Preston., ed. Latin America and the Enlightenment. Ithica: Cornell University Press, 1961.

White, Richard Alan. Paraguay's Autonomous Revolution 1810-1840. Albuquerque: University of New Mexico Press, 1978.

Wiarda, Howard J. "Corporatism and Development in the Iberic-Latin World: Persistent Strains and New Variations." In The New Corporatism. 3-33. Edited by Frederick B. Pike and Thomas Stritch. South Bend, Indiana: University of Notre Dame Press, 1974.

Wiarda, Howard J. Politics and Social Change in Latin America: The Distinct Tradition. Amherst: University of Massachusetts Press, 1974.

Wilgus, Curtis., ed. Argentina, Brazil and Chile Since Independence. Washington, D.C.: George Washington University Press, 1935.

Williams, Eric. Capitalism and Slavery. New York: Russell and Russell, 1944.

Williams, John Hoyt. The Rise and Fall of the Paraguayan Republic, 1800-1870. Austin: University of Texas Press, 1979.

Wolf, Eric; and Hansen, Edward. "Caudillo Politics: A Structural Analysis." Comparative Studies in Society and History IX (1967): 168-179.

Wolfe, Alan. The Limits of Legitimacy. New York: Free Press, 1977.

Wolfe, Alan. "New Directions in the Marxist Theory of the State." Politics and Society Number 4 (Winter 1975): 131-160.

Woodward, Margaret L. "The Spanish Army and the Loss of America 1810-1824." Hispanic American Historical Review XLVIII, Number 4 (November 1968): 586-607.

Woodward, Ralph Lee. Central America: A Nation Divided. New York: Oxford University Press, 1976.

Wright, Eric Olin. Class, Crisis and the State. London: New Left Books, 1978.

Wright, Winthrop R. British - Owned Railways in Argentina: Their Effect on Economic Nationalism, 1854-1948. Austin: University of Texas Press, 1974.

Zimmerman, Arthur Franklin. "The Land Policy of Argentina with Particular Reference to the Conquest of the Southern Pampas." Hispanic American Historical Review XXV (February 1945): 3-36.

Index

Abascal, José de, 99, 101, 102, 104
Absolutist State, 17, 18, 33, 35, 82, 167
  and the development of capitalism, 17-18, 167
  in Europe, 17
  in Spain, 33, 35, 68, 82
Alcabala (sales tax), 49, 72, 78-80
  Indians exempt from, 49
Alcaldes mayores, 42, 71, 72. See also Corregidores
Amin, Samir, 204
Anderson, Perry, 55
Argentina, 15, 16, 20, 56, 128-133, 179-189
  caudillism in, 157-158
  centralism (Unitarianism) in, 146-149. See also Unitarianism
  church-State conflict in, 153-154
  conservatism in, 143-144
  creation of the Viceroyalty of Río de la Plata, 70
  economy of, 128-133, 179-189 199-202
  export economy, 116-118, 179-189, 199-203
  Federalism in, 146-149. See also Federalism
  Indian slavery in, 47
  interior provinces, 70, 128, 131-133, 143, 146-148, 200
  liberalism in, 142-143
  littoral provinces, 103, 105
  ruralization of political

Argentina (cont'd)
  power in, 105, 128-130
  See Buenos Aires; Wars of Independence
Aristocracy, 17, 18, 35-37, 39, 40, 56, 69
  Spanish, 35-37, 69
Artigas, José, 104. See Uruguay
Audencias, 52-53
  decline of creole representation on, 74
  and intendants, 73
  See Bureaucracy
Aztecs, conquest of, 39
Balta, José, 174-176
Banda Oriental. See Uruguay
Belgrano, Manuel, 103
Beresford, William C., invades Buenos Aires, 95
Bolívar, Simon,
  and liberal reforms in Peru, 123
  liberates Peru, 105, 144
  liberates New Granada, 106
  mita abolished by, 125
  and the Peruvian clergy, 154
Bolivia. See Upper Peru
Bourbon reforms, 13, 55, 57, 67-82, 94, 97, 100, 118, 133, 142-143
  economic, 70-73, 76-78, 81-82
  political, 70-76, 145
  in Spain, 68-69
  See also Bureaucracy; intendants
Bourgeoisie, 17, 18, 47, 55, 204

229

Laclau, Ernesto, 7
La Fuente, Antonio Guittíerrez de, 150
La Mar, José de, 154, 149-150, 158
Landowners, 20, 43-44, 50-51, 72-74, 77-78, 81-82, 118, 122-133, 173-174
  and the Bourbon reforms, 77-80, 81-82
  and the church, 50-51, 152
  conflict among, 10, 13, 20, 133-134
  and labor, 10, 43-44, 122-127, 129-133
  rise of in Argentina, 105, 128-129
Lang, James, 36
La Serna, José de, 106
Las Heras, Bartolomé Maria de, 154
Lavalle, Juan, 147
Liberalism, 13-16, 106, 141-155, 158, 168, 171
  in Argentina, 143-144
  in Peru, 144-145, 149-158, 168, 171
Liniers, Santiago, 95-97, 99
Loans, foreign, 116, 203
  of Argentina, 180, 181
  of Peru, 168, 172, 174-178
López Jordán, Ricardo, 157
Luna Pizarro, Francisco Javier de, 154
Lynch, John, 73, 128, 141, 185
McAlister, Lyle, 48-49
Maríategui, José Carlos, 149, 170
Martínez de Rozas, Juan, 98
Marx, Karl, 6-8, 11, 16-17, 39, 47
Mecham, J. Lloyd, 15
Meiggs, Henry, 175
Mellafe, Rolando, 41, 48
Mercantilism, Spanish, 37, 117-118, 139-140
Merchant capital, 6-7, 18. See also Capitalism
Merchants, 42-46, 51-52, 73-74, 76-78, 117-118, 129, 143-144, 158, 179-181, 187
  and the Bourbon reforms, 73-74

Merchants (cont'd)
  creole, 52, 77-78, 117-118
  and independence, 128-129, 143-144, 179-181
  Spanish, 51-52, 76-78, 97, 117
Mestizos, 9, 43, 48-50, 81, 122
  and the Wars of independence, 10, 16, 156
  See also Castas, society of,
Mexico, 41-56
  and the Bourbon reforms, 74-78, 81-82
  conquest of, 38-39
  independence of, 100, 106
  manufacturing in, 22
Military, 49, 52, 75, 79, 156-158
  in Argentina, 95-97, 103, 104, 105, 129-131, 132-133, 157-158, 179, 181
  in Peru, 144-145, 149-151, 158, 169-172, 174, 176, 199
  Spanish army in America, 104, 106
Miners, 10, 13, 16, 20, 77
  and the Bourbon reforms, 80, 81
  difficulty recruiting labor, 125-126
  financial penury of, 45-46
  use of forced labor, 44-45
  See also Mining
Mining, 9, 10, 21, 40-41, 78
  in Argentina, 181
  and aviadores (money lenders), 46
  decline of, 56, 122, 125-126
  mercury, 44-46
  in Mexico, 41, 45-46, 53-78
  in Peru, 41, 44-46, 53, 78, 122, 125-126, 199-200
  silver, 41, 44-46, 53, 125-126
Mita, 40-46, 79-80. See also Indians; Mining
Mitre, Bartolomé, 148, 158, 200, 201
Mode of production, 6-8, 17, 40, 78
Modernization theory, 4-7
Montevideo, 95-96, 99, 104. See also Uruguay

233

Rosas (cont'd)
  and the church, 153-154
  defeated by the
    confederation, 148, 158
  economic policy of, 185-188
  and the gauchos, 130,
  land policy of, 184-185
Safford, Frank, 13, 141-142
San Martín, José de, 146,
  abolishes tribute, 168
  and the church, 154
  in Peru, 100, 105, 144
Santa Cruz, Andrés, 150-151
Sarfatti, Magali, 37, 74
Sarmiento, Domingo, 158, 200
Scholasticism, Spanish, 13
  and independence, 82, 95, 97,
    99, 100
  and liberalism, 142
Scobie, James, 132, 157, 180,
  201
Scott, James, 71
Seigniorialism, Spanish, 34, 37
  See also Feudalism
Skocpol, Theda, 130
Slatta, Richard, 130
Slavery, 47-48, 53, 126-127,
  173
  abolition of in Peru, 126-
    128, 173
  Black, 47-48, 49, 53
  Indian, 47
  trade, 47-48
Spain, 34-36
  aristocracy in, 34-35, 69
  Bourbon reforms in, 67-70,
    71-72, 76-78, 143
  bourgeoisie in, 18, 35-36, 69
  Constitution of 1812, 101-102
  decline of, 35-36, 68
  economy of, 18, 51-52, 67-70,
    71-72, 143
  French invasion of, 94-95, 96
  Junta Central, 94-97, 100
  reconquest of, 33-37, 55-56
  Regency in, 95, 99, 103
  war with Peru, 174
Spalding, Karen, 122
State,
  Argentine, 179-189, 200-202
  colonial, 9-10, 42-44, 50-57,
    69-83
  crisis of the, 19-21, 68, 78-

State (cont'd)
  83, 94-99, 100, 102-107,
  139-140, 146, 156-159, 189
  and economy, 12-13, 16-19,
    21-22, 51-57, 69-83, 118,
    133-134, 167-168, 199
  legitimacy of, 52, 54-55, 67-
    68, 82, 97, 102-103, 105,
    139-140, 145, 156, 159,
    169, 172, 189, 203
  Marxist theory of the, 11-13,
    16-19
  Peruvian, 168-179, 199-200
  relative autonomy of the, 11-
    12, 16-19, 55, 133-134,
    140, 189, 202-203
Stoetzer, O. Carlos, 55, 74
Suárez, Francisco, 82. See also
  Scholasticism, Spanish
Sucre, José de, 150
Tariffs,
  in Argentina, 181-182, 185-
    188
  in Peru, 168-169
  See also Revenue, State
Towns,
  function only as centers of
    administration, 54-56
Tribute, Indian, 20, 38, 39,
  40, 42, 44, 54, 123-124,
  168, 173
  abolition of, 149, 173
  and the Bourbon reforms, 72,
    78
Trade,
  of Argentina, 131, 132, 144,
    178-182, 184, 185-189, 201-
    203
  and the Bourbon reforms, 69-
    71, 73-74, 76-79
  colonial, 51-52, 54, 56
  contraband, 54, 104
  and the development of
    capitalism, 5-7, 17, 18
  export, 21, 115-18, 122, 129,
    170-172, 174-175, 177-189,
    199-203
  of Peru, 149, 158, 170-172,
    174-175, 177-178, 199-200
  slave, 47
  Spanish State control of, 37,
    51, 56-57, 68
Tucumán, 77, 79, 147, 201

Tucumán (cont'd)
control of labor in, 133
Tupac Amaru revolt, 10, 79-80.
See also Revolts
Ulloa, Juan de, 71
Upper Peru,
Argentina loses, 104, 128,
131, 143, 179
becomes part of the Vice-
royalty of Río de la Plata,
70-71, 78
and the Bourbon reforms, 70-
71, 173
independence movement in, 99
and the Peru-Bolivia Con-
federation, 149-151
revolts in, 79
Unitarians, 129, 147
and the church, 153
economic policy of the, 142-
144, 179-183
labor policy of the, 130, 180
land policy of the, 180
See also Argentina;
Centralism
Urquiza, Justo José de, 148,
158, 200
Uruguay, 118, 129
and Argentina, 104, 143, 187
See also, Artigas; Montevideo
Vagrancy laws, Argentine, 129-
133
Véliz, Claudio, 40, 108

Vicens Vives, Jaime, 34
Viceroyalty of New Granada. See
Colombia
Viceroyalty of New Spain. See
Spain
Viceroyalty of Peru. See Peru
Viceroyalty of Río de la Plata.
See Argentina
Vidaurre, Manuel Lorenzo de,
155
Vigil, Francisco de Paula
González, 155
Vivanco, Manuel Ignacio, 158
Wage labor,
and capitalism, 6-8, 12
lack of in Spanish America,
44-47, 53
See also Capitalism
Wallerstein, Immanuel, 204
War of the Pacific, 179, 199
Wars of Independence, 10-11,
20-21
in Argentina, 95-97, 102-105
and caudillism, 16, 50
causes of the, 67-68, 93-95,
115-116
in Chile, 97-99
in Peru, 100-102, 105-106
Weaver, Frederick Stirton, 102
Weeks, John, 7
Whitelocke, John, 95-96
World capitalist system. See
International economy
World systems theory, 204-205

236